CHRISTIANITY AND GESTALT THERAPY

Christianity and Gestalt Therapy is a unique integration written for psychotherapists who want to better understand their Christian clients and Christian counselors who want a clinically sound approach that embraces Christian spirituality.

This book explores critical concepts in phenomenology and how they relate to both gestalt therapy and Christianity. Using mixed literary forms that include poetry and story, this book provides a window into gestalt therapy for Christian counselors interested in learning how the gestalt therapeutic model can be incorporated into their beliefs and practices. It explores the tension in psychology and psychotherapy between a rigid naturalism and an enchanted take on life.

A rich mix of theory, philosophy, theology, and practice, *Christianity and Gestalt Therapy* is an important resource for therapists working with Christian patients.

Philip Brownell, MDiv, PsyD, is a clinical psychologist licensed in Idaho. He is a trained gestalt therapist, ordained clergyman, independent scholar, researcher, and author with over fifty years' experience.

CHRISTIANITY AND GESTALT THERAPY

The Presence of God in Human Relationships

Philip Brownell

NEW YORK AND LONDON

First published 2020
by Routledge
52 Vanderbilt Avenue, New York, NY 10017

and by Routledge
2 Park Square, Milton Park, Abingdon, Oxon, OX14 4RN

Routledge is an imprint of the Taylor & Francis Group, an informa business

© 2020 Philip Brownell

The right of Philip Brownell to be identified as author of this work
has been asserted by him in accordance with sections 77 and 78 of the
Copyright, Designs and Patents Act 1988.

All rights reserved. No part of this book may be reprinted or reproduced
or utilised in any form or by any electronic, mechanical, or other means,
now known or hereafter invented, including photocopying and recording,
or in any information storage or retrieval system, without permission in
writing from the publishers.

Trademark notice: Product or corporate names may be trademarks or
registered trademarks, and are used only for identification and explanation
without intent to infringe.

Library of Congress Cataloging-in-Publication Data
A catalog record for this book has been requested

ISBN: 978-1-138-47899-2 (hbk)
ISBN: 978-1-138-47900-5 (pbk)
ISBN: 978-1-351-01407-6 (ebk)

Typeset in Bembo
by Apex CoVantage, LLC

Permission to Quote

The text of the New American Standard Bible® may be quoted and/
or reprinted up to and inclusive of five hundred verses without express
written permission of The Lockman Foundation, providing the verses
do not amount to a complete book of the Bible nor do the verses
quoted account for more than 25% of the total work in which they are
quoted. Notice of copyright must appear on the title or copyright page
of the work as follows: "Scripture taken from the NEW AMERICAN
STANDARD BIBLE®, Copyright © 1960, 1962, 1963, 1968, 1971,
1972, 1973, 1975, 1977, 1995 by The Lockman Foundation. Used by
permission."

I dedicate this book to all seekers—people who want to know God and cohabitate with Him. Some of these people don't yet know it is He they desire. Others know but wish their desire for God were white hot with passion so that they might live more completely by faith and walk more closely in step with the Holy Spirit. Others I think resent God for how much they need Him.

But we are all seekers nonetheless.

I also dedicate this book to my wife, Linda. The partner in life God gave me as an answer to prayer. She is a true partner. She has enriched my life more than I could ever have imagined possible. I love you, dear.

Last, I dedicate this book to my children and all the other people God has providentially brought into my life, including people I've met in the church and in the gestalt community. To my children: no one is to me as you have been and continue to be. I love you and pray for you. I am privileged to be your earthly father. To my providential friends inside and outside the church, inside and outside gestalt therapy: thank you for both your agreement and disagreement. Thank you for integrity, intelligence, and a willingness to dialogue.

CONTENTS

Acknowledgments		*x*
Introduction		1

PART 1
Being Present 5

1	Existing and the Conditions of Contact	6
2	Being God	16
3	Being Present in Therapy	28
4	A Critical Realist Perspective on Presence	37
5	Non-Independence and Alterity—When People Meet People	44
6	Immanence and Transcendence—When God Meets People	53
	Story One A Private Lake	63

viii Contents

PART 2
The Pneumenal Field in Gestalt Therapy   69

7 Basic Field Dynamics   70

8 Atmospheres and the Organism-Environment Field   80

9 Enchantment and the Pneumenal   99

Story Two A Change in Atmosphere   108

PART 3
The Experience of Contact With God   115

10 A Basic Orientation to Phenomenology   116

11 A Phenomenology of Spiritual Life   126

12 Eavesdropping on Relationships With God   133

Story Three The Longed-for Peace   139

PART 4
Risk and Trust   145

13 The Ineffable and the Enigmatic   146

14 Risk and Trust   153

Story Four Obviously Not Obvious   158

PART 5
Change, Salvation, and Growth   165

15 Change Is Constant   166

16 Grace, Regeneration, and Salvation   174

17 Rules, Introjects, and Matters of Conscience   186

18	Growth in Spiritual Sensitivity	190
19	Growth in Availability	195
	Story Five Time for a Change	199
	Conclusion	208

Index   *210*

ACKNOWLEDGMENTS

I want to express my gratitude to Dan Bloom for his support, as always, and his critical mind as I have repeatedly shot snippets of this book to him for his perspective. He is a remarkable person, and I am blessed to have him in my life, but I don't think Dan is in my life by accident. God is not only the hound of heaven, He is the greatest loving father who provides and enriches, giving a life worth living, and Dan has been one of His gifts to me.

I also want to express my affection and respect for Margherita Spagnuolo Lobb, who, along with Dan, provided an endorsement for this book. People have, at various times, told me they marvel at my energy; well, I marvel at hers. More than that I sense in her a kindred soul.

Beyond that I acknowledge all my gestalt friends and the field of gestalt therapy that has been so influential. The overall impact is too large to delineate.

Similarly, are all the Christian friends and influences who have affected me from even before the day that I stopped running away from God and challenged Him to make himself known to me. Thank you. Some day we will reunite in the congregation of the redeemed known as the marriage supper of the lamb. At the head of the table will be Jesus, we will see Him as He is, and we will be like Him.

Of course, there are the people at Routledge. Thank you for your interest in this book and your willingness to give it a public opportunity. And thank you for your patience.

All quoted scripture comes from the New American Standard Bible (NASB).

INTRODUCTION

This week I mowed the weeds
And watered the trees.
They shoot up. They put out leaves.
Most will live a long time—
Longer than I.

Who
Will enjoy the trees I planted
After I'm gone?
What will it look like,
This forest I nurture?

It's the same question I have
About the things I've been writing.
Or my work as a therapist.
How will the people who've come into my life
Be affected because I was here?

I was entrusted with much.
I've been given a lot.
I asked God to make Himself known
To me,
And He did.

Then I lived
Forty-nine more years.

2 Introduction

So many people in so many places.
I have no way to know if I've been profitable to my King,
But someday.

Perhaps soon
I will know.
For now,
I hope my trees
Are growing stronger and taller every day.

We are in this world quickly. While finishing this book I received news that a friend had died. Sylvia Crocker was a gestalt therapist, consummate writer, Christian sister, and determined debater for her point of view. I met Sylvia in my early phase as a gestalt therapist, during my training years. She lived in Wyoming, and I lived in Oregon. We met at a conference of the Association for the Advancement of Gestalt Therapy (AAGT) and then began a long relationship online in which we discussed theory and practice. We argued. She was annoying in her detail, and I found myself studying just to meet her with any hope of holding my own ground. She made me a more careful thinker, and she, along with all the other dialogue partners at Gstalt-L (an online discussion group), forced me to face myself and modulate my own way of heating up the conversation.

There are not many outspoken, transparent Christians in the gestalt community. Sylvia was one. I did not share her theology, but I recognized her sense of being here on loan. She felt she had been given a mission to speak for the Christian perspective, and so when she wrote her book, *A Well-Lived Life: Essays in Gestalt Therapy*, she included a chapter about that.

Linda and I visited her this last summer, a few months, as it turns out, before she died. She showed us around her town. We ate together. She took us into her home. I am very thankful for that time.

We are in this world quickly—and then we are not. I wrote this book because it's been developing over the last ten years or longer, coming together as my own understanding of the issues grew. I am not like Sylvia. I don't believe I've been given a *special* mission; however, I do believe my way, the Tao of my life, has been transparency, and I do believe I've been called of God to simply be who I am. I am a child of God. I have been irritatingly direct with people because of that, the need to be who I am. I say what I think. What I think is a mix of where I've been, like all of us, and where *I* have been is what you will find in this book.

I am many things, but for the purposes of this book it's enough to say that I am a Christian and a gestalt therapist. So, this book is an integration of those two worlds. Hopefully, it will illuminate those worlds, one for the other.

It also needs to be stated that I am not writing this book from one particular theological or ecclesiastical perspective. I am protestant, but I have been affected by Catholic writers, and I find them interesting. For example, I have found the

Catholic attention to phenomenology, what has been called the theological turn in phenomenology, an extremely important development and one that serves the universal church. I attended a Conservative Baptist seminary, but I have outgrown the Conservative Baptist tendency to fight over miniscule tidbits of theology and then split people out because they don't appear "orthodox." Nobody in any branch of the church has it all correct. Humility goes a long way, and I have knocked off some rough edges that I hope make me more accepting of people and less abrasive. Having said that, I am pretty standard in my theology, all things considered, and I suppose one could say I'm more Reformed than not, although vestiges of dispensationalism still wave from the stands when "my team" has the ball.

I wrote a book previously on *Spiritual Competency in Psychotherapy*. It was not enough. This is not a book about spirituality in general. This is a book that can help gestalt therapists understand the Christian perspective, way of life . . . way of being. Not all Christians believe exactly the same things, but in this book you will find issues very relevant to what Christian patients come into therapy with. They may compartmentalize, minimize, deny, spiritualize, and they may have been influenced by the doctrine of separation of church and state (so that they feel intimidated to even mention their spirituality), but these chapters will, as the saying goes, open a window on what it's like to be a Christian, and perhaps that might serve the process of therapy.

Conversely, my hope is that this book will also show Christian counselors, psychotherapists, psychologists, pastors, pastoral counselors, and others what gestalt therapy is like. I believe it is a wonderful way of working with people that allows them to be authentic and to grow. As a gestalt therapist and a Christian, I have found the praxis of gestalt therapy helpful in doing what really amounts to pastoral counseling, not that that is what I was setting out to do, but on the occasion that a Christian person has come to me, and his or her issues and interests directed us, gestalt therapy as a method has facilitated the process quite well.

I need to say something else about the professional field of gestalt therapy and my depiction of it in this book. The gestalt therapy reader will notice that I do not cite frequent and long lists of many gestalt writers. That is not because they don't exist (as we know). I think it is because they have become more a part of me than a reference for me. God's Spirit is in me, and His word has shaped who I am and how I think, but now also the world of gestalt therapy has become almost second nature. I *could* have referenced numerous gestalt writers in making my various points about gestalt therapy (and I have certainly listed some). But let me say that Gary Yontef, Lynne Jacobs, Peter Philippson, Jean-Marie Robine, Margherita Spagnuolo Lobb, Dan Bloom, Gianni Francesetti, Dave Mann, Gordon Wheeler, and numerous others are in the current generation of writers that I associate with a more contemporary gestalt therapy approach; they could have appeared frequently in this book as authoritative references (I meant no disrespect from not listing them that way). Furthermore, this brief list does not even touch our

4 Introduction

foundational generation of writers, and I have made no reference to my gestalt research colleagues who are attempting to provide a needed research tradition in support of contemporary gestalt therapy (and for whom I have extreme affection and respect—they are consummate gestalt professionals). The point being that it was not my purpose to illustrate the rich literary field of gestalt therapy.

The reader will find that I have written stories rather than true case studies. I found it more interesting to do that, but also, it harmonizes with the fact that gestalt therapy is really about a way of life, a style of living. So, it's not just about therapy; it's about growth, about being alive, about being a living thing. It's not just a clinical modality; many people find themselves living and relating to others using what they have learned in gestalt therapy. Also, after having trained and practiced gestalt therapy, after having written about it, and taught others about it, I have found that it has become a natural way of being for me. So much so that, frankly, doing gestalt therapy is very much a matter of being myself with another person. So, I wrote stories that hopefully captured some of the living that people do relevant to the chapters that precede those stories.

Right now, as I write, my trees are covered by snow. I am in Idaho, living next to the Snake River, near the rim of the Snake River Canyon. Shoshone Falls roars in the winter air. I am about to put this book to bed. Then I will do the same for myself. I guess I'll be in this world for a little while longer.

December 2019
From Above Shoshone Falls

PART 1
Being Present

1

EXISTING AND THE CONDITIONS OF CONTACT

Sometimes like a mist upon the skin.
Sometimes like a scent I smell.
Sometimes like a rock that hits one in the face,
Is it there or can I tell?

What perceptions will I allow
To come to me as given?
What experience will I bid myself,
"It's only me and how I'm driven?"

Bear with me here at the start. I want to lay a ground for what it's like to exist and have the experience of living in a world among others.

In Christianity one must believe that God exists and that He rewards those who diligently seek Him.[1] Everything in Christianity follows upon trusting that God is not a fairy tale told to young children. The grand story of the Bible, the story of the experience of God in this world, is true. It is told from a phenomenological perspective, the experience of human beings, so it is related to questions of philosophy as well, but it is true.

In life philosophers have devoted themselves to thinking carefully about matters related to existing and having a life. In philosophy, for instance, the question of which takes precedence, existence or essence, has been debated at length. It matters to Christians as well, because the issue of what kind of God exists follows immediately the issue of His existence.

The topic of existence is of passing interest here, for my main concern is with contacting and experience, but existence does need to be acknowledged. If nothing actually exists, then contacting (an essential issue in gestalt therapy)

Existing and the Conditions of Contact **7**

doesn't happen and experience does not emerge. Existence is the condition of contact.

Unfortunately, I do not have the space to develop it at length. Follow these bulleted points:

- Some say a thing could not exist unless the logical composition, the essence of what that thing is, preceded its formation. The schematic of the widget comes before the building of the widget. Put that way, however, such a template would constitute a categorial intentional object—an abstraction or conception (such as "justice" or "grace") that exists as a construct but not as a physical object. Its conceptual existence precedes its corporeal existence, even if it has no actual physical existence. As such it still exists, posing another wrinkle in the issue.
- All categorial intentionality is a product of the rational thought of human beings who already exist. In fact, such categorial intentions are accidental and contingent, relative to the essential beings giving them life. Until the widget is made, the existence of the widget is entirely conceptual. After the widget is created, however, the existence of the widget is actual. It is then a physical object—not just a real thing (i.e. a real concept), but an actual thing (i.e. an objectively existing thing—an "extant").
- Put another, and more customary way, the essence of an extant is its existence. According to a summary by Edith Stein[2] (2002) of Aristotle's ten categories of being, the first, and essential category, is what the thing is, that is, *that* it is. The rest of the nine categories are accidental, being contingent on the first. Aristotle's term for essential existence is *ousia*, which has been translated "essence." Thus, the primary consideration is not really essence at all, because the essence of anything that exists is its existence. Essence is captured by existence.
- The real meaning of *ousia* is "being." *Ousia* is a form of the Greek word for being—*eimi*. I am. You are. He, she, or it is. That is our primary essence, and everything else about us follows. The same is true of God. When Moses asked God who he should say sent him, God replied, Yahweh (translated "I am that I am"); "tell them I Am has sent you."[3] I AM—the existing one.
- In John 8:48–59 Jesus is in conversation with Jewish leaders and He states that before Abraham came into existence, He (Jesus) existed in an ongoing state (ϖρὶν Ἀβραὰμ γενέσθαι ἐγὼ εἰμί = before Abraham was, I am). It is not just coincidence that those words harken back to Exodus 3:14. And the Jewish people in His presence understood His claims to deity based on the same infinite existence that Yahweh suggested to Moses; they started to stone Him. The essence of Jesus was His existence as equal with Yahweh.
- There is an important difference between the existence of God and the existence of every other thing that exists. The source of God's existence is found in Himself, but the source of our existence is found outside of ourselves, and

8 Being Present

in Christianity that is further defined as being *in* God. In God we live, move, and have our being—*esmen* (the present plural, active, indicative of the verb "to be," *eimi*, in Greek), exist.[4] The present tense indicates an ongoing existence. Gestalt therapists would put it "in the here and now," in the current moment we continue to exist in the sphere of God's existence—from one moment to the next, the primary consideration not really being time but the nature of an ongoing, continuing existence. Our essence is that we exist in Him; our existence is contingent on the existence of God.

- That last point is an important difference in perspective that will linger throughout this book. Heidegger claimed that human beings are concerned for our existence. At any moment we strive to exist, to live. That concern for existence is ontical, and it is also ontological (Mulhall, 1996), meaning that we build systems of meaning and think about our existence so that we live, move, and have our being in the evolving and continuous interpreting of our existence. I have described this as a process of interpreting our experience. However, for a Christian this meaning making is only a condition of the overall context of life that is living in the sphere of God's existence and His perspectives on our existence.

The Significance of Existence for Experience

In order to experience anything, one must exist. If one were totally alone, isolated, and there were no other things, one could not exist. So, there must be a sufficient environmental context to support life, and there must be a sufficient ground to support meaningful life. Thus, one must exist, one must be alive, and one must have contact with whatever is environmentally other in order to sustain the experience of living.

"Contact" is a technical term in gestalt therapy. It points to meetings, the fact of meeting, and the manner in which such meeting unfolds, including the aesthetic quality of that meeting. It includes the consequences of such meeting. Contact produces the experience of self, that is, the sense of being a person. Contacting generates experience.

These meetings are whole-person in nature. I used the term "person" here as when one says, "I see a person standing by the clock." The person is the whole human being, or, as often referred to in gestalt therapy, the "organism." So, meetings are whole-organism in nature. They are embodied physically and phenomenally. In a manner of speaking they can be physical before they are phenomenal, and they can be phenomenal before they are physical.

If you stand, for instance, in my "personal space," you are standing in proximity to my physical body, but you are likely not yet physically touching me. I sense you there, and that comes with a "feel." I start to make meanings about what is going on with you standing that close to me. I start to figure out what to do about it. In such an instance you would be in contact of my lived body—the sense I have of

Existing and the Conditions of Contact **9**

being a situated and embodied person in proximity to you, and my experience of self would be contingent upon contacting you, another person.

On the other hand, imagine you rounded a corner on a quick walk and ran full force suddenly into another person walking rapidly in the other direction. Your lived body (the experience of embodied self) would have to catch up to the physical collision, the physical meeting between your material body and the other's. The experience of self in that situation would be emergent. That is, consciousness that you (the subjective "I") had collided, and what you imagined that meant to everyone in that specific context would have arisen from the lower level physical functioning of your body and its sensory-motor pathways converging in the brain.

Self is a function of the situated organism contacting in the world. Here is an example:

Once Jesus was in a small boat crossing the Sea of Galilee with His disciples. A storm came upon them and the waves were crashing over the side of the boat. Jesus was asleep inside it, but the others felt the rain and wind in their faces, and they could see what was happening. They feared for their lives because they were in contact with the elements. They felt them physically, and their life worlds were filled with the knowledge of such storms. They woke Jesus and with some incredulity asked Him, "Don't you *care*?! We are perishing." Then Jesus rebuked the storm and it subsided. The men were thunderstruck, literally in awe. I have to ask myself, what must that have been like? I think the hair on my arms would have stood up. What kind of being is this, this one who commands the elements of nature? In fact, that is what they wondered. And this was all an episode of contacting the environment, being with others and meeting in the midst of a situation.

Gestalt therapists grow increasingly adept at monitoring the contacting styles of their patients and the concomitant support mechanisms they use to establish and maintain contact. Health is defined in gestalt therapy as the fluid ability to form figures of interest and to naturally pursue them in some way to satisfaction or resolution. That requires one to reach outward and toward an Other, whether that be an apple hanging on a tree when one is hungry, a smiling person when one is lonely, a burning bush that doesn't burn up when one is attracted to its mystery, or a Savior when one knows he or she is hell bent for destruction.

The Dialogue of Contacting

Contacting can be conceived of in dialogical terms. Imagine a circle drawn on the playground. At any given time two children can enter that circle. Imagine one does. Now she waits, available for whomever might also enter the circle. She imagines a space there for another. She makes room for that potential other in herself, anticipating that someone might likely enter. When someone does, they meet in various ways. They look at each other. They make facial expressions. They speak, so they also hear, and they listen. They see one another. They step back and then

10 Being Present

draw closer. They touch one another. All these actions are dialogical as there is a process and a sequence to their meeting in time.

In the clinical process of dialogue in gestalt therapy there is presence, inclusion, and a commitment to the process.

Presence

As a therapist assuming a dialogical attitude, I am there, present with my whole being—my existence. So, I feel free to self-regulate and self-disclose as seems best. I say some things and hold back others, but what I offer, what I make available is truly me. I do not assume a professional distance, erecting a buffer between myself and the client, and I do not pretend to be something I am not. I am genuinely present.

Inclusion

Furthermore, as a therapist practicing inclusion, I make room for the other to be with me without losing my own sense of self in the process. If the other is with me in the dialogical circle, I do not stiffen against them, walling them off with a polite but superficial smile. I let them in however they choose to manifest their own presence, and I take note of how that affects me. I pay attention to how they make themselves present. I respect how much or how little they choose to reveal themselves, and I ground myself in my own experience, allowing myself to experience them as they present themselves and without shutting myself down or demanding that they ramp themselves up.

Commitment

And then, still as a therapeutic stance, I commit myself to the process in which we meet. I remain there for what emerges in our meeting, paying attention to my own experience of emerging self as the process unfolds and how that is related to what I observe in their presenting.

That is dialogue. That is contacting. That is also what God desires in His relationship with people.

Even though God cannot be met physically through the typical processes, God can be met through one's lived body, through a proprioception of the spirit (Brownell, 2016). Like the automatic physical impression one has of being situated in space or of losing or attaining balance, the impression that one has experienced something directly from God is a definite meeting. It is contact with divinity. Dallas Willard (1999) described this contact as thoughts that are our thoughts though thoughts that are not from us.

Just as it is possible to shut down contact between people, it is possible to shut down contact between people and God. The Bible calls this "hardening the heart."

One simply stiffens. One holds back, reinforcing doubt rather than using doubt to explore enigma. The person will not. Whatever goes into that, the person will not. It is the opposite of what God describes as a "broken and contrite heart."

> For You do not delight in sacrifice, otherwise I would give it; You are not pleased with burnt offering. The sacrifices of God are a broken spirit; a broken and a contrite heart, O God, You will not despise.[5]

Notice that the text describes the contrast between a religiously willful person and someone whose heart is open to meeting God. We are not simply talking about atheists who don't believe, but also religious people who are set and satisfied in their religions. For some people Christianity can be just that—a satisfying rehearsal of abstractions and theological assertions, of rules for behavior, and formulas for bringing about what one wants to accomplish in his or her life. The genuine Christian life, however, is an ongoing practice of the presence of God— contactful relationship with the great I AM.

The Significance of Experience

On our property there is a rise where three ancient lava flows protrude above the ground. I planted trees and bushes among them where the depth of soil allowed. I walk there and talk to the trees. I wonder how tall the trees will get before I die.

One morning I walked up there before the sun came up. The sprinklers had watered the area the night before. I smelled the grass, the dead weeds, and the moist earth. Insects scratched nearby, and birds chirped. It was a community of life in the midst of my solitude, and there was a soft, cool breeze.

I often find myself in a parade of need and human suffering, but that morning I felt content, small in the face of creation and the vast passages of time that place had seen—at peace in that place. I was a part of it, just one recent part. I felt grounded.

Crisp (2018; cf. Hersch, 2015) identified six features of human experience: relatedness to a world, temporality, an interpretive perspective, care-fullness, embodiment, and being-with-others. The world goes on around us, and it was going on before we entered it. We "catch a ride" with it and try to understand our experiences and the people we meet in the course of our lives, always with the sense of passing time and our finite nature. We are embodied spirits, not spirits inside of bodies.

We know, and are known, through experience. The significance of experience is that it is the stuff of our lives. It's our living.

I once lived in Bermuda. Before moving to Bermuda, I had heard about it. I had imaginations about living on an island. I wondered what it might be like to reside outside the country in which my citizenship was located, to be a guest worker. There were many things I imagined or thought I knew because I had read

12 Being Present

or heard about that place. But I did not know what it was like to live on a sub-tropical island, six hundred miles into the Atlantic Ocean, to live in a British territory, to live as a racial minority, until I had been there about six years. You can't just visit Bermuda and know these things. You have to experience staying there through the seasons and watching the people who visit come and go.

My world at that time became an expanded one. I sat on the island and looked back at the United States, often hearing the interpretive stance of people from other countries. I was a professional, a psychologist and gestalt psychotherapist, and I interacted as before with people all over the world, but I did it from Bermuda. It was a rich, enlarging experience. It was a very productive phase in my life, but it was still insufficient. I did not achieve an exhaustive and absolute understanding of the place and its people, and I did not fully augment my perspective on the United States.

We are finite. Our experience is limited. We have a sense of eternity while living in the present moment, but we will not live forever, and our aging, our passing, is constantly in the process of emerging. We experience the giving up of one generation and the taking hold of another, the passing of one phase of life and the emergence of another. Nothing of this world lasts. Through experience we can only know in part.

We live and have our being in a current moment, the now, and are present to ourselves and others in that moment of experience. We live, move, and have our being in God, but it's in the now of God. The I Am of God (not the I Was or the I Will Be). God is infinite and there is no passing phase with Him. Although He may work in different ways in the various ages of human history, He himself does not change. Time has meaning for God only in as much as He is immanent within His creation.

In gestalt therapy the situational unit is a current moment with memory of the past and expectation of the future, but it is still the current moment. In that sense there is a similarity with the transcendent nature of God. In the current "I am" we pay attention to our awareness, meet others, and are affected.

Biblical Words and Their Significance

The Hebrew word עדי (*yada*) means to know by experience, to perceive, to discern, to recognize, to make known, to be known, or to make known, depending on the syntax of the context (Gesenius, Brown, Driver, & Briggs, 1978). It was used to convey the experience of the first people when they lost their innocence and realized, or came to know, that they were naked.

> When the woman saw that the tree was good for food, and that it was a delight to the eyes, and that the tree was desirable to make one wise, she took from its fruit and ate; and she gave also to her husband with her, and he ate. Then the eyes of both of them were opened, and they knew that

Existing and the Conditions of Contact **13**

they were naked; and they sewed fig leaves together and made themselves loin coverings.[6]

It was used to convey the idea of knowing a person intimately by experiencing a sexual union with another person. "Now the man had relations with his wife Eve, and she conceived and gave birth to Cain, and she said, 'I have gotten a manchild with *the help of* the LORD.'"[7] The words "had relations" in the text stand for *yada*. The man "knew" his wife.

The Greek word αἴσθησῖς (*aísthēsis*) means experience or perception by the senses. (Schutz, 1971, vol. 2, p. 391). Gestalt therapists chose that word to refer to an aesthetic criterion, which in gestalt therapy does not refer to the standards for judging artistic merit. It refers to a basic element in the gestalt approach:

> The aesthetic criterion is the basis for clinical knowledge derived from the immediate aesthetic (sensed) qualities of contact. That is, the brightness, clarity, rhythm, grace, and fluidity of the forming gestalt are directly experienced at the contact-boundary of the therapy session. "Disruptions" or "interruptions" of contacting are sensed as they affect the otherwise spontaneous whole figure/ground process. This is the basis for gestalt therapy's intrinsic rather than extrinsic evaluation of contact. Norms are not imposed, but experience is evaluated on its own terms, upon the aesthetic coherence of the forming figures.
>
> —*Dan Bloom, personal communication, August 4, 2018*[8]

The writer of the book of Hebrews used this word when he admonished his readers saying that the meatier elements of Scripture are for mature Christians, who have been trained by experience to discern good from evil.[9] Literally, who have had their senses trained by experience.

There is another word to convey the idea of knowing: γινώσκω (*ginōskō*). It means to "notice, perceive, or recognize a thing, person, or situation through the senses, particularly the sight . . . This leads to an intelligent ordering of the mind of what has been perceived in the world of experience" (Schmitz, 1971, p. 392). It also connotes a personal knowing, as in understanding another person. *Ginōskō* was often used to translate yada in the LXX.[10]

There is another word associated with knowing: οἶδα (*oida*). It is the perfect tense of a verb meaning to see; thus, it means to have seen with lasting effect, meaning to understand fully. The difference between *ginōskō* and *oida* is sometimes significant in a context.

Ginōskō frequently suggests inception or progress in knowledge, while *oida* suggests fullness of knowledge, e.g., in John 8:55 Jesus says in reference to God the Father, "ye have not known Him" (*ginōskō*), i.e., begun to "know," "but I know Him" (*oida*), i.e., "know Him perfectly."[11]

The Experience of Knowing God

J.I. Packer (1973) wrote that a person might know as much about God as Calvin knew and yet "hardly know God at all" (p. 26). Indeed, people have made entire academic careers out of studying the Biblical text but doing it as scholarship that has no corollary in experiential knowledge of God.

When I turned my life over to God, it was because He had made Himself known to me. It is impossible to give someone else that experience. I can tell them about it, describe it, and dissect it, but all they will get is a knowledge about me and perhaps something about God. They won't have the same experience that I have had; they won't have *my* experience. Each person must have his or her own experience of God.

When I turned around in my room in the Oakland hills of Northern California and said, "If you are real, make yourself known to me," the God who exists did.

Some people say we cannot talk about God because God is immaterial and we cannot have any empirical evidence that God is present. To speak of Him is "non-sense." But that is to misunderstand what it is like to have contact with God.

You can't touch Him, but He can touch you. Jesus said that God is spirit. He is like the wind that you cannot see. Although you cannot see the wind, you can see what the wind moves, and it can move you. This moving of God, this encounter with God, produces experience, but to discern contact with God requires an openness to what I have called "touch of another kind" (Brownell, 2016).

When God moves me, He and I do not exchange abstractions nor intellectualize. It's down to earth and personal.

> There is a conviction that one has encountered God, attested by an interoceptive-like experience. One is connected up with God by God's call. One knows the call of God in one's response. This all takes place in a world to which the person belongs and a world in which God is transcendent ontically yet immanent phenomenally.
>
> *(Brownell, 2016, p. 365)*

Conclusion

This is the beginning of the considerations of this book. I am forced by space to be succinct. The content becomes compact. This is the way it will be.

I trust that a reader exists. It is my experience that readers do exist. I get feedback that substantiates that fact. So, we meet, in print, but it is a truncated meeting. You will have an experience of me, but I am blind, deaf, numb, and ignorant of you. I don't like that.

Notes

1. Hebrews 11:6.
2. Edith Stein was born into a practicing Jewish family in Breslau in 1891. She abandoned her faith during adolescence and eventually became a student and an assistant for Edmund Husserl. She was described as Husserl's "favorite student." Stein wrote her PhD dissertation for him, *On the Problem of Empathy*, prior to World War II. She also came to a Christian faith after reading the life of St. Teresa of Avila and converted to Catholicism, eventually joining a Carmelite order and taking the name of Sister Teresa Benedicta of the Cross. She was murdered by the Nazis at Auschwitz in 1942, and she was later elevated to sainthood by Pope John Paul II in 1998. Today she is also known as St. Teresa Benedicta of the Cross.
3. Exodus 3:14.
4. Acts 17:28; cf. Colossians 1:17; John 5:26.
5. Psalm 51: 16 and 17.
6. Genesis 3:6 and 7.
7. Genesis 4:1.
8. Dan elaborated on this succinct definition in a chapter-long contribution: Bloom, D. (2003). Tiger! Tiger! Burning bright—Aesthetic values as clinical values in gestalt therapy. In M. Spagnuolo Lobb & N. Amend-Lyon (Eds.), *Creative license, the art of gestalt therapy* (pp. 63–78). Vienna: Springer Verlag.
9. Hebrews 5: 11–14.
10. The Greek translation of the Hebrew Bible, translated in the 3rd to 2nd century before Jesus was born.
11. Downloaded August 4, 2018 from Vines Expository Dictionary online, https://studybible.info/vines/Know,%20Known,%20Knowledge,%20Unknown.

References

Brownell, P. (2016). Touch of another kind: Contact with God and spiritual self. In J.-M. Robine (Ed.), *Self: A polyphony of contemporary gestalt therapists*. Bordeaux, France: L'exprimerie.

Crisp, R. (2018, July 9). An existential ontology for understanding the experience of psychosis. *The Humanistic Psychologist*. Advance online publication. doi:10.1037/hum0000096

Gesenius, W., Brown, F., Driver, S., & Briggs, C. (1907/1978). *A Hebrew and English lexicon of the Old Testament*. Oxford, UK: Clarendon Press and Oxford University Press.

Hersch, E. L. (2015). What an existential ontology can offer psychotherapists. *Philosophy, Psychiatry, & Psychology, 22*, 107–119. doi:10.1353/ppp.2015.0022

Mulhall, S. (1996). *Heidegger and being and time*. London, UK and New York, NY: Routledge.

Packer, J. I. (1973). *Knowing God*. Downers Grove, IL: InterVarsity Press.

Schmitz, E. D. (1971). γινώσκω. In C. Brown (Ed.), *New international dictionary of New Testament theology* (Vol. 2, pp. 392–406). Grand Rapids, MI: Zondervan.

Schutz, E. (1971). αἴσθησῖς. In C. Brown (Ed.), *New international dictionary of New Testament theology* (Vol. 2, p. 391). Grand Rapids, MI: Zondervan.

Stein, E. (2002). *Finite and eternal being*. Washington, DC: ICS Publications, Institute of Carmelite Studies.

Willard, D. (1999). *Hearing God: Developing a conversational relationship with God*. Downer's Grove, IL: InterVarsity Press.

2

BEING GOD

I pray—an attempt to talk with God:
"The more I know your creation,
the more I cannot completely know you, God.
How can I, Father?
I see what you've made and reason back to you, Creator,
But the universe looms larger and more complex
As I investigate,
And I tell myself, 'You must be like that.
Inexhaustible.'
Yet I aspire to know You, the Infinite Ineffable.
Perhaps there is a universe in your word.
Perhaps I will find you there if I explore.
Perhaps you might show me then?
What is it like
Being God?"

Philip Schaff documented the development of creeds, statements of belief with regards to various tenets of faith held by the church. He started with one of the earliest, in which the church affirmed, "We believe in one God, the Father Almighty, maker of heaven and earth, of all things visible and invisible, and in one Lord Jesus Christ, the only-begotten Son of God . . ." (Schaff, 1931/1985, p. 27). That was hammered out in opposition to various assertions of thought about the being and nature of Jesus during the first three centuries. One might ask why they bothered with that for over three hundred years, but perhaps it has to do with an observation by Abraham Heschel (1951/1976): "the mind is primarily concerned not with the problems of the nature of man—urgent and important as

Being God **17**

they are—but with God; not with the relation of the world to our categories but with the relation of the world to God" (p. 52).

I was talking with a friend, and we were discussing the contents of chapter one of this book. He asked, "Does the experience of God prove the existence of God?"

I responded, "Does talking with me prove that I exist?"

He went on, "Does the experience of God call God into existence?"

I responded, "Nothing will 'prove' the existence of God. To me, my experience does not determine anything about God or compel Him in any particular direction. Yet, my experience is of interest to Him. So, consistent with His nature, God will intercede in my life. My experience does not call God into existence, but it does call God into action."

Was my friend asking if my experience created God—for me? In other words, was my experience of God simply "my truth" but not *The* Truth?

This question of things existing outside of one conjuring them up, both the visible and the invisible (Merleau-Ponty, 1968), is relevant for therapists who meet with people, real people, but who can still imagine various things about them. In therapy two people interact. There is a back-and-forth, initiative and response. The response of one does not prove the other exists, is actually there, or that his or her issues are as they seem to be. The interaction shows that for one the other is real, but that does not prove that the other actually exists. I once watched a patient carry on a vivid conversation with someone I could not see, who not only was not real for me, but I contend did not objectively exist. Can I prove that that person did not exist? No. For the patient that other person was real and did exist. However, at some point the merely imagined breaks down and lets down. It is a shimmering mirage on a hot highway.

I am assuming that God does exist. There are others who have addressed the question of His existence (Swinburne, 2004; Spitzer, 2010; Nagasawa, 2011; Craig & Moreland, 2012), and I will leave the issue with them. There are also those who don't believe the issue of God's existence, His being, is of a first concern (Marion, 2012).

Does the experience of the client call the therapist into existence? It sounds absurd, doesn't it? But the experience of the client does call forth the therapist's response. It calls him or her into action. And the therapist knows the call of the client *in that response* (Chrétien, 2004).

So, we go back and forth here between the relationship with God and the relationship between gestalt therapists and their clients. Back and forth as well between the call to existence and the call to action. What are the implications if one's experience can call God into action? Does God learn about us in His response to us? Who is sovereign over whom? Can a person catch God unawares? Is God scrambling to keep up with us? Are we, like little children, running God ragged by our adventures and risky behaviors?

In gestalt therapy the patient has an effect on the therapist. Levinas (1999) established the transcendence of the client as one who is ultimately unknowable

18 Being Present

in their transcendence, yet, as one whose personal presence burdens the therapist with the ethical obligation to honor and respect that presence.

Does human existence and presence obligate God to act on our behalf? Is therapy any different from other processes and experiences in life such that it warrants separating it from the general consideration of God's relevance? Is God moved by what transpires between therapists and their clients? What is there about God's nature that might prompt Him to get involved in therapy?

Understanding the narrative of one's ongoing relationship or standing with God depends on understanding some basics regarding the nature of God. Those are only available in revelation, because the gulf between a finite creature and an infinite creator is too great to allow us to plumb, unaided, the depths of God.

Likewise, there is a gulf of transcendence between one human being and another, between a gestalt therapist and his or her client. Neither can read the other's mind. Neither possesses the other's experience and perspective of being in the world. Both must interpret the other.[1] But each must self-disclose, must reveal him- or herself and provide an interpersonal uncovering.

I have compared the inscrutability of God and the need for His self-disclosure to the experience of the dog who watches its master reading. There is no way the dog can grasp what the master is doing. The master's behavior is incomprehensive, impenetrable, inexplicable to the dog. Mystery is the dog's experience.

What is it about God that creates this enigma for us? When it comes to God, mystery is our experience.

To say that God is too big for us is not enough. J.B. Phillips (1952/1997) wrote that most people have too small a concept of God, but that is not quite the issue. There is something about God that creates unsolvable puzzles. How can there be three persons in one God? How can God be good and tell the Jews to wipe out whole villages and people during Old Testament times? How can two natures exist in the one person of Christ? Three persons, one God; two natures, one person. Infinite. Timeless. It swirls around in the mind and never comes to a complete resolution. God told the Israelites not to make any image representative of Him, and the reason was that no image could capture His essence, His nature. Every one of them would be less and so diminish in the minds of people what He is like.

Yet, God can be known. So, we do know some things about God, even if they seem mysterious and even though we have an incomplete knowledge of Him. That is because God wants to be known and has made Himself known. As Martin Buber (1952) put it, God is not indifferent to being known. We can meet Him. He invites us to interact. He says, "Come now, let us reason together . . ."[2]

Attributes

An attribute is a quality, some feature that is inherent and characteristic, an essential property, trait, or aspect of something under consideration. An essential property of water is hydrogen. There are two parts hydrogen and one of oxygen in water. Unlike such finite things as water, God's attributes are not in part, because one of His attributes (infinity) makes all His features without limit. The attributes interact, and, so to speak, the infinity of God expands the other attributes to an infinite degree. God's presence, for instance, "becomes"[3] omnipresence, His power omnipotence, and His knowledge omniscience.

There are many attributes of God that have been discovered by study of the Bible and reflection upon what the Bible says about God. Various theologians have organized them in diverse lists.[4] These are perspectives. In fact, there are many resultant taxonomies that list diverse attributes in overlapping categories. An exhaustive treatment of this subject could take volumes. Therefore, I will describe just a few attributes that especially relate to the use of gestalt therapy. These I am calling the "relational" attributes of God.

The relational attributes of God include those attributes facilitating God's relationship with people. They include elements of what have been called the communicable, transitive, and relative attributes of God. All of God's nature is important to God's relationship with people, but some of his ways are better understood as making contact with God more comprehensible. Put another way, when contact with God occurs, what elements of God's nature facilitate a meaningful contacting?

The Relational Attributes of God

Communicable Attributes of God

These are those attributes of God in which a counterpart in some measure can be found in human beings. God is true and God is truthful. Human beings have a love-hate relationship with the truth, often asking, as Pontius Pilate did, "What is truth?" Regardless, every time someone testifies in a court of law they swear to tell the truth; so, people innately understand the concept. Because God is true and truthful, and because we understand what that means in our own daily lives, we do in fact either trust Him or reject trust in him, and those who trust Him can rely on what He says. The communicable attributes of God create a common capacity and medium through which relationship with God can take place.

Transitive Attributes of God

I previously said that my experience calls God to action. He has mercy on me, because I am pitiful, but He has mercy because He is merciful as a being, not because I control the situation in some way and coerce it from Him. God would be merciful even if there were no transgressors. This aspect of His being emanates from Him to me. That is, His mercy is transitive and comes to rest on me. One way of looking at the being of God, then, is that some of His features are intransitive and some are transitive (Erickson, 1985). The transitive attributes of God create a common experience through which any given person might build a personal ground or history with God.

Relative Attributes of God

These are attributes that are manifest through difference, which is a key element of contact. Gestalt therapists understand contact to *be* the awareness of difference. It is a meeting through which the awareness of difference emerges. It is the realization, "Oh. I am not like that." This is what happens when people contemplate the nature of God. God is not just like people. God is omnipresent. While human beings can manifest presence, it is situational and spatial—limited. We are embodied, but God is spirit. We are here, not everywhere. The relative attributes promote what Rudolph Otto (1923) called the *mysterium tremendum* and the *mysterium fascinans* (respect and fascination, which are both aspects of worship). Worship is an appropriate response to contact with God, a being so far above us that we cannot fully grasp God's self-disclosing contact, a being who seems at once terribly disturbing and irresistibly attractive.

From Contact With God to Contact With Others

Humans are created in the image of God. God's nature, His ontic composition as such, is essentially relational. He is not only the I AM, He is also the triune being—the three-in-one. The very beginning of creation was a relational act. God said, "Let Us make man in Our image, according to Our likeness . . .".[5] Every member of the godhead was active in the creation, and they did it together. Creation is a joint project and the result of a relational purpose held jointly among the three persons of the one God. God created us to be like Him, to be relational. And His purpose was for us to enjoy a relationship with Him. That is also why God created human beings as male and female. The relational aspects of the human nature were hard wired, built in, from the very start. It is not accidental; it is essential.

If we start from the beginning, although God created us with the capacity and for the purpose of relationship with Him, evidently it was not enough. God said it was not "good" for the first human being to be alone. Of course, he was *not* alone. He had God. He had an untarnished, undiminished capacity for direct relationship with God, but God pronounced that situation to be not enough. Without the second human being created, the first was alone, and God said it was not good for that man to be alone. Just as we need contact with God, we also need contact with one another as human beings.

Contact in gestalt therapy is understood to be meetings of various kinds. Contacting is engaging with the world in which we live; it is meeting and connecting with something (Bloom, forthcoming), be that air, ground, food, or another person. For example, we have an Australian shepherd mix who rides in the truck with us. She was right up next to me in the cab, but she was excited with her front feet on the console and her eyes straight ahead, watching the road. When I made a sound like she makes when she whines, she jerked around, put her face close to mine and looked me right in the eyes. Then, not breaking with my own eyes, she cocked her head to one side as if to say, "Huh?!" In my judgement that was contact. We met. Such contact is not like the contact of synchronicity, where one person begins to copy the movements of another, repeating and matching what the other person is doing in simple gestures and body postures but without ever really paying conscious attention to the other. That is contacting, because without meeting, synchronicity could not happen, but it is a contacting that runs "in the back of one's head."

In a previous place I have discussed "touch of another kind," describing what contact with God is like. I claimed there (Brownell, 2016) that the "sense of being connected up to the world through contact, through smell, sight, hearing, and touch for instance, is augmented by the inner impressions of being a body that is alive and situated in that world" (p. 359). The inner sense of balance, for instance, is a proprioceptive and physical phenomenon; there is also a kind of proprioception of the spirit in which people are moved by God's Spirit and experience contact with God. We *can* experience the presence of God. We cannot prove to others it is what it is, and so it is more personal guidance than anything, but our faith in God is not hope against hope in something so ethereally thin as to be without evidence.

Internal Summary

Thus, these kinds of relational attributes make for the possibility that gestalt therapists, in turn, might meet their clients in an intersubjective process, one human being to another (Buber, 1947/2002), just as they make possible contact and relationship with God. We all share in a common humanity, made in the image of God. For gestalt therapists these attributes facilitate contact, a central feature of the relational aspect of gestalt therapy. However, because there is also a decided difference between the nature of God and that of other human beings, contact with God differs from contact with other human beings.

Examples of Relational Attributes

What follows are examples of some relational attributes as they play out in life, both in terms of relationship with God and in relationships between human beings.

God Is Spirit

What is that? God is immaterial. God is not extended nor bounded. By contrast human beings are both material and immaterial, but in our immateriality we share, in limited capacity, at least one aspect of God.

But this does not really show what spirit *is*. It is not physical, but what is it?

In a previous book (Brownell, 2015) I examined the issue of the nature of spirit, looking inductively at how the term is used in three major Abrahamic religions (Judaism, Christianity, and Islam). I concluded that spirit "is a human capacity of emotion and thought that animates the physical body and provides a

22 Being Present

conduit of communication and power between human beings and God" (p. 28). Some people would also call this personhood. It is the inner, immaterial life of a human being, but spirit, thus understood, is also an aspect of the nature of God.[6] Spirit includes thinking, feeling, valuing, purposing. So, both God and people share personhood and our process with God is interpersonal.

Spirit is intentional (Brownell, 2011). That is, there is an aboutness to the spiritual life that extends to the implications and connections between what we focus upon and that to which it is related. So, the Holy Spirit, the One Jesus called the helper who would be with us after Jesus was lifted up to heaven, and who would be in us through indwelling, is the personification of such spirit. When God suggested He would give people the desires of their heart,[7] He was talking about the effect of the indwelling Spirit of God who yearns for the things of God, who desires intimacy with God, and who subordinates to the will of the Father. That is a total package of thinking, feeling, and wanting. When we warm to the Word of God, it is our spirit communing with the Holy Spirit. At such points we are in sympathetic vibration with the being of God. Conversely, when we ignore the still small voice of God, rush past the yearning for God in order to indulge ourselves in some enticing distraction, we darken and diminish our own spiritual experience and limit our spiritual capacity. Our thinking becomes confused. Our emotions become troubled. Our desires are misplaced, and we waste our time here in this world, a world into which Christians have been placed for God's purposes.

Gestalt therapists can tap into the spiritual dimension in their clinical work. Whether a person believes in Jesus or not, assuming Christianity to be true (and this definition of spirituality to be reliable), both client and therapist have been created in the image of God and share a spiritual nature. It's not that there is no spirit in the human being prior to faith in Jesus. It's that the spirit that is there is characterized by blindness but is renewed, redeemed, enlightened, and invigorated through faith in Jesus. It is regenerated. Then it is safeguarded and continuously impacted by the residency and companionship of the Holy Spirit, who is a guarantor of the completed redemption to come.

When therapists of any kind start exploring the thoughts, emotions, purposes, values, and motivations of their clients, and when they experience the impact of the client as those elements resonate or reverberate in their own set of thoughts, emotions and so forth, the therapist and the client are in the realm of the spirit. Theirs becomes a spiritual process.

God Is One, a Whole, and Not the Sum of Parts

This observation is known as the oneness or simplicity of God. This wholeness or oneness is also true of human beings. The persons of the godhead are not components that added together comprise the fullness of God; likewise, the cognitive, emotional, physical, and spiritual aspects of any given human being are not separate from the person who thinks or feels them. Touch one and you touch the whole

Being God **23**

person. Touch my body, and you touch me. Criticize what I think, and you criticize me. Deal with the Holy Spirit, and you deal with God. Contemplate the works of the Son or the words of the Father, and you may experience contact with God.

When gestalt therapists interact with clients, we meet whole people. We do not simply apply leverage to the way a person thinks, as if thought process is the primary consideration. Just so, one cannot take a cognitive approach alone to understanding God. God is a whole Being who defies our logic, meeting us in various ways such as the emotional gush of a worship song, a sunset, the cuddle of a soft cat, or the anguish and suffering of defenseless children. The Spirit of God is present in and with believers, and He is active in the world to convict of the need for change. For example, shortly after coming to faith in Jesus, I felt a physical pain in my throat. I had been smoking a pack of cigarettes a day at that point, and God impressed upon me the need to stop. I experienced contact with God *in the pain*. God is whole as we are whole; therapy of the whole person requires meeting, contacting, and the time doing that resulting in relationship.

God Is Love, Loving

God's love is not exactly like the love that human beings understand. However, we rise to an understanding of God's love by appreciating some of the words in the Bible used to address the subject of love (see Table 2.1). Further, I want to include here the subject of concern. God is concerned with us, and He has

TABLE 2.1 Biblical Words for Love[8]

Word	Definition	Biblical References
agapaō	In classical Greek synonymous with *phileo*, but in the New Testament specifically for a person's love of God, love for other persons, and of God's love for people (GLB; BAG).	Ephesians 5:25 & 28; Romans 8: 35 & 37.
eraō	Longing, craving to take possession, sexual desire (GLB).	Not appearing in the New Testament
phileō	In classical Greek the most general word meaning "to regard with affection"; it includes concern, care, and hospitality (GLB).	
stergō	To feel affection as in the mutual love between parents and children.	Not appearing in the New Testament
'āhēḇ	Affection, both pure and impure, divine and human (BDB); spontaneous force driving one to something or someone over oneself (GLB).	Genesis 22:2, 24:67; Leviticus 19:18; 1 Samuel 18:20;
ḥeseḏ	God's kindness; loving kindness in condescending to the needs of his creatures (BDB); loyal love, grace, enduring self-sacrificial love (GLB)	Genesis 39:21; Deuteronomy 7:9; Psalm 40: 10–11; Hosea 11: 1-4.

24 Being Present

accommodated Himself to our limitations, our developmental capacities, and our sociocultural contexts of life in order to self-disclose Himself to us in ways that we might comprehend.

Concern

God is concerned with us. He is not merely in the world with us, but in and *toward* us. As an example of both His love and His desire for relationship, He has accommodated Himself to us in various means of revelation or self-disclosure.

> *God, after He spoke long ago to the fathers in the prophets in many portions and*
> *in many ways, in these last days has spoken to us in*
> *His Son, whom He appointed heir of all things,*
> *through whom also He made the world.*
> *And He is the radiance of His glory and*
> *the exact representation of His nature.*[9]

How did He do this? Jesus emptied Himself of the prerogatives of divinity and assumed a human nature.

> *Have this attitude in yourselves which was also in Christ Jesus, who,*
> *although He existed in the form of God, did not regard equality with God*
> *a thing to be grasped, but emptied Himself, taking the form of a bond-servant,*
> *and being made in the likeness of men. Being found in appearance as a man,*
> *He humbled Himself by becoming obedient to the point of death,*
> *even death on a cross.*[10]

Hebrews spoke of God's self-disclosure in many ways. God used the Sumerian and Semitic societies and cultures, utilizing their forms (i.e. cutting a covenant with Abram and using the Suzerain-Vassal Treaty format as a template for the giving of the law to Moses). In the Old Testament God talked as if human in order to communicate to humans. "On the one hand, He is utterly other than the stuff of the world or its laws ... at the same time, this being of total nondependence is portrayed in the Bible as having qualities that can only be described as human" (Muffs, 2005, p. 55).

The God portrayed in the Bible is a relational being in His nature and His actions. Although being wholly other, set apart in a class all His own (the definition of holiness), He accommodated Himself to the limits of humankind in order to establish and facilitate relationship with us—to be known by us, because He cares *for* us.

Mercy

This concept takes different nuances moving from the use of *ḥeseḏ* in the Old Testament to the use of *eleos* in the New Testament. The first is influenced by a

Hebrew/Semitic understanding of loyalty among participants to a covenant, in other words commitment. Some writers have used the term "loyal love." The second goes more clearly to the emotional and psychological phenomenon of pity or being moved emotionally at the difficult plight of another. Thus, Jesus, in his sermon on the mount, said, "Blessed are the merciful, for they shall receive mercy" (Matthew 5:7), and later He referred back to 1 Samuel 15:22 and Hosea 6:6 to assert that God does not require religious sacrifice but compassion on those who fail to measure up. If you put the two together you have a basis for forgiveness. God is merciful, committed to his promises and assertions toward people, and graciously forgiving.

> *God, being rich in mercy,*
> *because of His great love with which He loved us,*
> *even when we were dead in our transgressions,*
> *made us alive together with Christ*
>   *(by grace you have been saved)* ...[11]

Conclusion

There is no other being like God. Why He would be concerned with human beings is amazing and lost to us. We cannot comprehend it outside an earnest searching of the nature of God. Because God desires us, wants relationship with us, and is utterly committed to developing that relationship we know what we know about Him and even about ourselves. Gestalt therapists, who are especially concerned with the relational aspects of our approach to psychotherapy, can find a solid spiritual rationale for doing what we do, and they can find it in the being of God.

Notes

1. This relates to the subject of hermeneutics, which is not only about the interpretation of sacred texts but also the interpretation of experience (cf. Brownell, 2018; Zimmerman, 2015; Porter & Robinson, 2011).
2. Isaiah 1:18.
3. It is not that God's nature or character "becomes" in the sense that it was lacking or that it was one thing and then changed and became something else. This is a manner of speaking to communicate the effect of one attribute on another. They are mutually influential. Or, as a gestalt therapist might say, they are parts of a whole that is simply larger than the sum of those parts.
4. See for instance Strong (1907/1976), Charnock (1797/1977), Feinberg (2006), Erickson (1985), and Horton (2011).
5. Genesis 1:26.
6. Most people view contact with God to be surpassing the mundane. The experience of the numinous, resulting in fear and attraction, is regarded to be transcendent. The issue of God's immanence and transcendence, though, can be found in chapter six.
7. Psalm 37:4.

26 Being Present

8. Table constructed by referring to Günther, Link, and Brown (GLB) (1976), Bauer, Arndt, and Gingrich (BAG) (1957/1975), and Brown, Driver, and Briggs (BDB) (1907/1978).
9. Hebrews 1:1–3a.
10. Philippians 2:5–8.
11. Ephesians 2:4, 5.

References

Bauer, W., Arndt, W., & Gingrich, F. W. (1957/1975). *A Greek-English lexicon of the new testament and other early Christian literature*. Chicago, IL: The University of Chicago Press.

Brown, F., Driver, S. R., & Briggs, C. (1907/1978). *A Hebrew and English lexicon of the Old Testament*. Oxford, UK: Clarendon Press.

Brownell, P. (2011). Intentional spirituality. In D. Bloom & P. Brownell (Eds.), *Continuity and change: Gestalt therapy now* (pp. 236–260). Newcastle upon Tyne, UK: Cambridge Scholars Publishing.

Brownell, P. (2015). *Spiritual competency in psychotherapy*. New York, NY: Springer Publishing.

Brownell, P. (2016). Touch of another kind: Contact with God and spiritual self. In J.-M. Robine (Ed.), *Self: A polyphony of contemporary gestalt therapists* (pp. 351–370). Bordeaux, France: L'exprimerie.

Brownell, P. (2018). Hermeneutic coaching. In S. English, J. Sabatine, & P. Brownell (Eds.), *Professional coaching: Principles and practice* (pp. 175–184). New York, NY: Springer Publishing.

Buber, M. (1947/2002). *Between man and man*. New York, NY: Routledge.

Buber, M. (1952). *Eclipse of God: Studies in the relation between religion and philosophy*. Amherst, NY: Humanity Books.

Charnock, S. (1797/1977). *The existence and attributes of God*. Minneapolis, MN: Klock & Klock Christian Publishers.

Chrétien, J.-L. (2004). *The call and the response*. New York, NY: Fordham University Press.

Craig, W. L., & Moreland, J. P. (2012). *The Blackwell companion to natural theology*. Oxford, UK: Blackwell Publishing Ltd, John Wiley & Sons, Ltd.

Erickson, M. (1985). *Christian theology*. Grand Rapids, MI: Baker Book House.

Feinberg, J. (2006). *No one like him: The doctrine of God*. Wheaton, IL: Crossway.

Günther, W., Link, H.-G., & Brown, C. (1976). Love. In C. Brown (Ed.), *The new international dictionary of New Testament theology* (Vol. 2, pp. 538–551). Grand Rapids, MI: Zondervan.

Heschel, A. (1951/1976). *Man is not alone: A philosophy of religion*. New York, NY: Farrar, Straus & Giroux.

Horton, M. (2011). *The Christian faith: A systematic theology for pilgrims on the way*. Grand Rapids, MI: Zondervan, Harper Collins Publishing.

Levinas, E. (1999). *Alterity and transcendence*. New York, NY: Columbia University Press.

Marion, J.-L. (2012). *God without being*. Chicago, IL: University of Chicago Press.

Merleau-Ponty, M. (1968). *The visible and the invisible*. Evanston, IL: Northwestern University Press.

Muffs, Y. (2005). *The personhood of God: Biblical theology, human faith, and the divine image*. Woodstock, VT: Jewish Lights Publishing.

Nagasawa, Y. (2011). *The existence of God: A philosophical introduction*. New York, NY: Routledge, Taylor & Francis Group.

Otto, R. (1923). *The idea of the holy*. Oxford, UK: Oxford University Press.

Phillips, J. B. (1952/1998). *Your God is too small*. New York, NY: Touchstone.

Porter, S., & Robinson, J. (2011). *Hermeneutics: An introduction to interpretive theory*. Grand Rapids, MI: William B. Eerdmans Publishing Company.

Schaff, P. (1931/1985). *The History of Creeds: Vol. 1. The creeds of Christendom with a history and critical notes* (Vols. 3). Grand Rapids, MI: Baker Book House.

Spitzer, J. (2010). *New proofs for the existence of God: Contributions of contemporary physics and philosophy*. Grand Rapids, MI: Eerdmans Publishing Co.

Strong, A. H. (1907/1976). *Systematic theology*. Valley Forge, PA: Judson Press.

Swinburne, R. (2004). *The existence of God* (2nd ed.). Oxford, UK: Clarendon Press, Oxford University Press.

Zimmermann, J. (2015). *Hermeneutics: A very short introduction (very short introductions)*. Oxford, UK: Oxford University Press.

3

BEING PRESENT IN THERAPY

Present to One and then to others
Here and with.
First to one and then another
Then and since.
One whose presence rends and shatters
Now and hence.
Here and all within my matters
Times commence.

Many people, at some point in their lives, have been in a room with a number of people when a person showed up with a clipboard and yelled, "Sing out when I call your name." Then he or she started calling names and people responded "Here," or "Present." I contend that while all the people responding may have been there, not all of them were present.

Have you ever tried to communicate with someone whom you realized suddenly was staring off over your shoulder at nothing in particular, and you stopped to ask them, "Are you with me?" Such a question is appropriate because although there in body, they were not tracking you, not actually *with* you.

Presence as a term refers to the experience of being situated, forming and satisfying figures of interest that arise from the process of contacting, not only existing physically in an environment, but also aware that one's experience is one's possession and that it matters. Being involved—living—is not simply taking in and breathing out air, but also attending to what matters, what is interesting, what is needed, what one wants or does not want. Presence is a grounded, tangible sense of being there. According to Greenberg and Geller (2012), "Therapists claimed that when in presence, they are intensely focused, aware, and alert in their

Being Present in Therapy **29**

involvement with the client and the therapy session" (p. 119). Silsbe claimed that "Being present is observing the self, others, and the context as if from a balcony perspective, and having full awareness in the moment, rather than thinking about the future or rehashing the past" (2019, p. 120).

I believe what these people have been doing is describing mindfulness and then applying that to the relationship (therapeutic and coaching). Awareness in gestalt therapy, however, is not simply mindfulness. It's not watching oneself, the client, and the context as if from a balcony overlooking these things. It is, after all, being *there . . . being* there—not somewhere else looking in that direction. So, with all I am at a given moment, I am *there*. Awareness surely plays a part but there has to be an awareness of something and if presence is all about a *person's* presence, then I think the starting point must be the sense of embodiment and situation.

The person desiring to intensify presence must do something with regard to his or her embodiment in the given situation. Relatedly, Dorothy Siminovitch (2019) contrasted presence with use of self. My paraphrase of what she said is that presence is being while use of self is doing. Presence is being there, situated as a being, but use of self, use of one's presence, is a purposeful action. It is doing. What we evoke in others is "an interior response to our being, our presence" while what we provoke or influence by what we do—"that impact is the result of our use of self" (p. 139).

Accordingly, I believe presence, or use of self, is basic. I have called presence the first experiment; the therapist enters the crucible of the therapy session and opens up to what may emerge, something that cannot be scheduled or manufactured, but something that can be experienced. Presence must be what gestalt therapy describes as healthy functioning—the fluid identification and satisfaction of figures of interest. Presence is contacting. Presence must also include intentionality—the aboutness of experience, including intentional objects and their natural associations, often found in abiding life themes (so also personality function). It must be whole-self kind of phenomena—that is, including id, ego, and personality function. It must approximate who a person is. One must show up, be there: Identity "is a construct we build to make ourselves feel at ease and at peace and reasonably stable in the world. But *being* is not a construct. Being is just being. In being, there's a whole variety of wild and untamed things that remain in us" (Springsteen, 2018).

Being present leads to unpredictable consequences. Being present to God, for instance, can lead to awakening, what some call revival. When I was on staff at a large, multi-staffed church in Sacramento, California people frequently said that we needed to pray for revival. One day our Senior Pastor, Lee Toms, said, "I don't know if you want revival. Revival is messy." He meant that it is unpredictable and uncontrollable. In the same way that the presence of God exceeds our expectations and is unpredictable and uncontrollable, being present to other human beings often causes a stir.

Presence Is Fluid, Not Static

To be fully present means to focus the attention on the other person, on oneself, and on the ongoing process that is emerging in the moment. "This focusing of attention on multiple aspects of experience involves multileveled cognitive, emotional and somatic awareness . . ." (Atkins, 2014, p. 70). Lynne Jacobs describes presence as an attitude that "induces one to include the otherness of the other as fully as possible while being present to the other—a kind of porous, vulnerable nakedness" (2018, p. 37). It is intentional, personal, dialogical, and field dynamic.

Presence Is Manifest in the Middle Voice

One's presence is something he or she makes evident; a person presents him or herself. As such it is not something that happens to them. It is not passive. They offer themselves as phenomena, an appearing, for others. So, the person does appear, and they are not a phantom. They are actual and not simply real. You can see them, hear them, touch them, or taste them (not all of which would be appropriate in therapy). They are within one's grasp. You can affect them and be affected by them; so, in good therapy clients do, in fact, affect their therapists, and, of course, the therapist affects his or her clients.

All of this activity is conducted in the middle voice of intentionality. Intentionality is the phenomenological construct associated with figures of interest. As I said, it is the aboutness of experience and its associated concerns and issues (Brownell, 2010). The middle voice can be understood as active process that comes with clear and prominent self-interest. I hit the ball *for* myself. I don't just hit the ball myself; I hit the ball in some way because I am interested, invested, organized around hitting the ball.

The therapist grounds him or herself in the moment, the place, and the sense of what is emerging by intensifying personal observation and permitting unbridled interest and curiosity, which are inherent to dialogical inquiry. This is not merely a reflexive process, as in types of mirroring.

Presence is like a creature that prowls with excitement and stalks its prey with enthusiasm. But presence is not just the pounce; it can also be the pause. And sometimes it's the pity.

The therapist exceeds the obvious and the immediately familiar to wait on the situational moment, that is, the impact of atmosphere (see chapter eight) and emergent field effects. It is the sense that "something" is "going on here" that one cannot fully figure out, but that it has captured one's attention and imagination. The therapist self discloses his or her own place, their *sense* of place and their experience of the moment in a paradoxical move of revelation that tethers the therapist's being to a concrete time in space where phenomena can be shared among persons.

Presence lives.

Presence Is Personal

Presence must be *of the person*. A person is a thinking, feeling, choosing being. A subjective being. A person is an embodied and situated being—situated in geographical, political, socio-cultural contexts that influence his or her understanding and values.

The philosophical consideration of personhood exceeds the scope of this chapter; however, let me assert that there is a difference between knowing facts about a person and having first-hand experience of that person. Surely, the facts, if they are facts, come along and adhere to one's sense of the person, but being in the presence of the person him or herself far exceeds knowing things about that person.

That is why therapists need to do more than gather "data" when they are doing diagnostic interviews; one cannot get a sense of the person by writing down the demographics, the history of their previous treatments, or what medications they take. If they are living, one contacts their person and then constructs a sense of their personhood. It's more an impression of the other than it is a "history" of the other.

An impression can be an idea or feeling that emerges apart from conscious effort, and it can be the mark left on a surface when something is pressed into it. A signature ring leaves an impression when pressed into warm wax. Just so, contact leaves a mark on people. Punch someone in the arm and it will likely leave a bruise; come to another person with great presence and it is likely to affect, or impress. This does not mean to necessarily make others think well but simply to affect, to leave one's mark on others.

In personal presence, when it is experienced, facts about the person recede. They are not figural. Rather, it is the person him or herself that looms large. Consequently, personal presence communicates a quality of personhood that lends itself to impressions. Is the person in whose presence I am an assertive, imposing person or a retiring, self-effacing person? That is illustrating with a simple polarity, but it shows that presence lends itself to an impression of the person, and then to a knowledge of their personhood.

Presence Is Dialogical

The process of presenting oneself to another is dialogical in nature although often it is non-verbally so. Thus, presence does not necessarily indicate a running verbal self-disclosure of every current awareness or sensory experience. It's not just revealing one's id function in an indiscriminate manner. It's not simply "emoting" in the presence of the client. It is certainly not a ritualized performance for the sake of the client in order to elicit an emotional response. That would be making the other into an object to be changed. Dialogue is an exchange at the contact boundary and an offering, a self-sacrifice of one's vulnerability. There cannot be

32 Being Present

an intimate exchange in dialogue when someone is hiding from or using the other.

Presence Is Field Dynamic

Presence in terms of field dynamics leads to a consideration of influence. Change something in a field, and it nudges everything else into a new organization of that field. Perhaps another way of thinking about this is to realize that fields are in constant flux. Everything is always changing. So, the issue is how such change occurs, and one way that interpersonal fields change is through contact, which cannot occur apart from presence.

That is speaking from a strategic perspective about how to affect change in a field. There is another perspective, and that is how the field affects or impresses any given person who is "of the field." In speaking about atmospheres, for instance, Tonino Griffero (2017) asserted that atmospheres have a presence. "As an influential 'presence'—inextricably linked to felt-bodily processes and characterized by a qualitative microgranularity that is inaccessible to a naturalistic-epistemic perspective—an atmosphere is, in short, more a 'spatial' state of the world than a very private psychic state" (n.p., Kindle edition). Schmitz, Müllan, and Slaby (2011) described this process as the world showing up "not as a neutral realm of already separate entities but as the atmospheric fields of significant situations, opportunities or quasi-corporeal forces or 'opponents' that in the first instance become manifest to the conscious person in form of the 'internally diffuse meaningfulness' of holistic corporeal impressions" (p. 244).

Atmospheres are concerned with the pathic and aesthetic quality of any given space that impresses itself on those who enter into it. The pathic (from *pathos*) refers to what we feel immediately and passively. "We are seized by the pathic; we do not choose it, we are moved by it. . . . The pathic dimension . . . is situated at the root of the emerging of the subject, when the subject has yet to be formed, moving it by calling it to respond, incessantly" (Francesetti, forthcoming). This is what Chrétien was describing in his development of call-and-response. We can only know the call, the pathic, in our response to it, after the sense of self has fully emerged from the pre-reflective call itself and can reflect upon it.

As such, an atmosphere is a quasi-thing or half-entity such as wind, the emotional quality in a human voice, musical melodies, gravity, and weather fronts. As quasi-things emotions can fill lived, public space. This is different from the perspective that people project upon their surroundings, constructing an associational strata to the spaces they inhabit.

The word *atmosphere* comes from the Greek roots *atmos*, meaning "vapor" or "steam," and *spharia*, meaning "sphere." "The Greek *atmos* derives from the proto Indo-European *awet-mo-*, from base *wet*—'to blow, inspire, spiritually arouse.' In everyday language, the word atmosphere is used interchangeably with mood, feeling, ambience, tone and other ways of naming collective affects" (Costa,

Carmenates, Madeira, & Stanghellini, 2014, p. 352). Costa and his colleagues used it to refer to the "elusive and almost indefinable 'air' that imbues and envelops a given situation and participates in the global awareness of that situation."

Put that together with the derivation of the word "spirit" (*pneuma*) out of the Greek (which means "breath" or "wind") and these are concepts that are cousins. An atmosphere is, in classical understanding, a spiritual concept, a spiritual manifestation. It's part of the pre-modern worldview and central to the re-enchantment of many fields currently underway (outside of religion, by the way) in a rejection of modernism/enlightenment and related principles.

How atmospheres form is beyond the limits of this chapter, but the reader can pursue the subject through Griffero, Schmitz, Costa, and others.

Reflections on Presence in Clinical Practice and Training

Therapists are supposed to know themselves. Just as a musician learns his or her instrument, the therapist's "instrument" is his or her own self, and they need to learn to "play" it. They need to know the effect of various kinds of clinical phenomena on their experience of self in order to use their subjective experience as a clue to the clinical process under way at any given point between themselves and their clients.

I have learned that in listening to people in therapy if I perceive very common meandering or what seems to be a seeking of secondary gain, such as not being serious about the therapy but wanting me to supply notes and so forth that might support a seeking of disability, then I tend to drift and fall asleep. While the patient is droning on, I am going away, getting away from it as best I can. Since I can't simply get up and walk out of the room, I reduce my presence in another way. This is not a conscious choice; it's something that overtakes me. And there certainly emerges a circularity to it. As my presence becomes smaller, it evokes an absence in the client, and then the client feels lost or perhaps alone, which increases the meandering, which tends to magnify the pointlessness of the process.

I used to try to fight it as soon as I noticed my drowsiness or my daydreaming. However, then I was present to myself, preoccupied with my professional responsibility to *listen* when I could not stand what the patient was doing. Then I was still not present to the patient; I was struggling with my own dilemma, trying to trick or force myself to be alert. But I was not present *to* the patient. The intentionality of my presence was directed inward. The solution was to redirect it outward, toward the patient and to deal openly with what it was like for me to be with them while they were doing what they were doing.

In such a situation, does one say, "You are boring me"? Rather than that I turn up the brightness of my curiosity and the intensity of my observation.

"I notice that as you talk to me it comes in a monotone that lacks much energy." Or, "What do you really want me to do about this?"

34 Being Present

Sometimes I bring myself into this newly directed light by self-disclosing, but self-disclosing that links my observations of the client with my experience of self. "As you talk, I am wondering what you really want. What are you hoping to get out of coming here?" I try to be direct.

When I am doing therapy, I am often seeing one client after another. The atmosphere can become stale and claustrophobic as I sit in the same room and just switch out people. I have to purposefully do something to interrupt the sense of an endless parade. Each person is actually different; so, I need to allow that difference to fill the space. Such a thing does not happen by quickly jumping into the treatment plan and asking about the goals we discussed last week. I have to let the room come to me, the new room that is new because there is a new inhabitant there, and I have to let that new person and the new atmosphere envelop me.

Essentially, I have to pay attention and point my awareness not only to the client, but also to the event. I have to allow my curiosity and senses to lead me. I have to be consciously invested. I have to practice living in that moment with that other person in that specific place.

Present to One and Then to Others

The room was a large amphitheater, with theater-type seating. There was a sound mixer board in the far back and the trainees gathered here and there in the seats all over. Most chose to be down front and not far from the stage.

The stage was elevated. It had hardwood flooring and a rounded face. There was a podium to one side, but we sat in chairs toward the center. I sat next to someone who interpreted what the trainee said, translating from Korean into English. Across from me, next to the trainee, sat the son of the professor who had organized our conference. He translated from English into Korean for the trainee, a young woman who was in training for gestalt therapy and who had volunteered to work with me as a demonstration for others to observe. There were about 200 people watching.

The son of the professor was a young man in his late twenties who was, himself, enrolled in a graduate program of clinical psychology in the United States. He happened to be home and available for the conference. He volunteered to translate. He knew something of American culture. He seemed relaxed, being familiar with his father's work and being a doctoral student. I felt drawn to him. I was dependent on him to communicate my expressions to the trainee. I was oriented toward him as of first recourse when I spoke to the trainee. I tried to keep my eye contact with her, but I was keenly aware of my translator.

I spoke noticing both the trainee and the translator. I watched the trainee listen to words of a different language, and I watched as recognition lit up her face as the translator spoke. I watched the translator listen to what I said, and I wondered how my words and thoughts were being put into a different language. At first, I spoke naturally, as if I were simply talking to another person without any need of translation, and I noticed that the translator was spending a long time giving the translation. So, I adjusted. I began to speak in shorter segments, and I noticed that he did not take as long to give the translation. He also appeared less stressed. When I made the first shorter statement, the translator waited as if he expected me to say more, so I gestured for him to go ahead and translate. He did. Then I continued my thought in the next shorter phrase and gestured with it. He translated. We were watching each other intently. I noticed that there was an "echo" in the whole room as well in that often the 200 people watching would respond with a laugh or a sigh or some kind of movement that told me they were tracking, but they did that in response to the translator and not to me as of first order. It was a once-removed, delayed reaction to me that became part of the rhythm of our interaction. I timed myself to it. I began to feel it as if it were a natural part of me.

That process became interesting, and I noticed that when a new trainee volunteered to work, and someone else took the translating role from the son of the professor, it wasn't the same. The other person had their own pace and manner of interacting with me while translating. It felt awkward, because I had become accustomed to the other person. I am sure that what I evoked in others was my sense of uneasiness. The work became more difficult. I began trying harder, and the work became less satisfying. As soon as the son of the professor returned to translating following a break and with a new trainee I felt much better, more at ease, and the work felt more fluid.

It would have been a mistake, I believe, to have attributed the uneasiness of the second demonstration to the trainee. I also believe it would have been a mistake to have blamed the translator. I was the same person. The room was the same room. The general situation was the same. The only variables that were different were the trainee and the translator. Rather, what makes most sense to me is to admit the influence of my own presence and use of self.

References

Atkins, S. (2014). The courage to meet the other: Personal presence in the helping relationship. In H. Eberhart, S. Atkins, & P. Knill (Eds.), *Presence and process in expressive arts work* (pp. 59–84). Philadelphia, PA: Jessica Kingsley Publishers

Brownell, P. (2010). Intentional spirituality. In J. H. Ellens (Ed.), *The healing power of spirituality: How faith helps humans thrive* (pp. 19–40). Santa Barbara, CA: ABC-CLIO.

Costa, C., Carmenates, S., Madeira, L., & Stanghellini, G. (2014). Phenomenology of atmospheres. The felt meanings of clinical encounters. *Journal of Psychopathology, 20*, 351–357.

Francesetti, G. (forthcoming). Neither inside, nor outside. In G. Francesetti & T. Griffero (Eds.), *Psychopathology and atmospheres* (n.p.). Newcastle Upon Tyne, UK: Cambridge Scholars Publishing.

Greenberg, L., & Geller, S. (2012). *Therapeutic presence: A mindful approach to effective therapy.* Washington, DC: American Psychological Association.

Griffero, T. (2017). *Quasi-things: The paradigm of atmospheres.* Albany, NY: State University of New York Press.

36 Being Present

Jacobs, L. (2018). Comment to my other's keeper: Resources for the ethical turn in psychotherapy by D. M. Orange. In M. Spagnuolo Lobb, D. Bloom, J. Roubal, J. Zeleskov Djoric, M. Cannavò, R. La Rosa, . . . V. Pinna (Eds.), *The aesthetic of otherness: Meeting at the boundary in a desensitized world, proceedings* (pp. 37–39). Siracusa, Italy: Istituto di Gestalt HCC Italy Publ. Co.

Schmitz, H., Müllan, R. O., & Slaby, J. (2011). Emotions outside the box—The new phenomenology of feeling and corporeality. *Phenomenology and the Cognitive Sciences, 10*, 241–259. doi:10.1007/s11097-011-9195-1

Silsbe, D. (2019) Coaching as a coaching meta-competency. In S. English, J. Sabatine, & P. Brownell (Eds.) *Professional coaching: Principles and practices* (pp. 119–133). New York, NY: Springer Publishing.

Siminovitch, D. (2019). The coach as awareness agent: A process approach. In S. English, J. Sabatine, & P. Brownell (Eds.), *Professional coaching: Principles and practices* (pp. 135–147). New York, NY: Springer Publishing.

Springsteen, B. (2018, November 27). "Beneath the surface of Bruce Springsteen," an interview with Michael Hainey. *Esquire.* Retrieved November 28, 2018, from www.esquire.com/entertainment/a25133821/bruce-springsteen-interview-netflix-broadway-2018/

4

A CRITICAL REALIST PERSPECTIVE ON PRESENCE

Is air real?
We can't see it, taste it, or touch it.
If you smell it,
You're not smelling air
But
What's in it.
So, is air itself real?

Four Takes on Realism

This chapter could easily spin on the subjects of ontology and epistemology. Indeed, it will touch these subjects, but it won't come close to exhausting them. Rather, the goal here is to point out some general perspectives with regards to the trustworthiness of religious belief, because the same perspectives arise in working with people in therapy. There are, for instance, faith commitments among gestalt therapists regarding the nature, the reality, the process of people meeting in a therapeutic relationship.

For this section I am in debt to Andrew Collier (2004) and others.

Non-Realist View of Belief

This is the view that the stories in the Bible, for instance, are stories, and that is their main value. It does not matter if any of the people in those stories actually existed. What matters are the values and principles taught in those stories. The same is true for the stories one's clients tell.

38 Being Present

The problem here, though, is that one cannot trust nor love—one cannot have a relationship with—a fictional character out of a story in the Bible. And the answer to the question of "What is going on here?" with one's client surely depends on questions of reality. What, for instance, do I (as therapist), believe my client's diagnosis to be? Does such a "thing" (insert process) actually exist? How can I talk about it, if there is no truth to be had, and what are my reasons for believing that that is the nature of my client's presentation? Can I believe what my client tells me? Can I believe the pastor of my church when he makes claims about God? If all that matters is the telling and what it means to me in the hearing, then I think we lose something important and find ourselves adrift.

Realism Without Rational Judgment Between Beliefs

Realism, a broad category of which there are several types, simply refers to the belief in a reality of something, "an existence that does not depend on minds, human or otherwise" (Chakravartty, 2007, n.p.). When that says "reality," I take it to mean actuality, and not simply a relative truth that can be real for one person but not for another. That is what is meant by the qualifier in Chakravartty's statement that it does not depend on minds. It's not dependent on a perspective, a "take" on a given situation that is socially constructed.

The realist perspective touches ontology, semantics, epistemology, and rational judgment—the evaluation of arguments and evidence. It asserts an existence outside what anybody believes or thinks about it. Claims can be made about this existence that have truth values. That which cannot be observed can also be described in the language of truth values, and it is possible to build knowledge about this existence through investigation.

Having a belief about reality but not having much of a reason for believing such a thing, however, would be realism without rational judgment. A person could say, "I believe that unicorns once roamed the prairies of North America," but when pressed for what makes them believe that, they could not come up with any evidence, no arguments offered by others, etc. They could just believe it. The converse would be if a fossil of a unicorn had been found, then they could point to support for their belief. Realism *with* rational judgment allows for the discussion of supports and evidences and arguments back and forth over the issue of the existence of any given "thing." In realism with rational judgment there can be debate, but in realism without rational judgement there can be none.

Non-Critical Relativism

Non-critical realism borders on delusion or prejudice, but non-critical relativism privileges one's beliefs as being untouchable. One does not question one's relativism, simply assuming what is believed. One does not even suspect that something resides in the subtle sub-strata of one's belief system. In that sense the belief is not subject to rational judgment.

A Critical Realist Perspective on Presence **39**

One form of non-critical relativism could be called "perspectivalism," or as some of my colleagues call it, "perspectival realism" (just to make things all the more convoluted). What is meant here relates to truth statements in which truth is relative to the person's point of view, the way they see or experience the world and specifically the situation in which they find themselves. You know this form of relativism when you hear people say something like, "Well, that's the way you see it; you're entitled to your opinion."

Here is an actual example. I see the basic anthropology in gestalt therapy, extrapolating from the relationship between organism and environment that is described in Perls, Hefferline, and Goodman (1951) (PHG) to be caught by the term "organism-environment." My friend, Dan Bloom, sees it as "organism/environment." The first captures the idea that the entity in question is an organism-environment kind of organism. When put in terms of a human being, it refers to the fact that any human being is ontologically of the environment in which he or she lives. You cannot separate organism from environment and still have a living human being. The nature of that human being is a hyphenated nature. Dan, however, sees the construction to be referring to the contact boundary and the actions that take place at it. He does not see organism/environment to be referring to the type of being, the anthropology, but to the nature of the contact boundary, that it's a "place" where organism meets environment. My truth is as good as his truth, but they are different. Is PHG talking about the nature of the human-field or the contacting of the human being in his or her field? Is the human being *of* the field? Is that it's nature, or does that term refer to the interactions in that field? There are two perspectives; there are two ways of knowing. So it is with many things in human experience where people do not inhabit the same physical space and understand events and processes diversely. Some things are true for one person, but not for another.[1]

Do terms refer to what is ontologically real or simply epistemologically relative? Because they are perspectival, they are protected from rational judgment with respect to ontological truth claims.[2]

Another form of non-critical relativism is similar. This is where people bracket subjects, categories, terms, and so forth with quotation marks. An example is so-called "white privilege." Does that actually exist? Or is it simply "so-called"? Putting brackets around it sidesteps a discussion of actuality and makes the term a subject for discussion, even while privileging its existence—as if to say, "For the sake of discussion, let's assume . . ." Indeed. The item in brackets is assumed with regard to ontological realism. But it is relative to the discussion and otherwise unassailable.

Relativism is often presented as "respecting people's freedom, but what it actually is, is treating that freedom as a matter of arbitrary taste rather than rational deliberation which requires grounds for deliberation" (Collier, 2004, p. 44).

Another form of relativism is called epistemological relativism. This is the recognition that any body of thought, any collection of theories, any belief system is bound to include a measure of error, or false beliefs. With regards to Christian

40 Being Present

theology, for instance, I am an epistemological relativist. How do I know that my theology is flawed at some points? I know that because I know that *I* am flawed (at many points). I am not omniscient. I do not know all things. I do not know with the same infinite capacity that God does. I am bound to be wrong somewhere, at some point, with some conclusion and even with elements of theology that I believe whole-heartedly. Does this mean that I am skeptical with regards to what people can know, with regards to what I can know from my study of the scriptures? No. It means that my ontology is tempered by my rational judgment and that of others. Of such an understanding, it's a reflection on "the products of our inquiry into 'reality,' so that our assertions about 'reality' acknowledge our own provisionality" (Porter & Pitts, 2015, p. 2).

Critical Realism

In my writing and teaching on the subject of research in psychotherapy, I have referred to the concept that a philosophy of science in psychology is comprised of a three-legged stool (Machado, 2007): systematic observation, mathematical analysis, and critical thought. Just so, my understanding of critical realism is that it is comprised of ontological realism, epistemological relativism, and rational judgmentalism.

N.T. Wright describes this approach as an attitude acknowledging "the reality of the thing known, as something other than the knower (hence 'realism'), while also fully acknowledging that the only access we have to this reality lies along the spiraling path of appropriate dialogue or conversation between the knower and the thing known (hence 'critical')" (p. 35).

The Big "So What?"

If you are a theologian or a philosopher, then discussions of ontology, what does and does not exist, are certainly relevant. If you are a psychotherapist, ontology has not been so interesting. More to the issue for gestalt therapists is the way clients make sense from experience and the fixed structures of their commitments, that is the foundational beliefs they have about themselves, others, and the way things work for them in the world. So, gestalt therapists usually will admit to there being a world that exists outside of the ways in which we think about it, but they often say that we can't get to it as it is. So, they leave questions of ontology behind and focus on the relative phenomenalities they encounter when they work with clients. The world exists; so what?

Whether or not the world exists outside of what I think about it could be seen as an academic question. Whether or not my client exists outside of what I think about them is a very practical question. The implications reinforce, for instance, Levinas's concept of alterity. The alterity is actual, because the other person really exists. And they do so on their own merits. They transcend one's relative ways of

A Critical Realist Perspective on Presence **41**

knowing (epistemological relativism). I can sit there with them rehearsing various theories about how therapist and client navigate contact, and I can remind myself of the atmosphere and that we both belong to a field, and I can recall how Husserl and Heidegger wrote about phenomenology, and so on. I can try to understand the client through some kind of reduction, applying a philosophical method to a clinical process, but in the end, if I do not meet that other person on his or her own terms in a simple dialogue, I'm missing a great deal. Dialogue in gestalt therapy cannot take place if there is not an actual other. Such a thing would not be dialogue. It would be monologue.

Beyond that resides the question, "What is going on here?" This has to do with case conceptualization. Consider the following examples:

1. John is 55 years old, and he's been drinking. He drops by your office unannounced. He is intoxicated. He has mentioned a few times that he likes to frequent a local bar where he meets his friends. He says he lost his job, because he blew up at the boss, and nobody can help. His wife walked out when she learned it, saying, "That's it. I can't live like this. I'm outta here. You finally killed it. Our marriage is over." You know that he struggles with depression. You know he's been suicidal in the past and that he's had a plan to hang himself. The depression is what he's been seeing you for. You ask, "Are you suicidal?" He stops for a moment. He looks your way. He says, "I don't know what I came here for. You can't change things. You can't change the scumbag I am." You say, "Have you been thinking about killing yourself?" He mimics you, "Have you been thinking. . .' bout killing yourself?" Then he says, "Do you think I'd tell you?"

    a. Question: Is he seriously thinking of killing himself or is this a drunk talking; is there a difference? What is going on here?
    b. Question: Does he want to talk with you about "the scumbag" he thinks he is, or does he want you to stop him from killing himself?
    c. Question: Is he an alcoholic? Did you miss that?
    d. Question: How should you document this encounter, and are there any amendments to the treatment program that are necessary?

2. It is the third session with Mr. Oswald. He enters and sits in the farthest corner of the room in a chair you put in the room mostly for decoration. You feel irritated. He always sits there. You purposefully created a little nook at the other end of the room where you can sit more intimately with your clients. It's more well-lit from light streaming through the window, and it's especially warming on this bright autumn day. You keep the blinds open to let that light in. You keep the pillows fluffy in the nook, but it's darker where Mr. Oswald chooses to sit. Once again he looks irritated. You smile in his direction and say, "Welcome," but you realize you don't really feel welcoming. Immediately you wonder how that distancing takes place. You realize it seems like a fixture

42 Being Present

of Mr. Oswald's presence, at least it's a feature of the way you two seem to be getting along. It is difficult to be with him. You wonder if this is what he experiences with other people, and you say, "Why don't you come over here closer and sit with me by the window," but he says, "No thanks." Then there is silence. You hear the clock ticking. Mr. Oswald shifts in his seat. You hear the wind rustling the leaves on the trees just left of the window. You finally make an observation. You say, "Mr. Oswald . . ." He preferred you address him that way rather than call him by his first name, Jerrold. You say, "Mr. Oswald, you told me that you have a hard time making friends, and I notice that you keep a distance from me right here." That is when Mr. Oswald rolls his eyes, grimaces, and then gets up and walks out. Stunned, you watch the door close behind him, and you sit back in the chair and let the fluffy pillow and the warm light soften the rejection. After a few moments your receptionist opens the door, and she is obviously annoyed. She says, "Pardon me. That man is the most irritating person. The first time he came he didn't have his insurance card with him, and I told him he should have come prepared, because after all it's a doctor's office. He came early and I told him he'd have to wait. The second time he came it was raining and he was all wet and he just sat with his wet coat on the couches. I told him right away to get up and take his coat off. I told him to hang it up and let it drip over the air vent in the floor. And today of all things. He asked me to shut the blinds on the windows because he's very sensitive to sun light. Well, I shut them but what an inconvenience!"

a. Question: Was the pattern developing between you and Mr. Oswald a function of what was going on inside your office or outside of it?

b. Question: Did Mr. Oswald sit in the shadows at a distance because he did not feel comfortable with you as his therapist or because the nook was too well lit?

c. Question: Why did he get up and leave, ending the therapy before it could really get much off the ground?

d. Pick one of the following that best accounts for what is going on in this situation:

    i. Mr. Oswald has adopted a cold and distancing posture as a way of protecting himself from people he has learned can be hurtful in their judgments of him

    ii. You, the therapist, want a "cozy" intimacy to develop with all your clients and you become irritated when you can't get that with someone.

    iii. Your receptionist has skewed the therapeutic relationship by being too compulsive and demanding with Mr. Oswald before he ever gets a chance to relax into his sessions with you.

    iv. The situation is a mix of all these things

Notes

1. In my example of the difference between the terms organism-environment and organism/environment there is another alternative. That is semantic realism. These two grammatical structures each point to two different concepts. They are each real as linguistic indicators of categorial intentional objects that are different. Be that as it may, semantic realism is not my main concern here.
2. Having said that, it is also true that Dan and I have made this a matter open to rational judgment; we have debated it, but when we have, we have debated it on the level of semantic realism. That is, we have each advocated our preference for either the backslash or the hyphen, and in our debates it has become clear, at least to me, that we are talking about two different concepts. When addressing such differences at the level of ontological relativism, this is not done.

References

Chakravartty, A. (2007). *A metaphysics for scientific realism: Knowing the unobservable*. Cambridge, UK: Cambridge University Press (kindle version).

Collier, A. (2004). Realism, relativism, and reason in religious belief. In M. Archer, A. Collier, & D. Porpora (Eds.), *Transcendence: Critical realism and God* (pp. 41–47). New York, NY: Routledge, Taylor & Francis Group (kindle version).

Machado, A., & Silva, F. (2007). Toward a richer view of the scientific method: The role of conceptual analysis. *American Psychologist, 62*(7), 671–681.

Perls, F., Hefferline, R., & Goodman, P. (1951). *Gestalt therapy: Excitement and growth in the human personality*. New York, NY: The Julian Press.

Porter, S., & Pitts, A. (2015). Critical realism in context: N.T. Wright's historical method and analytic epistemology. *Journal for the Study of the Historical Jesus, 13*, 1–31.

Wright, N.T. (1992). *The New Testament and the people of God (Christian origins and the question of God)*. Philadelphia, PA: Fortress Press.

5

NON-INDEPENDENCE AND ALTERITY—WHEN PEOPLE MEET PEOPLE

No one knows You as I do.
Emerging from the shadow of my occupations,
Touching like a feather floating faintly to the straw.
Speaking to the center of my being.

No one knows our love affair.
I yearn; You care.
There is a You. There is a me.
But no one knows how we are we.

I find antinomies, apparent paradoxes, in much of life. In this way the universe may be "bisexual." Look at it one way and it looks female, but look at it another way and it looks male. Particles—look at them one way and they do indeed look like particles, but look at them another way and they look like waves. The sovereignty of God but the free will of human beings. Salvation—look at it one way and salvation is by faith, not by works, but look at it another and faith without works is dead. Salvation is both "male" and "female." In the same way people in relationships are joined by non-independence, but when you look at that relationship another way, you realize that they are separated by alterity. And that's the way it is when people meet people.

Of course, the analogy breaks down when people embrace a poly-gendered perspective, but here I just want to focus on these two aspects of contacting: non-independence and alterity.

I use the term "meet" in a particular way. I don't mean bumping into one another in a crowd and then moving on to the next bump. I am referring to contact in which there is a significant meeting. I am referring to the kind of meeting

Non-Independence and Alterity **45**

in which the other becomes subject to one's own subjectivity (Levinas, 1999). That is not the same thing as the other becoming subjected to one's subjectivity!

Non-Independence

Non-independence manifests itself when two people have a third factor in common (Kenny, Kashy, & Cook, 2006). If I go to the same market and check out with the same checker over a period of time, then it is not simply that we meet over time, but that we have the market and its environment in common. We have a market kind of non-independence. We are joined by the commonality of that particular market and by market dynamics in general. But there are also more specific ways in which non-independence is evident.

Therapists doing couples work are working with non-independent people who usually have in common living in the same house, sharing the economics of joint finances, and sleeping in the same bed while contributing to the intimacies of a mutual sex life. Non-independence involves commonalities in contacting.

> Contacting has been described as the awareness of difference, and in non-independence there is no awareness of difference but there is no awareness of sameness either.
>
> Non-independence is not a general consideration. It results in rituals and routines in which each extends into the environment through the other, effecting change and taking care of business with selective focal points and objectives, in specific regions of the lifeworld of each of them.
>
> *(Brownell, 2018, p. 102)*

Non-independence is a field dynamic that exerts influence without calling attention to itself. This is not the same as being unconscious. People can be made aware of the non-independent features of their relationships, but those features don't shout and demand attention from the start.

Countertransference is an example of non-independence. Hayes, Gelso, Goldberg, and Kivlighan (2018) proposed an integrative definition of countertransference in which the unresolved conflicts of the therapist become stirred by some aspect of the presence, the presenting, the transference, the appearing (or phenomena) of the client. They then become useful to treatment. It is the substance of these enduring themes, triggered in the commonality between therapist and client, that forms the non-independent nature of countertransference. Cvetovac and Adame (2017) referred to this saying, "the therapist's capacity to heal others is directly related to his or her own experiences of wounding and healing. However, the therapist's wounds must be adequately examined and understood for them to benefit rather than hinder work with clients . . ." (p. 349). Whether or not one agrees with the idea that the therapist "heals others," the non-independence in question is not a negative nor a positive; it just is. Its potential is bi-directional.

46 Being Present

In gestalt therapy non-independence should not be confused with confluence. The confluence of a river is where two tributaries join to become one. At Pittsburgh, Pennsylvania there is a confluence of the Allegheny and Monongahela rivers to form the Ohio. From the point of that confluence these two rivers cease to exist as individual rivers and the water coming from the Allegheny is indistinguishable from the water that was in the Monongahela. From that point on there is only the Ohio. Confluence in gestalt therapy is not as extreme as that, for surely there appears to be two different people but the contacting between them gets obscured in the blending of individual differences. The experience of confluence is that of joining, of communion, of union, and the classic example of a positive form of confluence is sexual intercourse.

By contrast, non-independence maintains individual differences. There is a you. There is a me. These differences can even provoke disagreement and conflict. Rather than precluding contacting, though, non-independence offers a channel along which contacting most easily runs. It is what two people have in common and that which forms the mutual ground of their meeting.

As I write, it is winter in Southern Idaho, USA. There has been snow flying sideways in the wind today. The temperatures are dropping again, and soon it will be 15F/−9C. This is usually an arid climate, being high desert almost four thousand feet above sea level. It's a mountain state. The water comes from aquifers below the dry ground, but those aquifers are fed by melting snow. When I meet with people here, they typically laugh off the snow, but they need it, because that water is used to irrigate crops.

I used to live, by contrast, in Bermuda, where it *never* freezes. Bermuda is a sub-tropical island toward the middle of the Atlantic ocean, about six hundred miles off the coast of North Carolina. The people there collect water as it runs off their roofs and store it in tanks below their houses. If the island goes very long without a significant rain ("tank rain"), the people have to purchase water from businesses, and that can be expensive. They look forward to the rain and feel relieved when tropical systems blow through from the south.

Both places rely on precipitation because of the climate. They are non-independent by virtue of concern for and reliance on a source of water, but this non-independence appears in different ways, and the perspective on water is quite different. In terms of reliance on water and concern for water, Bermuda and Southern Idaho are non-independent, but the people in Idaho don't gather water from their roofs, and the people in Bermuda don't have to shovel snow or try to drive on ice.

In Christianity the ground of meeting is common partnership with the Holy Spirit. There may be other elements of non-independence such as belonging to the same local church, being Catholic, Orthodox, or Protestant, and belonging to the same small group or home Bible study; however, the greatest non-independence that unites Christians is the experiential knowledge of God. J.I. Packer (1973) contrasted knowledge about God—Biblical facts and points of theology—with knowledge of God—the ability to hear from God through contacting (Willard, 2012). It is this that produces the sense of being in relationship with God.

In psychotherapy the non-independence between therapist and client can be seen in the common belonging to a social community such as a city or neighborhood, often common involvement with an integrated health organization or mental health/counseling organization, shared participation in an HMO/insurance company, or the simple and obvious fact that they meet together for the purposes of psychotherapy. The informed consent, then, is a negotiation that establishes important elements of non-independence.

Alterity

How can someone else become subject to a person's subjectivity?

That question doesn't refer to becoming the subject of an investigation such that one grasps another, comes to a theory about them, strives to understand them from one's own frame of reference, digests them, or assimilates them to one's own experience. That would not really be as much about the other as it would be about the one creating such a model *of* the other. In a sense it would be using the other to reinforce one's models, one's views of the world.

Being subject to a person's subjectivity also doesn't mean to be put through a process by which one becomes bound by or dependent upon someone else. In the 1950s some were subjected to questioning by Senator Joe McCarthy, as he imposed upon them a form of brutalizing intimidation that was actually stylized by the House Un-American Activities Committee, which was started in 1938 to look into supposed disloyalty and subversion by private citizens and public officials—anyone suspected of being a communist. A more contemporary and relevant form of subjection is conducted by controlling persons in relationships who subjugate their partners, forcing them to conform to values, goals, emotions, and behavior that is not actually their own. Doing so, in their conformity, they end up acting in bad faith.

In cultural anthropology and ethnography, *alterity* is the conceptualizing and behavior directed at an unfamiliar, foreign other who is made into a model, a facsimile or pattern which is a representation, a re-presenting of the person to one's ways of knowing, and as such is also related to colonization—the use of the other for one's personal gain (Marti, 2014). That is one sense of alterity.

So, is that all there is to the concept? Not in the hands of Emmanuel Levinas; he coupled transcendence to simple otherness and came up with a special form of separateness. Writing of this, Critchley (2002) said that in Levinas "there is something about the other person, a dimension of separateness, interiority, secrecy or what Levinas calls 'alterity' that escapes my comprehension" (p. 26). Dealing with the issues of transcendence and immanence, Levinas said "the identity of the identical and the non-identical in self-consciousness" marked the return of transcendent thought in philosophy to itself, and that constituted immanence—presenting

48 Being Present

what is otherwise separate from oneself (transcendent) *to* oneself so as to make its presence (immanence) comprehensible. "All externality reduces to or returns to the immanence of a subjectivity that itself and in itself exteriorizes itself" (Levinas, 1999, pp. 11–12). Levinas is saying we cannot help seeing what is non-identical with identical eyes.

There are other aspects to Levinas's appreciation of alterity. The other is accepted on their own terms (Treanor, 2006). They are honored as a subject in the same standing as one's self, but not summed up by one's "take," one's thematization. To tell oneself a story about another based on one's own frame of reference and fund of information is to never escape the solipsistic picture of another person, making them the same (same as one's self), thus, not other at all. "Encountering the other on our terms rather than *as other* profoundly affects ethics, politics, theology, and all the other relationships between the self and an other" (Treanor, 2006, p. 5).

So, rather than do that, to approach others with a respect for alterity is to perceive the other person as a distinct other who transcends one's ways of knowing and defies grasping, thematizing, and assimilating. Alterity is a celebration of difference. Further, alterity requires an ontological other, an actual other person. Without the ontical field, there is no alterity.

Divine Alterity

Referring to Derrida quoting Levinas, Critchley (2002) pointed out that Levinas was truly interested in "the holy, the holiness of the holy" (p. 27). Going to Levinas's keen interest in the holiness of the holy, it is possible to see how important his religious ground was. Although he did not write in strictly religious terms, he thought in terms of Biblical concepts.

Alterity, in connection with God, is one aspect of His transcendence, which will be dealt with in greater detail in the next chapter. The word "holy" originally comes from a consonantal root (שדק) that takes verb, noun, and adjectival forms. As such it can mean to set aside or consecrate (i.e. to God), that which is so set aside or consecrated, and the separate nature of that which has been set aside (Brown, Driver, & Briggs, 1907/1978). To be holy is to be separate. As such, God is separate, sacred, and His people are to be likewise set aside (for His purposes).

Alterity is also a relational construct. Compared to me God is different. In a relationship with me, I follow. That may seem simple, but the alterity of God sneaks up on people. Religious people are often criticized for "creating" an image of God that is a mere projection of humanity. Instead of God creating human beings in His image, Christians are often described as creating God in their image.

When people find God puzzling, confusing, or troubling—when people judge God and find Him wanting—that is their annihilating subjugation of God, their presenting of God to themselves as "same," creating an expectation of God which is ultimately disappointed. When people yield to the mystery, the enigma of

God, even though puzzling, confusing, and troubling, that is when God becomes another subject to their own subjectivity.

In some ways God *is* like human beings of course, because we have been created in His image, but there are important ways in which He is dissimilar. Does God have emotions like us? What does it mean when God seems to be unresponsive? If we were to experience silence from another human being, we might imagine that person to be upset, to have grown cold, or to have abandoned us. It is not that way with God.

When we attribute human qualities to God, when we anthropomorphize, we are thematizing God and making Him the same (i.e. the same as us). Every thematization of God will fall short, and that is why God forbade making images of Him. Nothing can suffice. Everything will fail to grasp Him absolutely, and every attempt to reach an exhaustive understanding of Him is ultimately an attempt to control Him by assimilating Him to our experience and comprehension.

Human Alterity

These observations about how people thematize God and make Him over in their images can also be applied to how we operate with other human beings. We do not have the omniscient capacity that God does; so, we do not know what it is like to be any other person. Unlike God, we do not discern others' thoughts from afar, but we can imagine (and we do).

Alterity, though, is when the other's ontology exceeds my epistemology. It's when their existence exceeds my imaginations about them. For Levinas that set up an ethical obligation to respect the otherness that transcends one's ways of knowing and to refrain from constructing stories about the other based on one's own frame of reference. But that poses another question: does this transcendent alterity make it impossible to know the other at all?

For Marion the transcendence of the other does not preclude the other having effect; so, abstaining as much as possible from thematizing the other, one is prepared to receive the other as given, which can be surprising. Marion might say this opens the way for a saturated phenomenon. "A saturated phenomenon is one that cannot be contained wholly within concepts that can be grasped by our understanding. It gives so much in intuition that there is always an excess left over. Thus, it is saturated with intuition" (Mackinlay, 2010, p. 1). Intuition can be understood as a sensing. The resulting intentionality[1] is mystery, wonder, enigma.

Perhaps a tame version of the saturated phenomenon is that which emerges from the chiasm, Merleau-Ponty's conception of contacting in which one bumps into the actual world, from which experience provides the raw material of interpretation. "Chiasm is therefore a crisscrossing or a bi-directional becoming or exchange between the body and things that justifies speaking of a 'flesh' of things, a kinship between the sensing body and sensed things that makes their communication possible" (Toadvine, 2019, n.p.). Of this Hass (2008) stated, "perceptual experience is a field of contact with things, but it is a contact with things and a world that opens up, eludes, and limits our exploration" (n.p.). Merleau-Ponty himself described the chiasm as not just a me-other exchange, but a process by which there is an "exchange between me and the world, between the phenomenal body and the 'objective' body, between the perceiving and the perceived: what begins as a thing ends as consciousness of the thing, what begins as a 'state of consciousness' ends as a thing" (p. 215).

Thus, we interpret our experience from an interaction with what is there, but it is not completely fabricated from pure imagination, which would entirely leave behind what is there. Again, for alterity to be possible there must be an actual other, but to have any meaningful relationship with an other, we must accept the presence of the other as given.

Summary

If alterity is when the other's ontology exceeds my epistemology, non-independence is when the other-and-I form an ontological unit in which the phenomenality of each exceeds our relative transcendence. The intentionality of non-independence is with-ness, which can be loathsome and hindering or enchanting and exciting. The intentionality of alterity is otherness. The alterity of God is holy in nature.

When People Meet People

My wife, Linda, is a very creative and resourceful person. She is what I have called a "make-it-happen" kind of person. And she does make things happen. She is action oriented.

When we bought our house in Twin Falls, we immediately realized we needed to make several changes. Thus, I settled into a construction zone. Further, Linda found a series of vendors—craftsmen who could also make things happen, but according to their relative spheres of expertise. Some were carpenters. Some were plumbers, some were electricians. And then there was Frank.[2]

Frank was slender with longish, unkept straight, sandy hair. His front teeth were gone because he'd been using too much methamphetamine, but Frank was clean and had been off drugs for some time when Linda found him. Frank could do a little bit of everything, but his primary expertise was in tile. And we needed to replace old carpet with new tile.

I could not understand Frank when he spoke. Invariably he would say something, it would sound like nonsense syllables tumbled in the dryer, and I would say, "What?" He would repeat himself, and I would say, "What?" He would try again, and I would *still* not get it, but I would smile, say, "oh," and move on. Sometimes I would have to drive him back from our property to his house and all the time we were in route he would be talking, but I would be smiling, nodding my head, and wondering what he was talking about, hoping he would not catch that I was totally lost.

Linda and I both liked Frank, but it seemed I had nothing in common with him. I had not lost all my teeth. I had not been addicted to any drugs. I had a respectable job and made a reasonable living. Frank had lost his driver's license, but I still had mine. Frank had no car, but I had a new one. Frank was a master of many crafts, and he could paint, do electrical work, carpentry, and of course Frank could do the tile work that we wanted done. I could not. He did odd jobs around the property as well when Linda had something else that needed to be done. I liked gardening and landscaping. Frank was not a gardener.

Frank lived in a house that he rented from the man who employed him. He was routinely opening his house to people in need, usually people with criminal and substance abuse records, and they were consistently stealing his things.

One day Frank brought us a gift. He had been out in the town and seen someone selling puppies by the side of the road; so, he bought one. They were Australian Shepherd mixes. He knew we had cats, but he thought we needed a dog. It was a Christmas present and utterly impossible to refuse, even though we took the dog with a groan. As the puppy grew, she learned to herd basketballs in our pasture. Then she started retrieving them and rolling them back to me after I had kicked one several yards away. "Bailey" is now one of our family, and every time Frank comes over to work he greets her. I love that dog, and I sometimes marvel at the kindness and generosity, the intuitive knowing about what would add to our lives, of a man who exceeds my theories about him.

As therapists we are involved in non-independent relationships with our clients, because the process of psychotherapy unites us, and these are all people who exceed our theories about them. We may have to give them diagnoses, but those are simply tags, markers that make it efficient to deal with them in a mental health system. In actuality there are no such things as schizophrenics, depressives, and borderlines. These things do not exist in space. Rather, people do. Beyond the intersubjective dynamic that is captured in contacting, the set-up of psychotherapy links us to these persons and makes both client and therapist non-independent.

Although I don't believe Levinas ever said it this way, I believe psychotherapists are obligated to honor the non-independence that unites us with the client through our common creaturehood, created in the image of God, while we owe every person respect for their otherness, the kind that understands an infinite creator forms people so that no two are the same.

Notes

1. Intentionality is a construct of phenomenological philosophy. Its concern is the aboutness of experience, including that which is logically and/or experientially related to a figure of interest.
2. "Frank" is a fictional name for a real person.

References

Brown, F., Driver, S. R., & Briggs, C. A. (1907/1978). *A Hebrew and English lexicon of the Old Testament*. Oxford, UK: Clarendon Press.

Brownell, P. (2018). *Gestalt psychotherapy & coaching for relationships*. New York and London, UK: Routledge, Taylor & Francis Group.

Critchley, S. (2002). Introduction. In S. Critchley & R. Bernasconi (Eds.), *The Cambridge companion to Levinas* (pp. 1–32). New York, NY: Cambridge University Press.

Cvetovac, M., & Adame, A. (2017). The wounded therapist: Understanding the relationship between personal suffering and clinical practice. *The Humanistic Psychologist, 45*(4), 348–366. doi:10.1037/hum0000071

Hass, L. (2008). *Merleau-Ponty's philosophy*. Bloomington and Indianapolis: Indiana University Press.

Hayes, J., Gelso, C., Goldberg, S., & Kivlighan, D. (2018). Countertransference management effective psychotherapy: Meta-analytic findings. *Psychotherapy, 55*(4), 496–507. doi:10.1037/pst0000189

Kenny, D., Kashy, D., & Cook, W. (2006). *Dyadic data analysis*. New York, NY: Guilford Press.

Levinas, E. (1999). *Alterity and transcendence*. New York, NY: Columbia University Press.

Mackinlay, D. (2010). *Interpreting excess: Jean-Luc Marion, saturated phenomena, and hermeneutics*. New York, NY: Fordham University Press.

Marti, J. (2014). Music and alterity processes. *Humanities, 3*, 645–659. doi:10.3390/h3040645

Merleau-Ponty, M. (1968). *The visible and the invisible*. Evanston, IL: Northwestern University Press.

Packer, J. I. (1973). *Knowing God*. Downers Grove, IL: InterVarsity Press.

Toadvine, T. (2019). Maurice Merleau-Ponty. In E. Zalta (Ed.), *The Stanford encyclopedia of philosophy* (Spring 2019 ed.). Retrieved March 31, 2019, from https://plato.stanford.edu/archives/spr2019/entries/merleau-ponty

Treanor, B. (2006). *Aspects of alterity: Levinas, Marcel and the contemporary debate*. New York, NY: Fordham University Press.

Willard, D. (2012). *Hearing God: Developing a conversational relationship with God*. Downers Grove, IL: IVP Books.

6

IMMANENCE AND TRANSCENDENCE—WHEN GOD MEETS PEOPLE

Why do you bother?
Why do you care?
When you come close, you want closer,
But how close makes you there?

You're not like the others,
Transcending us all
With an immanent transcending
In a mysterious call.

Forgive me, O God,
For my frivolous aims,
Those wasteful amusements
That make me ashamed.

I want to adore you,
To become as undone
In the thought of your presence—
Camaraderie with Your Son.

Jeremiah, the prophet, warned people that God was quite able to see what they were doing in His name, claiming to prophesy, claiming to have had authoritative dreams, while all the time not really practicing the presence of God that would have allowed them to really hear from God. Jeremiah said,

> *"Am I a God who is near,"* declares the Lord,
> *"And not a God far off?*

> *"Can a man hide himself in hiding places*
> *So I do not see him?" declares the Lord.*
> *"Do I not fill the heavens and the earth?" declares the Lord.*[1]

God *is* "near" and "far off." He is right here and as far away as I could ever get. He is everywhere, but there is another way to understand this than it being a matter of physical distance. God is commensurate (similar) and incommensurate (different). He is with us in that He is like us, and so near, but He is also utterly beyond us in that He is dissimilar, and so far. The words for these categories are immanence and transcendence; God is immanent and transcendent.

There are what some call "small" immanence and small transcendence. Small immanence would be the philosophical sense of the concept, dealing with commonality in conceptualizing or one's phenomenality—a reference to personal experience. In that way the philosophy is shared and the experience is mine, what it is like to be me. Big immanence would be the theological—a reference to the presence of God. Small transcendence refers to such striking experiences as a mountain vista, the sunset, or the smile on a new-born baby that transports one beyond the mundane. These experiences contrast with "big" transcendence, which is the kind that has to do with the ontical nature of God (Nelson, 2009) and the wholly ineffable.

I don't like these designations of small and large, because they don't communicate well enough. They can be used to point to one thing or another, but they don't help people understand the nuances of transcendence and immanence. The distinction has nothing to do with size.[2]

Transcendence as a term refers to a form of knowledge often considered to be not based on empirical experience or observation and not accessible through experience and research (Oprea, Oprea, & Oprea, 2016). It is beyond this material world and its physical laws, and it contrasts to *immanence*, which refers to something that *is* of this world and accessible by others. The meeting of these two in a world currently influenced by the immanent frame of exclusionary naturalism (Slife, Möller, & Chun, 2019) can be described as enchantment (Taylor, 2007; Smith, 2014).

Because transcendent entities are thought to be beyond human experience, some believe it is impossible to speak about a transcendent God. Certainly, nothing can capture the essence of God and provide an exhaustive knowledge of God, but is it possible to have an immanent experience of the transcendent? Or like matter and dark matter would they cancel one another out? What happens when the transcendent intrudes upon our world? That is the crux of the issue when God meets people. What is it like when something so utterly other appears? Would not the presence of the transcendent cause a ripple on the quiet surface of one's immanent pond? Or would the "take" of a closed system, what Taylor (2007) calls an imminent frame, cause an a priori exclusion of the transcendent, an interpreting away and out of consideration of the call of that which exceeds one's horizon? As a related curiosity, in the presence of revelation is it possible to harden the heart to the degree that one resists contact with God and then cannot appreciate the saturated phenomenon, the enchantment of one's life world?

Evidently so.[3]

Immanence

Psalm 139 affirms both the omnipresence and omniscience of God, both of which are also subsets of His immanence. He is "with" His creation, both in personal presence and intentional concern. Thus, He is *not* the deistic clockmaker who resides solely in His transcendence, having set the clock to run on cosmic time according to the design that He gave it but making no current intervention with it.

The Bible is filled with instances in which God intrudes upon the flow of human history and upon the personal history of individuals. Table 6.1 provides just a few examples of God's immanent presence.

Transcendence

God knows all about me. He knows when I sit down and when I stand up. He discerns my thoughts while they are still forming in my own mind and knows what I'm going to say before I say it. There is no place I can go that He will not be. Even in my darkest moments that darkness does not shut Him out, and He knows exactly how long I have to live, as He determined my last day before I even had my first.[4] This kind of presence is omnipresence, and this kind of knowledge is omniscience. They are ways in which He transcends our plane of experience. He is so far beyond us that He is inscrutable. If He had not revealed Himself to us, we could never have conjured up such a being as Yahweh. If he had not spoken to us in various ways by various means, if He had not fully revealed Himself in His Son, Emmanuel ("God with us"), we would not know Him. We would not have imagined Him. The evidence is in the contrast between the God of the Bible and the gods of Olympus.

> *"For My thoughts are not your thoughts*
> *Nor are your ways My ways," declares the Lord.*
> *"For as the heavens are higher than the earth*
> *So are My ways higher than your ways*
> *And My thoughts than your thoughts."*[5]

I referred previously to the illustration of one of our cats or dogs watching me read. They have no possible way of comprehending what I am doing. They can see me there, and they can see the book in my hands, and they can see me looking at it in what seems to them to be silence and stillness. They cannot

56 Being Present

TABLE 6.1 Examples of God's Immanence

Reference	Description
Genesis 3:8	God was walking in the garden of Eden, and Adam and Eve heard Him and hid themselves "from the presence of the Lord God among the trees of the garden."
Genesis 6–8	God interacted with Noah and was present with him during the time of a vast flood.
Genesis 12:1–4ff	God called Abram to leave his country; God made promises to him
Genesis 15	God spoke to Abram, and the formula "the word of the Lord came" to Abram was used repeatedly to convey the idea that God spoke directly to him. Further God "cut a covenant" with him to commit to promises He made to Abram.
Exodus 3: 2–15	God appeared to Moses in the burning bush, spoke to him, and commissioned him to bring the Jewish people out of bondage in Egypt. He told him to tell them "'I Am' has sent me to you."
Exodus 12: 1–32	God gave Moses the structure of the Passover and the Feast of Unleavened Bread as both the contents of an event He would bring to pass and a memorial of that event for all generations.
Exodus 40:34–38	The presence of God by day and night filled the tabernacle.
2 Chronicles 7:1–2	The glory of the Lord filled the house of God that Solomon had built—the temple.
Isaiah 6	Isaiah was given a vision of God and he received a commission from God as a prophet of God.
Isaiah 7:14 (cf. Matthew 1:18–25; Luke 1:26ff)	God gave Isaiah a prophecy concerning the birth of Jesus, who was characterized as being Immanuel, meaning "God with us."
John 8:54–58	Jesus stated, ". . . before Abraham was I am . . ." Which was a reference to the statement made to Moses at the burning bush.
John 14:6–11	Jesus claimed that He and his Father are one so that those seeing Jesus also perceive His Father—God.
Hebrews 1:1–3	Jesus was God's presence, the radiance of His glory, among the people with whom He lived.
John 14:16–30	Jesus made several statements about living with people, and He promised to send the Holy Spirit of God to reside within people and to be a "helper" who would teach people concerning the things of God.
Acts 2	The promised Holy Spirit came to reside with and in those believing in Jesus.
Galatians 5:25	Believers in Christ live and conduct their lives in step with the abiding presence of God through the Holy Spirit.

understand that my mind is active, and I may be transported to another place, with other people, or contemplating an idea, a conceptualization. They don't know the pleasure of such abstraction. In this act of reading I transcend them. Yet, I am still with them.

I think surely that one would not appreciate the transcendent nature of something unless it were showing, presenting, given. But at the level of mere appearing to another it is not transcendent as much as it is simply a phenomenon—an appearance. What makes it transcendent is the phenomenality of the experience of the appearance—that in the appearing one realizes it's beyond in some way. Beyond the normal. Beyond the mundane. Beyond the natural and possibly *from* beyond. This was Moses's experience upon seeing a bush that was burning but not burning up. As he drew closer, he was transfixed and encountered God. The whole experience was certainly a showing, an epiphany, but also just as surely not a customary thing. Marion calls this kind of phenomenon a "saturated" phenomenon, and it is saturated with intuition. So, it is also an effective revelation. It *is* a showing, but a showing of something that would not be suspected because the saturation exceeds one's horizon. Thus, the showing is from beyond the horizon. It transcends the horizon. It intrudes on the lifeworld. That is the nature, for me, of "big" transcendence.

The Immanence and Transcendence of God in the Hypostatic Union

Heresies emerge when one fails to find a balance while forming theological positions. For instance, the "one-sided insistence of the immanence of God, to the exclusion of His transcendence, leads to Pantheism, just as the one-sided insistence upon His transcendence, to the exclusion of His immanence, leads to Deism" (Ciocan, 2016). The early church had to work out some basic theology in its first three to four hundred years, and they faced down several imbalanced heresies in the process. The equipoise between immanence and transcendence is perhaps best considered in the doctrine of the two essences in the one person of Christ (Istodor, 2016), and the church forged a position on this that became known as the hypostatic union.[6]

At the Council of Chalcedon in 451 the church affirmed the following:

- The true incarnation of the Logos (second person of the Godhead) in which the two natures formed an "abiding union of the two in one personal life" (Schaff, 1931/1985, p. 30).
- The distinction between nature and person, in which *nature* (*essence, ousia*) is the sum of the powers and qualities constituting a being and *person* (*hypostasis*) is the ego, the self-conscious, self-asserting, and acting subject. The person is the one who says, "me."

58 Being Present

- The result of this incarnation is a God-man, being both divine and human (not a double being with two persons nor some kind of third thing that is never quite divine nor human).
- The divine intentionality and purpose remain divine and the human intentionality and purpose remain human, but they share one, common life and "interpenetrate each other, like the persons of the Trinity" (Schaff, ibid., p. 31).
- The union of the two natures in the one person of Christ is inseparable.
- The whole work of Christ is completed by His person rather than to one or the other nature.

Because Jesus is both divine and human, He communicates to humans the divine nature. The book of Hebrews asserted that after revealing Himself in many ways prior to Jesus, finally God revealed Himself more directly *in* his Son, of whom the text says, that "He is the radiance of His glory and the exact representation of His nature . . ."[7] Jesus is the radiance (ἀπαύγασμα) and the representation of His glory (χαρακτὴρ τῆς ὑποστάσεως αὐτοῦ). *Radiance* means "illumination," "effulgence," while the word χαρακτὴρ (or character) means the impress that reproduces and represents, and in this case it is that which is the impress of God's substantial nature, essence, actual being (ὑποστάσεως αὐτοῦ).

Jesus made the invisible God visible. This is what Christians believe.

When he met the woman at the well and they started talking about worship, He told her, "God is spirit," meaning, among other things, no one can see Him. However, the one-of-a-kind (μονογενής, meaning "only," "unique") Son of God has ἐξηγήσατο (meaning "explained," "interpreted," or "described") Him.[8] This explaining is the same word used in referring to what a pastor does when he studies the Bible in order to draw out its meaning and give that to his congregation. He exegetes. Jesus, in His very being and presence, exegeted the Father for people with whom Jesus resided (Bauer, Arndt, & Gingrich, 1957). He was able to do that because the transcendent nature of God was present, immanent, in the person and experience of the immanent man named Jesus.

When God Meets People

God is always present, but God does not always meet people. That is, God does not constantly engage in contacting with individuals. That is something special. Regardless, the presence and contacting of God always have consequences.

The Immanence of God Creates a Pneumenal Field

The presence of God, His "with-ness," creates a pneumenal field. God is spirit.[9] The word for spirit in the New Testament is πνεῦμα (*pneuma*). The emphasis in the Greek text is on spirit; so, it does not say that God is *a* spirit. It says, literally, πνεῦμα ὁ θεός, "God is (by nature) spirit." That is God's substance. Since God is also infinite, His presence, His immanence, transforms the ontical field into a pneumenal field. All that exists yields to His immanence, and all things having effect are influenced by God's spiritual nature.[10]

Understood another way the ontical field is all that actually exists, everything that is. I assume here that God does, in fact, exist. Since God is involved with and *part of* such a field, one cannot avoid being influenced by His spiritual nature (Brownell, 2012), because any given person also exists and is part of the same field.

It would be possible to simply refer to the ontical field and describe what the phenomenality is of encounter with God without using the term "pneumenal field," but I think there are overlapping fields in life, fields within fields, and the things of God are not mundane. They are sacred. They are the ontical and phenomenal fields viewed within a spiritual attitude, and they give life to one's spiritual horizon, populating one's spiritual-life world.

Pargament (2007) claimed "the sacred is the heart and soul of spirituality" (p. 32). He referred to a sacred core constituted by ideas of God and transcendent reality and around that a ring filled with various elements of life. "Surrounding the sacred core is a ring of other aspects of life that become extraordinary, indeed sacred themselves, through their association with the sacred core" (Pargament, 2007, p. 32). That is an example of the pneumenal field.

Contacting the Transcendent God Creates the Experience of the Numinous

Rudolph Otto (1950) wrote about the sacred, but he called this *the idea of the holy*. He asserted that contact with God gives rise to a kind of experience, and he called that the numinous. "The numinous is the nonrational component of the Holy that is experienced when a religious 'object' activates it" (Nelson, 2009, p. 127). The activating is through personal encounter, or what gestalt therapists know as contact. When contact with the sacred occurs, according to Otto, it brings about three kinds of experience:

1. Humility—an intuitive understanding of one's creaturehood in contrast to the presence of the Creator.
2. The *mysterium tremendum*—a sense of awe or dread, the awareness of an overpowering and consuming presence.
3. The *mysterium fascinans*—a sense of fascination and yearning that attracts and draws one in.

The Indwelling Holy Spirit Creates the Experience of a Superlative Immanence

What is the "superlative" immanence of God? What about it makes it superlative?

In human experience one cannot get much more intimate physically than sexual intercourse. One person penetrates the other. One person goes into another.

In working with women in psychotherapy I have frequently heard them say, in talking about rejecting a man, "I no longer wanted him inside me." The Bible talks about marriage as a kind of picture of the relationship between Christ and the church, or if you would between God and those who trust in Him. To be sure, it is more than this, but one thing that is sure is that He penetrates them. He goes into them by imparting the Holy Spirit to indwell them. Therefore, I carry God with me wherever I go. I am never alone, and it's not because God is omnipresent; it's because He is present with and in me. We endure events in this life together. That is an intimate and personal presence and a superlative immanence. You cannot get more immanent than that; my experience is infused by the Spirit of God.

- Ezekiel 36:27 "I will put My Spirit within you and cause you to walk in My statutes, and you will be careful to observe My ordinances."
- Ezekiel 37:14 "I will put My Spirit in you and you will live, and I will settle you in your own land. Then you will know that I, the LORD, have spoken, and I will do it, declares the LORD."
- John 14:16–18 "I will ask the Father, and He will give you another Helper, that He may be with you forever; that is the Spirit of truth, whom the world cannot receive, because it does not see Him or know Him, but you know Him because He abides with you and will be in you."
- 1 John 3:24 "Whoever keeps His commandments remains in God, and God in him. And by this we know that He remains in us: by the Spirit He has given us."
- Romans 8:9–11 "However, you are not in the flesh but in the Spirit, if indeed the Spirit of God dwells in you. But if anyone does not have the Spirit of Christ, he does not belong to Him. If Christ is in you, though the body is dead because of sin, yet the spirit is alive because of righteousness. But if the Spirit of Him who raised Jesus from the dead dwells in you, He who raised Christ Jesus from the dead will also give life to your mortal bodies through His Spirit who dwells in you."
- 1 Corinthians 3:16 "Do you not know that you are a temple of God and that the Spirit of God dwells in you?"
- 1 Corinthians 6:17–20 "But the one who joins himself to the Lord is one spirit *with Him*. Flee immorality. Every *other* sin that a man commits is outside the body, but the immoral man sins against his own body. Or do you not know that your body is a temple of the Holy Spirit who is in you, whom you have from God, and that you are not your own? For you have been bought with a price: therefore glorify God in your body."
- Ephesians 5: 28–32 "So husbands ought also to love their own wives as their own bodies. He who loves his own wife loves himself; for no one ever hated his own flesh, but nourishes and cherishes it, just as Christ also *does* the church, because we are members of His body. For this reason a man shall leave his father and mother and shall be joined to his wife, and the two shall become one flesh. This mystery is great; but I am speaking with reference to Christ and the church."

Implications for Gestalt Therapy

When we meet people, anywhere at any time for anything, are we meeting them in a naturalistic, immanent frame in which our self is buffered and hardened against enchantment, or do we meet in a pneumenal field where novelty and enchantment surprise? This is an important consideration for gestalt therapists. What is actually going on?

There are four possibilities.

1. A Christian patient meets with a Christian gestalt therapist.
2. A Christian patient meets with a non-Christian gestalt therapist.
3. A non-Christian patient meets with a non-Christian gestalt therapist.
4. A non-Christian patient meets with a Christian gestalt therapist.

In the first case both patient and therapist will recognize the Spirit of God in the other. This commonly takes place in the wider world in which one walks away saying to him or herself about the other, "That person knows the Lord." They have a commonality, a sharing, a community with one another that the Bible calls κοινωνία (*koinonia*).

Koine Greek is that form of the Greek language that became the common language of the Hellenistic world that formed from the conquests of Alexander the Great. Like English today, it was the common language of commerce and diplomacy back then. And that is why the New Testament, a collection of books and letters produced by people speaking many languages, was written in Koine Greek. So, the Christian patient meeting with the Christian gestalt therapist will fluidly enter into the ways in which God, through the indwelling Holy Spirit, makes a difference in both of their lives. They will speak a common language. And that will become a rich resource not usually covered in standard descriptions of gestalt therapy but very relevant to a phenomenological field theory.

In the second case the Christian patient will not sense a common language of the Spirit. They will have commonality as two human beings, but there will always be something missing, ways of looking at the world, ways of understanding experience, that the Christian will not be able to communicate adequately to the non-Christian because spiritual matters are spiritually discerned and the non-Christian does not have the resource of the indwelling Holy Spirit. This is not to claim that there would be no benefit for meeting with a non-Christian therapist, but the two would have to find common ground, and that would be in keeping with the naturalistic frame that is common to our secular age.

In the third case both are of that naturalistic frame. They share a common, naturalistic perspective on life and in many ways speak that same language.

In the fourth case the non-Christian patient may sense something odd about the Christian therapist, and the Christian therapist may experience insights into the non-Christian patient that require finesse in response.

62 Being Present

In all four cases the therapeutic method and process of gestalt therapy could be applied. It's just that the specific nature of that process, with regards to a spiritual horizon, would differ for each case.

Notes

1. Jeremiah 23:23–24.
2. Having said that, there is no way to be exhaustive of this subject in a chapter so short. I can merely point in the direction of more complexity and hope to stir the imagination.
3. Psalm 95:8; Hebrews 3:15.
4. Psalm 139.
5. Isaiah 55:8–9.
6. There is another good illustration in the doctrine of the economic trinity, but in this short chapter there is not room to explore it.
7. Hebrews 1:3.
8. John 1:18.
9. John 4:24.
10. Romans 1:20; Isaiah 55:12; Luke 19:40.

References

Bauer, W., Arndt, W., & Gingrich, F. W. (1957). *A Greek-English lexicon of the New Testament and other early Christian literature*. Chicago, IL: University of Chicago Press.

Brownell, P. (2012). Spirituality in gestalt therapy. In T. Bar-Yoseph Levine (Ed.), *Gestalt therapy: Advances in theory and practice* (pp. 92–103). New York, NY: Routledge.

Ciocan, C. T. (2016). The philosophic paradigm as basis for early Christian doctrine of God's immanence. *Dialogo (The Dialogue Between Theology and Philosophy)*, 2(2), 133–150. doi:10.18638/dialogo.2015.2.2.12

Istodor, G. (2016). Transcendent and immanent in orthodox theology. *Dialogo (The Dialogue Between Theology and Philosophy)*, 2(2) (Suppl.), 45–54. doi:10.18638/dialogo.2015.2.2.4

Nelson, J. (2009). *Psychology, religion, and spirituality*. New York, NY: Springer.

Oprea, E., Oprea, C., & Oprea, A. (2016). Transcendence of theology, philosophy and science in Russian cosmism. *Dialogo (The Dialogue Between Theology and Philosophy)*, 2(2), 71–80. doi:10.18638/dialogo.2015.2.2.6

Otto, R. (1923/1950). *The idea of the holy*. London, UK: Oxford University Press.

Pargament, K. (2007). *Spiritually integrated psychotherapy: Understanding and addressing the sacred*. New York, NY: The Guilford Press.

Schaff, P. (1931/1985). *The creeds of Christendom, with a history and critical notes. Volume one: The history of creeds*. Grand Rapids, MI: Baker Book House.

Slife, B., Möller, E., & Chun, S. (2019). Perspective three: The excluded other in psychological research: Diary of a probing theist. In P. Brownell (Ed.), *Handbook for theory, research and practice in gestalt therapy* (2nd ed., pp. 65–87). Newcastle upon Tyne, UK: Cambridge Scholars Publishing.

Smith, J. K. A. (2014). *How (not) to be secular: Reading Charles Taylor*. Grand Rapids, MI: William B. Eerdmans Publishing Company.

Taylor, C. (2007). *A secular age*. Cambridge, MA and London, UK: The Belknap Press of Harvard University Press.

Story One

A PRIVATE LAKE

It was a bell he had heard ring, and he couldn't pretend he hadn't heard it.

His eyes opened on a new day. Another day. Still another day.

He swung his legs out over the edge of the bed, grabbed the side of the mattress with his hand, and pulled himself up. His back stiffened. He reached beside and slightly behind himself and pushed against the bed to brace against the pain. What started in his lower back grew to the point that his muscles usually seized him late in the day with a burning that grew until night when he would collapse in exhaustion.

So, still another day.

Bret had been a carpenter for over thirty years until he fell from a roofing job and broke his back. They fused his spine. It worked well enough, but he was never as productive, and eventually he started staying home instead of trying to find new work. In carpentry one is always working oneself out of a job, and Bret simply stopped trying to get another new one.

His wife died two years after the accident. Now, he was tired of being alone. Tired of hurting. Tired of fading memories. He was lonely and tired of fading.

He stood at the sink washing the dishes left there the night before, and he gazed out the window at the lake. That lake, and the house that sat next to it, had been her passion. They had found the house in need of repair and worked together to make it her treasure. They were alone with each other there, the nearest neighbors being on the far side and then one person off to the right about two miles away.

64 Being Present

She used to stand at that sink and sing while washing the dishes. She used to watch the lake in its changing patterns. They used to run naked down to the water.

Now he was alone there, and he could not sing. He did not run. There was no point to being naked.

The lake was motionless. Silent. There was no wind. There were no waves. It was flat.

Bret began to stare. His mind went to sleep. His eyes lost focus.

A western bluebird appeared on the ledge outside the window. He hadn't seen it come in. Its head moved quickly to survey the place, and that took Bret out of his trance. The bird's head was deep blue, and so were his neck and wings. There was a touch of gray where his beak joined his head, and it looked like he was trying to grow a beard—an old-man, bluebird's beard. He wore a brown vest of feathers over his chest to keep himself warm and it joined over his back. He was alone.

The old bluebird caught sight of Bret on the other side of the window, and he cocked his head so he could peer at him with one eye through the glass.

Bret peered back. They held each other's gaze.

"You're not afraid of me at all, are you?" he said.

Bret raised his hand into the air. The bird did not move. He kept watching.

Bret tapped on the glass, but the bluebird did not move.

Bret said, "Okay. Right. Somebody locked up the idiot in his house." He tapped on the glass again. The bird did not move. He kept still and his eye fixed on Bret.

Bret said, "You're alone." The possibility settled down upon him.

Western bluebirds usually mate for life, and they build nests in convenient locations like boxes that people put out for them or hollow places in trees.

"Well, old man, I guess we're both alone," he said.

The bird flew off, but he returned quickly, and he came to rest in the other direction; so, he looked at Bret with his other eye. Still the same steady gaze.

Bret saw him. He said, "Hello again."

He finished the dishes, dried his hands, and looked again at the lake. It sat a football field beyond the bluebird, and his little boat was in the water next to the small dock. He picked up his cup of coffee and stepped outside on the deck, sat down in a chair that overlooked the lake and rested his head against the back of the chair.

The bluebird flitted around and came to rest about twelve feet away on the railing of the far side of the deck.

"What are you lookin' at?" said Bret. "Can you tell what's on my mind?"

He took a breath and sighed. Today was a good day. Might as well be today.

After two years of being alone, he still yearned for her presence. He and his wife used to sit on the deck and enjoy the woods and the animals. They used to take the boat out onto the lake. He would drop a line in the water, and she would read. He put a seat with a back to it on the boat so she could lean back and enjoy

A Private Lake **65**

her books. He never cared all that much about catching any fish. It was just relaxing and peaceful being together on what seemed like their private lake.

Now he looked across to the dock and considered taking the boat out again. The water would still be very cold. He did not like cold water.

He finished his coffee and went down to the dock. He glanced across the still water and saw that nobody else was out. He would have it all to himself. As he stepped into the boat it swung away from the dock and he scrambled back to keep from falling in. He swore at the boat. She would not have liked that.

Once in the boat he began to untie the knot in the rope that kept the boat from drifting. It was tight. It had not been undone for months. He peeled at it with his fingers. It would not yield. His fingers hurt. He kept working it. He swore at the rope.

The rope finally gave up, and he undid it from the boat and pushed away from the dock with an oar. The oar locks were stiff in their sockets, and the oars kept jumping out of them, because the locks were open ended. He had meant to replace them with closed locks but had not gotten around to it after his wife became ill. Now he was irritated with himself and losing patience. He knew what he had in mind, but ropes and oarlocks and worn out boats did not seem to be cooperating.

He put the oars in the water and began making his way from the dock. He watched the house recede. He watched mountains rise above the trees. He watched the shoreline grow smaller.

Out near the middle of the lake the water was deep and dark. He pulled the oars in and laid them in the bottom of the boat. He leaned over the edge of the boat and peered into the water. It was stygian, a kind of gloomy sanctum. The light from the day sank away inches below the surface. He saw no fish. There were no bubbles. The surface of the lake seemed peaceful, but it was deceptive. Below the water was an abyss, an abhorrent solitude. It was a lifeless, veritable vacuum.

He imagined leaning over the edge of the boat until gravity took him all the way over and then sinking down deeply until he could no longer hold his breath. Then bringing the water into his lungs. He could see this in his mind's eye. He played it over again and wondered what that moment, just as consciousness gives up, is really like.

He sat up and leaned against the back rest. He looked around as if to say good-bye. He draped his hand over the side of the boat to feel the water. It was as cold as he thought it might be. He reminded himself of that. How long would he have to endure the cold? Would water rushing into his lungs feel cold or be painful? How long would that last? Did it matter? How long might this terrible loneliness go on? How long did he have to yearn for the only person he ever loved?

He searched the shoreline of the lake all around, but nobody could be seen. The quiet solitude of the place stirred him. He had felt loneliness before meeting her—when he was younger. Back then he did frantic things to be with people, and when he could not find anyone with whom to eat food, watch a movie, or share his bed, he felt abandoned, desolate, and dismally empty.

66 Being Present

He did not feel abandoned now. She did not have a choice. She had not abandoned him. She had been taken. "Ah," he said. "Angry." Angry at God for taking her, if God even existed. Somehow it hurt less to think of God taking her than pure random, chaotic nonsense coincidentally slicing her out of his life. How hopeless. How senseless. What a waste. What a crime, but if there is no cosmic criminal to commit the crime, how meaningless. Her death was absurd.

"What a wonderful person she was," he said. Some people paint on a canvas, but the whole house was on her easel. She found things that other people threw away, and she put them uniquely together in configurations that amazed him. She turned his living space into a space that lived.

She was constantly meeting new people whenever they went into town. She dragged him along to church. She asked him periodically if he could hear from God. "What did you hear in that service?"

He never heard anything. Oh, he heard the preacher, and he heard the music. But he didn't hear anything riding atop all that. He knew what she was getting at, but he never heard from God.

And he was alone. The water was calm and the surface a glassy plain. He imagined his body falling over the edge of the boat like a pebble and ripples going out as a testimony to his passing.

The place was so still it made up its own noise. Every time he moved in the boat the sound he made carried out across the water, shouting that he was there, but he found himself not wanting people to know. He tried to be more careful. He tried to be quiet. He did not want people to interfere with what he intended to do.

He turned again toward the water at the side of the boat and peered into the deep of the lake. He found a penny in the bottom of the boat and dropped it over the side. He watched it disappear into the darkness. He leaned over the edge a little at a time. A little more and a little more. He felt himself following the penny. He could go. He could go now.

A little more and almost there. But then. . .

"Don't."

"Don't?" The thought was his, but it had not come from him.

He said, "Say again."

There was nothing. Just their private lake. And he was sitting in the middle of it.

Then the bluebird landed on the far end of the boat.

"That was not you!" he blurted. And he understood immediately that it wasn't himself or nature, or the solitude. Neither could he pretend that he had not heard it.

"Heard it?!" he marveled. "Yes."

"Don't." That was all? No explanation of why not? No repeats. No sentences? Just "*Don't?!*"

He put the oars back in the water, turned the boat toward his house and the dock, and started rowing. When he got back, he stashed the oars, set the oarlocks down, tied the boat up, and made his way to his house.

"Don't" was everywhere inside. He was no longer alone, but now there was something, perhaps someone, with whom to argue. He hated that. "Don't?! Don't tell me anything!"

He could not erase it from his mind. It was a bell he had heard ring, and he couldn't pretend he hadn't heard it. Nothing was the same.

PART 2

The Pneumenal Field in Gestalt Therapy

7

BASIC FIELD DYNAMICS

All there is
Or just for me?
If all there is
Is just for me
Then all's
Not
All there is
To me.

Perls, Hefferline, and Goodman (1951/1980) claimed that contacting takes place *at* the surface boundary, what they called at times the contact boundary, *in* "the field of the organism/environment" (p. 303).

They put it that way instead of saying between the organism and the environment, because "the definition of an animal involves its environment. . . . The definition of an organism is the definition of an organism/environment field; and the contact-boundary is, so to speak, the specific organ of awareness of the novel situation of the field . . ." (ibid., p. 303).

What kind of field? An organism-environment field.[1] The anthropology of gestalt therapy is of a certain type of being. O'Neill and Gaffney (2008) recognized this when they said that PHG outlines "a view of the self as intrinsically part of an overall organism-environment field" (p. 239) and pointed to PHG affirming that it is always to such an interacting field they refer and not to the actions of an isolated animal.

The authors of PHG went on in the context cited above to refer to the contact boundary and the action there as manifesting this dual nature of the organism-environment field. In taste, for instance they say that it is impossible to experience taste of something without one's mouth tasting it. The thing tasted, the mouth, and the taste are one in the act of tasting. So, the contacting at the boundary brings together the thing tasted and the thing tasting, and they merge in one phenomenal experience of taste. "Outer" and "inner" become one at the contact-boundary in the organism-environment field,[2] and this brings together ontical and phenomenal properties of one, unified experience.

Field dynamics are essential to gestalt therapy theory, but there are diverse terms, as already seen, that various people use to describe similar or overlapping concepts in the field theory of gestalt therapy. Yontef (1993), Parlett (1991), and Wheeler (1991, 2000) have all written about the field, often turning to the application of field theory to the social sciences that was observed in Kurt Lewin (1951). Francesetti (2019a) cited twenty-one references for various authors in gestalt therapy who were writing something about field theory.

As a beginning consideration of field dynamics in gestalt therapy and Christianity this chapter is limited to three types of fields, or three ways to conceptualize "the field": ontical, phenomenal, and pneumenal.

The Ontical Field

This is all that actually exists. This is the tree that stands in the forest and falls whether anyone perceives it or not. This is the world that acts regardless of our thoughts about it. This is the array of forces that act upon me, whether I like it or not. This is what is. This is what happens (Brownell, 2018).

The ontical field includes the existence of God. It includes what many people call the "spiritual realm," or the "kingdom of God." It is the material and the immaterial, the realities that exercise influence whether they are forces of nature that can be seen and measured or those of thought, intention, and motivation, of values that cannot be seen or measured except in the effect they have on people.

This is not to say that everything is everything. I'm talking about actualities that are glimpsed in part but sensed in one way or another as being connected to other "parts," and if one shifts one's gaze, these other parts come into view as figures of interest. We do not have absolute knowledge of the ontical field, because we are limited, finite.

In the office which is my study there is a window. Through that window I can see sagebrush and pine trees. The morning light is cool, and colors look more vibrant before noon. In the afternoon sun the colors appear hot and relatively faded. Is that what the trees and the sagebrush actually do—change color? Are they cool and vibrant in the morning, but then fade, loose their vibrancy, and wilt in the afternoon? I am sure something like that happens; something like that actually takes place, but I am also sure that the experience of looking out the window in the morning as opposed to the afternoon is affected by the way I look, by my abilities to see, by my disposition at such moments as well as by the physical conditions residing between me—the observer—and the sagebrush and trees—the observed. Is what I perceive all just my construction so that I never see what actually exists or am affected by the conditions that actually surround (and therefore the idea of an ontical field is a useful fantasy but a pragmatic absurdity)? I don't believe so. I think we actually have contact in a real world with things as they are (even if they are constantly changing), but we don't have an absolute knowledge of them from our encounters. We interpret our contact.

The Phenomenal Field

When the house is very dark at night and I get up, I walk without seeing where I'm going or what is around me. I open my eyes wide, but that doesn't help me see. It just makes the darkness deeper. I put my arms out in front of me to prevent myself from bumping into a wall. That's when I step on something with my bare feet. The pain shoots up into my legs and I lift off and shift my weight so I don't fall down. Automatically I say something representative of my pain and displeasure.

The phenomenal field is the arena of our experience while navigating the ontical field. It emerges through contacting. As such the phenomenal field "is generated by all that is relevant and extends into space and time *as far as it can produce a difference in experience*" (Francesetti, 2019a, p. 272). It is the field of one's experience and as such it is intrinsically linked to the real world, all that actually is. Our experience, and the perceptions we have, is not simply the dream of some kind of consciousness. We do not make it all up out of nothing. Our experience is dependent on contact with an actual reality that is going on and of which we have become partakers. "The phenomenal field is something that emerges between us and around us in our encounter" (Francesetti, 2019a, p. 272).

This field of experience that extends beyond the physical confines of any individual's body, any one person's self, their emotions, their values in play, their intentions, their preferences and interpretations of meaning all swirling in one phenomenality, is at once also actual and an aspect of the ontical field. "The phenomenal field is not material, it is not a 'thing.' Nevertheless, its existence is real and perceptible in time and space" (Francesetti, 2019a, p. 276).

Phenomenal fields evoke new experience. They are the artifacts of experience, if not experience itself going on, but they are not just "contained" within individuals. They are not simply my experience hermetically sealed within my vessel. I am not a clean room wandering untouchable and untouching in this world. I have effect. I affect others through my extension, my extensiveness. My energy warms my wife in bed at night when all around us the winter cold lays down heavy on the blankets over us. My emotions extend into the room and influence the experience of others in that same space. We cannot see such things taking place. We cannot measure the emotional tone of the room, but we can sense it. In its nascent phase such experience is atmospheric, not fully formed, not completely emergent and differentiated (Francesetti, 2019b).

Some people believe that all phenomenal fields begin as such atmospheres (see chapter eight for more on atmospheres), understood as quasi-things and being neither subject nor object. As such they are neither simply resident inside the person and his or her constructions of meaning nor outside the person, existing separate in and of themselves. Rather, they are emergent of what happens, and "what happens" is not simply what happens between two persons, as in the case of a therapist and client, a pastor and parishioner, a teacher and student, or between the Savior and His disciples. It is the mix of all that actually exists and the degree to which the persons involved are in contact. Jani (2018) describes this in her study of Edith Stein's approach to the ontic aspects of social life, writing, "from the view of the individual, the internal relationship between the communal life and the individual life is a circular one, in which the communal life is a part of the individual life, and the individual's own share of the community contributes to the understanding of the individual's personal life" (Jani, 2018, p. 50). The term "community" here is analogous to the ontic field itself. With regard to circularity, one cannot have a contributing part in any of it without being in contact; thus, it is the contacting that carries influence. It is contact that has effect.

The Pneumenal Field

The word for *spirit* in the Old Testament is רוּחַ (*ruah*) and in the New Testament it is πνεῦμα (*pneuma*); they both refer to the wind, to breathing (and have come also to refer to the vital life force of a human being). Thus, the pneumenal field is a spiritual field.[3] That begs the question "What is spirit?"

In the book *Spiritual Competency in Psychotherapy* (Brownell, 2015a), following an inductive study of the word spirit in the Old Testament, I concluded that in a person's spirit "is a human capacity of emotion and thought that animates the physical body and provides a conduit of communication and power between human beings and God" (p. 28). Because we live, move, and have our being *in* God,[4] we cannot escape Him. We inhabit His creation and the things He created constantly speak of Him.[5] These affect us, and we have spiritual experience.

The pneumenal field exists and operates in certain ways. If you would, there is a Tao to it.[6] It is infused with life, driven by spirit itself, perceived as transcendent, recognized through intuition, characterized in story, and congruent with the kingdom of God.

Infused With Life

When God created the first human being, He first fashioned the physical body out of dust, the elements of the earth, and it was an inert form. At that point it was not yet a human being. When He blew into it the breath of life, that physical body became a living being, a human being[7]—Adam, a man.

It has become fashionable for Christian thinkers to use the philosophy of emergence and non-reductive physicalism to explain the connection between

74 The Pneumenal Field in Gestalt Therapy

physical body and immaterial soul or mind. But that is starting to tell the story after it has already begun. What unites body and soul (soma and psyche), brain and mind, is life. It is human life that is the starting point and only when one is living does emergence kick in. Something must have life or else there is nothing going on and no emergence possible. Further, according to Genesis, it was not until that life was breathed into the body that it became a human being—a being at all. Therefore, it is artificial to dichotomize, to split up that being into parts and then to consider the relationship among those parts. It is like taking a part of the human body out of the body and looking at it in the laboratory. Such a lab is not where and how the real human physiology occurs. This is what Goldstein (1995) noted when he said that people cannot understand the reflex arc outside of the brain in which it occurs (nor the brain outside of the body in which *it* occurs). The whole organism *is* the being.

Since the pneumenal field is characterized by life, it includes the experience of one's lived body and life world. It is what I think, feel, intend, value, dream about, and long for. It's the horizon of my intentionality. So, it includes my figures of interest, their logical extensions, and the enduring life themes that seem to matter over time. It is the risked edge of my existence.

Driven by Spirit

The pneumenal field is filled with yearnings. When Paul, for instance, describes the internal struggle he experiences in which he sins but is disgusted by his sin and finds aspects of himself abhorrent in his desire to follow God, he is a point of awareness for the pneumenal field, the energetic waves of God's influence in his life as a believer.

> *I find then the principle that evil is present in me, the one who wants to do good.*
> *For I joyfully concur with the law of God in the inner man,*
> *but I see a different law in the members of my body,*
> *waging war against the law of my mind and making me a prisoner*
> *of the law of sin which is in my members. Wretched man that I am!*
> *Who will set me free from the body of this death?*
> *Thanks be to God through Jesus Christ our Lord!*
> *So then, on the one hand I myself with my mind am serving the law of God,*
> *but on the other, with my flesh the law of sin.*[8]

We have this yearning for the things of God because God has put it inside of us;[9] we have this disgust because we desire to satisfy our appetites (and become disappointed in ourselves when we do). It's not just that one is spiritual and the other is natural;[10] they both reside in a pneumenal field, because they are at odds with one another in the life of human beings. Questions of spiritual sensitivity or spiritual dullness, degrees of spiritual discernment, responsiveness to God—these are all push-pull dynamics in a person's pneumenal field.

Perceived as Transcendent

When people become aware of the pneumenal field *as pneumenal* it often seems other-worldly, ephemeral, numinous, or transcendent. One becomes aware that *something* is going on around them which is of another dimension. Beyond that, however, the pneumenal field transcends the binary of ontical vs phenomenal fields. It brings them together. The unseen but imagined or hoped for actually exists. I remember when it dawned on me that the story I was reading in the Bible was true. It seemed astonishing.

Recognized Through Intuition

The pneumenal field is recognized through intuition and results in a different kind of knowing. In Matthew 12, Jesus told a story about Jewish religious leaders disgruntled because Christ's disciples were picking grain and eating it on the Sabbath. Jesus told them that something greater than the Sabbath was at hand (namely Himself). They had not comprehended. They did not have the spiritual capacity to sense what was taking place right in front of them; so, they looked to what did make sense, and that was concrete, obvious, and "visible" statutes—religious laws and rules to govern virtually every circumstance. They could not perceive the kingdom come upon them, because it takes a different kind of knowing to detect it.

I have described this way of knowing elsewhere as an interoception or proprioception of the spirit—touch of another kind (Brownell, 2016b). It is a knowing, a whole-body recognition perceived in one's core that then dawns upon the mind. People refer to it as knowing in one's gut or one's heart, because that is where it is first felt. It is a knowing prior to knowing. Jesus referred to this when He often said, "He who has ears let him hear,"[11] which is echoed in what the Spirit says to the churches in Revelation 2:7 and 11.[12] Having ears means having the ability to comprehend, to know intuitively, to recognize the spiritual significance of something.

Characterized in Story

The pneumenal field exists outside of what anyone thinks about it, and it includes a whole realm of existence we cannot evaluate with a naturalistic epistemology. It is not simply intrapsychic. It is not simply the collective unconscious. It is not fantasy or science fiction.

However, it *is* characterized by narrative, drama, story. Spiritual conflict is one of the ontical features of the pneumenal field. The pneumenal field is a place of struggle. The story of Job illustrates that something is going on around us that we are not always aware of but which occurs nonetheless. We are in it and of it. We do not simply construct or imagine it.

76 The Pneumenal Field in Gestalt Therapy

In Daniel 10:10–14 an angel is obstructed in ministering to Daniel until Michael, one of the chief angels, comes to help him. The two battle against a fallen angel referred to as the "prince of the kingdom of Persia." Thus, the pneumenal field is not just a sub-category of the phenomenal field, not simply our religious consciences affirming or condemning us.

It also manifests through the influence of God directly, as in the presence of the Holy Spirit, and indirectly through people indwelt of the Holy Spirit. One often senses the spiritual as a call, a calling, or a presence.[13] One can detect that *something is going on here* when there is no concrete and tangible correlate for trepidation or presentiment.

One can sense the presence of the Holy Spirit; likewise, one can sense evil (Brownell, 2015b, 2016c).

The call of God in a person's life is a personal experience that is not really known outside of one's response to it (Chrétien, 2004). It is a purposeful leading, and it is likely given as a saturated phenomenon. "A saturated phenomenon is one that cannot be wholly contained within concepts that can be grasped by our understanding. It gives so much in intuition that there is always an excess left over, which is beyond conceptualization. Thus, it is saturated with intuition" (Mackinlay, 2010, p. 1).

Jesus said, "I will ask the Father, and He will give you another Helper, that He may be with you forever; *that is* the Spirit of truth, whom the world cannot receive, because it does not see Him or know Him, *but* you know Him because He abides with you and will be in you."[14] Therein resides the essential conflict of the world into which Christians are cast—the difference between a life world including God and one without.

Congruent With the Kingdom of God

The pneumenal field is consistent and congruent with what the Bible calls the kingdom of God. When Jesus said "the kingdom of God has come upon you,"[15] He meant it had done so in His person, in His actual presence and in His actions, which He ascribed to the works of God done through Him in their presence. The kingdom of God cannot be physically measured, and it is without bound.

Psalm 103:11–19

For as high as the heavens are above the earth,
So great is His lovingkindness toward those who fear Him.
As far as the east is from the west,
So far has He removed our transgressions from us.
Just as a father has compassion on his children,
So the Lord has compassion on those who fear Him.
For He Himself knows our frame;

He is mindful that we are but dust.
As for man, his days are like grass;
As a flower of the field, so he flourishes.
When the wind has passed over it, it is no more,
And its place acknowledges it no longer.
But the lovingkindness of the Lord is from everlasting to everlasting on those who
fear Him,
And His righteousness to children's children,
To those who keep His covenant
And remember His precepts to do them.
The Lord has established His throne in the heavens,
And His sovereignty rules over all.

A Contemporary Illustration

Mary rolled up her clothes, tied them, and then hid them just outside the house. Then she went to where the staff keys hung on the wall, opened the door to the office, found the key to the locked medication cabinet, and emptied all her medications into a sandwich bag. She took some of another resident's medications as well. She found some money in a desk drawer, and then she took her files and the staff mobile phone.

Mary left the building, found her clothes, and walked across town to the local crisis center. She told the people that she had escaped from a Jesus cult where they refused to let her see an outside counselor and would not let her eat full meals. She told them the staff were all "crazy." She texted her friends out of state, and she told them the same thing. She said she would catch a bus as soon as she could, the next day, and she'd be back home with them soon. That is what she did.

The people at the crisis center knew the staff at the recovery house. As soon as Mary arrived and unloaded her story they called. They told the staff what Mary and done and what she had been saying. The recovery house staff felt betrayed. They wondered if the crisis center staff believed her. Yes, they were faith-based in their approach to recovery from addiction, but they did not refuse meals to anyone and they weren't "crazy." They still felt slandered and scandalized. After the initial shock wore off, they also began lamenting, grieving that Mary had left, and wondering if they had failed her. Did they do something that offended her; did they not do enough? Where was God in all this? The staff at that recovery house donated their time out of a sense of mission and calling. They believed God brought Mary to them. How could she have come through the place and not been affected for the kingdom of God? Was she? Was there some kind of positive effect that took place, and providentially, then, that was all that was necessary from them in her life? They wondered, but they suspected they would never know.

78 The Pneumenal Field in Gestalt Therapy

In this story there are the facts. There is the experience of living in the influence of those facts, and there are the spiritual considerations relevant to the working of God in peoples' lives—ontical, phenomenal, and pneumenal field dynamics.

Notes

1. Change from / to — explained in the next footnote.
2. This is why I wrote (Brownell, 2016a) that the integrating factor, the central mechanism of integration in the theoretical integration that formed early gestalt therapy, was PHG's anthropology: "The organizing center for the integration that became Gestalt therapy is its anthropology—the concept of the person as emerging from the organism—environment field through contacting. That is, the human being in early Gestalt therapy was conceived of as an organism—environment entity, not just an organism in an environment" (p. 220). The human organism is an organism-environment kind of "thing." I continue to write it this way, with the hyphen, to make it clear that it is not either an organism or an environment, but one new thing: an organism-environment kind of thing, kind of organism. This way of viewing the contacting involved, then, has implications for the consideration of what Francesetti (2019b) and others call a phenomenal field. The contacting is *in* the organism, but the organism is already a hyphenated kind of being. It is already linked to the environment. It's not that it has to touch the environment to become an organism/environment, it is already an organism-environment field. The contacting is manifest *in* its being. That is what makes it at once both an ontical (because it is really happening and the entity actually exists as it is) and a phenomenal (experienced) consideration. It is both an object and an experience in the process of happening.
3. There are other words that convey the same basic idea of wind, breath, etc. I use this one because it is dominant.
4. Acts 17:28.
5. Psalm 19:1–6; Romans 1:18–20.
6. Tao is a Chinese word signifying way or path. It is considered to be the natural order of life that is not reduced to a concept and can only be known, or learned, through experience.
7. Genesis 2:7, cf. Genesis 7:22.
8. Romans 7:21–25.
9. Psalm 37:4.
10. 1. Corinthians 2:14–3:3.
11. Matthew 11:15; 13:9, 43; Mark 4:9, 23; Luke 8:8; 14:35.
12. cf. 3:6, 13; 13:9.
13. Hebrews 3:7ff, cf. 1 Kings 19:11–13.
14. John 14:16–17.
15. Luke 11:20, cf. Matthew 12:28.

Resources

Brownell, P. (2015a). *Spiritual competency in psychotherapy*. New York, NY: Springer Publishing.

Brownell, P. (2015b). *Jean-Louis Chrétien's call and response: Therapeutic implications of contact with divinity*. Presentation to the Psychology and the Other Conference, Cambridge, MA.

Brownell, P. (2016a). Contemporary gestalt therapy. In D. Cain, K. Keenan, & S. Rubin (Eds.), *Humanistic psychotherapies: Handbook of research and practice* (2nd ed.). Washington, DC: American Psychological Association.

Brownell, P. (2016b). Touch of another kind: Contact with God and spiritual self. In J.-M. Robine (Ed.), *Self: A polyphony of contemporary gestalt therapists*. Bordeaux, France: L'exprimerie.

Brownell, P. (2016c). Jean-Louis Chrétien's call and response: Therapeutic implications of contact with divinity. *The aesthetic of otherness*. Meeting at the Boundary in a Desensitized World—A Joint AAGT and EAGT Gestalt Conference at the Crossroads of Civilization, Taormina, Sicily.

Brownell, P. (2018). *Gestalt psychotherapy and coaching for relationships*. New York, NY: Routledge, Taylor & Francis.

Chrétien, J.-L. (2004). *The call and the response*. New York, NY: Fordham University Press.

Francesetti, G. (2019a). The field perspective in clinical practice: Towards a theory of therapeutic phronesis. In P. Brownell (Ed.), *Handbook for theory, research, and practice in gestalt therapy* (2nd ed., pp. 268–302). Newcastle upon Tyne, UK: Cambridge Scholars Publishing.

Francesetti, G. (2019b). A clinical exploration of atmospheres. Toward a field-based clinical practice. In G. Francesetti & T. Griffero (Eds.), *Psychopathology and atmospheres* (pp. 35–68). Newcastle upon Tyne, UK: Cambridge Scholars Publishing.

Goldstein, K. (1995). *The organism*. New York, NY: Zone Books.

Jani, A. (2018). The ontic-ontological aspects of social life. Edith Stein's approach to the problem. In S. Luft & R. Hagengruber (Eds.), *Women phenomenologists on social ontology: We experiences, communal life, and joint action* (pp. 45–59). Cham, Switzerland: Springer Nature Switzerland AG.

Lewin, K. (1951). *Field theory in social science: Selected theoretical papers* (D. Cartwright, Ed.). Oxford, UK: Harpers.

Mackinlay, S. (2010). *Interpreting excess: Jean-Luc Marion, saturated phenomena, and hermeneutics*. New York, NY: Fordham University Press.

O'Neill, B., & Gaffney, S. (2008). Field theoretical strategy. In P. Brownell (Ed.), *Handbook for theory, research, and practice in gestalt therapy* (1st ed., pp. 228–256). Newcastle upon Tyne, UK: Cambridge Scholars Publishing.

Parlett, M. (1991). Reflections on field theory. *British Gestalt Journal, 1*, 68–91.

Perls, F., Hefferline, R., & Goodman, P. (1951/1980). *Gestalt therapy: Excitement and growth in the human personality*. New York, NY: Bantam Books.

Wheeler, G. (2000). *Beyond individualism*. Hillsdale, NJ: Analytic Press, GIC Press.

Wheeler, G. (1991). *Gestalt reconsidered*. New York, NY: Gardner Press, Inc., GIC Press.

Yontef, G. (1993). *Awareness, dialogue, & process: Essays on gestalt therapy*. Highland, NJ: Gestalt Journal Press.

8

ATMOSPHERES AND THE ORGANISM-ENVIRONMENT FIELD

Like a cloud, a mist descending.
Like a sound, but just beginning.
Like a thought that comes while fading
Or a tear that falls while fainting.

Like a touch that lingers touching.
Like a kiss of fragrance tempting.
Like the mourning of a lost love longing
Or a room that keeps on haunting.

C.S. Lewis was a professor and Christian writer of the last century. He is widely known for his fantasy books as well as his clear analyses of life and Christianity. He was a contemporary and friend of J.R.R. Tolkien. Those two and their friends used to meet at the Eagle and Child pub (also known as the Bird and Baby pub) in Oxford, drink beer, and discuss their various writing projects. About the mysterious that seems to elude us beyond the boundary of our natural surroundings, Lewis once claimed that experience by itself will not provide all the answers:

> If anything extraordinary seems to have happened, we can always say that we have been the victims of an illusion. If we hold a philosophy which excludes the supernatural, this is what we always shall say. What we learn from experience depends on the kind of philosophy we bring to experience. It is therefore useless to appeal to experience before we have settled, as well as we can, the philosophical question.
>
> *(Lewis, 1947/2002, p. 303)*

That is a good thought to keep in mind as we move into thinking about atmospheres and the kinds of pathic experiences people endure.

In gestalt therapy the various tenets of its theory are not modes that can be entered or left as one traverses a therapeutic landscape. They overlap, inhering one another to form a unity. Thus, elements of this chapter will find more development and application in the next section on phenomenology. Here, although we have very limited space, we need to understand the ontology of things in order to comprehend the nature of quasi-things, for atmospheres are quasi-things and atmospheres are the ontical beginnings of phenomenal fields.

Things

We live in a world of things, and these things speak for themselves (Bloom, 2019a). Husserl thought things have an essence that could be ascertained by setting aside the natural attitude, the ordinary way of seeing things, in a transcendental reduction (i.e. transcending the natural attitude). Heidegger believed the importance of things was in their being, for instance either present-at-hand, as an object of contemplation, or ready-to-hand, as a tool useful for practical purposes. Griffero said, "Things are roughly taken to be tangible and well-determined entities with a regular shape that, being three dimensional, cannot be exhausted by their representations" (2017, p. 4). Nevertheless, people do ascribe representations to them.

When we experience, we experience things. In a post-representational perspective life and thought are more centered in practice than abstracted through discourse, "the basis of meaning is commonly situated in actions, interactions and bodily experience, rather than discourse, semiotics and representation" (Buser, 2014, p. 230). Thus, one is most commonly engrossed in the experience of things rather than in theorizing about them. This, I have claimed, is also true of the process of therapy, where therapists are involved with their clients and the most effective process is interrupted when they begin to reduce them—transcend the natural attitude in order to ascertain the true essence of the patient, which is what we also do in case conceptualization and diagnosis.[1]

Sometimes I think we lose nothing by taking a bottom-up approach to therapy in which one focuses on process rather than a top-down approach in which one focuses on pathology and diagnoses, "prescribing" various interventions to change, heal, alter the constellation of symptoms that then comprises the therapist's thematization of the patient.

It has become fashionable for gestalt therapists to escape thing ontology by going to the relatedness of all things in constellations and the verbs that emerge from process, both of which comprise situations. Indeed, clinical field theory has been conceptualized as situational. Consequently, we speak of psychotherapy as an approach to a situation (Robine, 2016; Wollants, 2012). However, there is no given situation apart from the things that are in it and how they are affected by the

82 The Pneumenal Field in Gestalt Therapy

processes of the situation. The whole is larger than the sum of its parts, but there is no whole without them.

Things (Phenomena) Are Given

The reality we experience is given. "It is given . . . in the fact that it is emergent" (Robinson, 2015, p. 90). It may emerge from the interaction of the various elements involved, and so reach the level of awareness, but it is not simply constituted by a subject. Phenomena don't depend on someone's creativity—as if they were simply products of the sense of need or of social propriety.

Relatedly, constructivism is a re-presenting to oneself of what has already been given, what has emerged and been presented. It is a thematization of the perceived that leaves behind the original givenness of the experience.

But there is a simpler way to consider this. A phenomenon is basically an appearing in which the phenomenon shows itself. In other words, phenomena are *perceived* rather than *created*. And there is a logic here to be followed. If they show themselves, they must first give themselves because if they do not *give* themselves there is nothing showing.

This is Marion's logic. Jean-Luc Marion (2002) asserted that phenomena are given. If "the phenomenon is defined as what *shows itself* in and from itself (Heidegger), instead of what admits constitution (Husserl), this *self* can be attested only inasmuch as the phenomenon first *gives itself*" (p. 4). He also asserted that givenness organizes phenomenality. In thick lines of philosophical language he stepped over Kant's confines of possibility and said that possibility depends on phenomenality. In other words, the phenomenal horizon is always expanded by experience, and experience depends on givenness. Givenness, then, is tantamount to revelation—self-disclosure, purposeful transparency, deliberate presence. Thus, the construct of a saturated phenomenon, one that is in excess of the horizon and overwhelms intuition, is not such an impossible hurdle. It is simply an extension of the norm in which that which exceeds the horizon must be given.

Kinds and Qualities of Things

When we experience things, we can experience them in their essential nature but also in their accidental features. There are things considered as a set of essential characteristics, and there are features that adhere to them, that come and go without altering the basic nature of a given thing. A house is a thing in itself, but its blue color only adheres to it. The blueness is a property of the house but not its essential presence.

When we function in the world of things it seems that we are separate from them, observing them, and as such they appear as bounded, and we ascribe values, magnitudes, temperatures, and other descriptive qualities to them. It seems as if

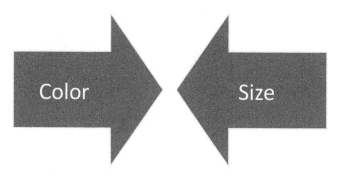

FIGURE 8.1 Qualities Ascribed to Things

these characteristics are contained within the surface boundary of such objects (see Figure 8.1).

One kind of thing to which we commonly ascribe qualities is an inanimate thing. Features of architectural space and the aesthetics of art are such inanimate things. They may depict life yet be without it themselves.

Inanimate Things

Our property is on the high desert at 3,743 feet above sea level. It's in Southern Idaho where ancient volcanic activity has left the place full of rocks. The Snake River Canyon is a monumental rock formation carved out of that landscape. I jokingly tell people that I am a farmer because we have some acreage, and we grow rocks. They come up in places where I have previously harvested others, and they continually emerge out of the dirt. I would love to have a time lapse video of their emerging, but the fact that they seem to move up from deep in the ground to peek through the grass and weeds and then steadily raise up into a new crop does not mean they are living. They are inanimate things that are acted upon by physical forces. They are cold in the night and get hot in the day because the sun beats down on them. In themselves there is no neurological activity; they are "brain dead." There is no heartbeat. Even though the rocks seem to move by being pushed up and out of the ground, they don't grow in their own stature. If you put a rock on the floor in your kitchen and scratch chalk on the wall at its height, you will never see the rock get taller. It's not just that it is dead. It was never alive. It is of a different kind of order from a living thing, and we can only ascribe qualities to such inanimate things; they lack the life necessary to exude them.

Other kinds of things do indeed exude qualities. Instead of having characteristics ascribed to them, they transmit value, evincing qualities for the perceiver (see Figure 8.2). These qualities, such as passion and presence, emanate from them.

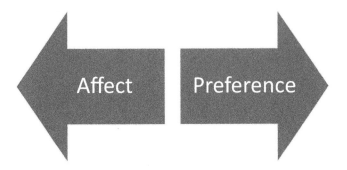

FIGURE 8.2 Qualities Perceived as Emanating From Things

Animate Things

Aristotle (2004) claimed that living things are characterized by movement and sensation. His treatise on the soul (*De Anima*) is the namesake for modern animation. Animation is the process whereby still pictures are manipulated to appear as moving objects. The pictures are not actually living because their content seems to move; animation is only the illusion of life. Truly living things, though, are intrinsically animate. Their capacity to move is inherent to their being as *living* being.

Living things don't just move from one spot to another; they also grow. So, I include in this definition all the metabolic processes by which living organisms do grow and are moved. Thus, they have heat, body temperature, and they have neurological activity. The heart beats and pumps blood around in the body. A living body has all those things (and more), but without them the physical body is not a living thing any longer but a corpse—the decomposing physical remnants of a living thing.

In addition, of course, animate things are also sensate. To various degrees they are sentient (having sentience—the capacity to feel, perceive or engage in subjective experience) and they show various degrees of sapience (practical knowledge of how things work, even the intuition that tells them how to act in their own best interest).

Living things display awareness, sensation, and knowing. "This idea opens a window into phenomenology; that is, to the 'how,' the 'what,' and the 'as' of experience within our human horizon" (Bloom, 2019b, p. 21). Indeed, phenomenology is based in an ontology of things.

Living human beings display life through both their physical bodies (*Körper*) and their lived bodies (*Leib*). Through the physical body they have sensory experience and perceive various phenomena. For instance, a thing can be present-to-hand for the physical body, but not be ready-to-hand if the lived body is lacking the background and understanding to realize how that thing is relevant and useful

The Organism-Environment Field **85**

in the life world of the person who is aware of them.[2] Bloom (2019b) described a continuum of awareness and consciousness, how awareness relates to consciousness, and I believe that awareness is more a function of the physical body and its mechanisms while the intentionality of knowing, or consciousness, is more a function of the lived body and the process of meaning making, of interpreting that raw, physical perception and experience. A living person is a consciousness—a conscious being, a living thing that has awareness.

> *There is a difference between what is reflected upon (awareness),*
> *and that which reflects (consciousness),*
> *even though in the process itself it is one whole contacting process,*
> *one whole stream of experience in which both are equally essential.*
> *This stream of experience is the awareness-consciousness continuum.*
> *Gestalt therapy attends to the structure of experience,*
> *and to the qualities of contacting, of this continuum.*
> *(Bloom, 2019b, p. 23)*

It is the living thing as person that embodies this consciousness. Titus, Vitz, Nordling, and DMU Group (forthcoming, n.p.) asserted

> *Each human exercises pre-rational*
> *sensory perceptual-cognitive capacities*
> *as a body-soul unity.*
> *These pre-rational capacities serve as*
> *important foundations for the rational human linguistic,*
> *interpersonal, and moral dimensions, and the higher cognitive capacities*
> *so central to the unique character of human life.*

Thus, both awareness and consciousness are aspects of a living thing, and they reside, as Bloom indicated, on a continuum. Likewise, both *Körper* and *Leib* are required for an animate thing to truly be considered living,[3] and they interact to produce the whole experience of living.

Animate things, living things, also have the capacity for extension of cognition and affect. Just as body temperature exceeds the surface boundary of the physical body, thoughts, motives, values, emotions, and intentions exceed what people might consider the surface boundary of the person. A person's influence in the field is a function of such extension (Clark & Chalmers, 1998; Rowlands, 2010). This is easy to understand if we consider the influence one's ideas might have through writing, but extension is not limited to products produced by the person; it includes one's presence. Thus, when someone regarded to be "larger than life" walks into the room, he or she seems to take up a lot of space, more space than the physical body actually requires, and that sense of the person is a perception of their lived body.

86 The Pneumenal Field in Gestalt Therapy

In either case (inanimate and animate) we might say that things are given to us as the kinds of things that they are.

Givenness, Hermeneutics, and the Middle Voice

As stated, phenomena do not simply appear; they are given. Let me come at givenness through the eyes of Shane Mackinlay (2010), who wrote that in place of "phenomena appearing as objects (Husserl) or beings (Heidegger) within the limits of horizons imposed by a constituting subject, Marion envisages phenomena as appearing without conditions or limits, given by themselves alone" (p. 11).

That sets up things in the sense of Günter Figal's (2010) use of the term *Gegenständlichkeit*. A *Gegenstand* is something that stands in opposition to or in tension with. It is opposed; it is different. Thus, the transcendent Other in Levinas (1999) is an ethically challenging Gegenstand. The other in a gestalt dialogue does not stand against as in the sense of a conflict but as an actual other, an ontologically necessary second (for without a second, the dialogue becomes a solipsistic monologue). In gestalt therapy the "second" gives him or herself to the "first" as he or she is, revealing what could not be known outside of this givenness, and thus also establishing a wondrous excess of intuition—a saturated phenomenon.

Yet, there is a problem. If givenness and revelation were all there were to the process, then we would have absolute knowledge of everything that is given. What would prevent it? But we don't. Conversely, if constitution and representation were all that is involved in dealing with the things in our lives, then the world would always function as we imagine and nothing would frustrate or surprise. But it does.

We are always situated, experientially, in a middle state. With reference to a person whose experience is in question, givenness could be conceived as involving a passive process (we receive what is given). Representation could be conceived as an active process (we create the imaginals we need, what makes sense, symbols that fit within the confines of our horizons). The givenness surprises, but the imaginals feel more familiar, because they make sense. The arbiter, the moderator of this seeming impasse (active or passive) is the middle voice of reflexive self-interest in which we interpret our experience of the actual world and find the middle ground that enlarges our life worlds. Do our representations fit the conditions of sensing what is given? Do phenomena exceed our imaginals?

This is what Merleau-Ponty considered in his construct of the chiasm. We bump into a world of things that have been given, among which we've been thrown, and with self-interest we make sense of our experience. This making meaning out of experience people call *hermeneutics*.

Quasi-Things

In talking about things we have distinguished animate and inanimate things, and we've followed some phenomenological philosophers of no small standing who claim

The Organism-Environment Field **87**

phenomena give and show themselves. That is, both animate and inanimate things are present according to what they are and they appear to us in experience. They are not simply imagined. They are not fictional. They exist and, as it were, pass before us having given and shown themselves through their presence to us. As such they are perceived.

There is another class of things which are at once not quite things. They could be called "almost things" but they *have* been called quasi-things. Atmospheres are quasi-things that refer to a feeling or mood that

> exceeds an individual body and instead pertains primarily to the overall situation in which bodies are entrenched. The concept of an atmosphere thus challenges a notion of feelings as the private mental states of a cognizant subject and instead construes feelings as collectively embodied, spatially extended, material, and culturally inflected.
>
> *(Riedel, 2019, p. 85)*

Atmospheres

Thomas Fuchs (2013) asserted that the intrapsychic view of mental illness is inadequate because we do not live in a merely physical world and we are not simply encased in a skull or a brain; the spaces we experience—the spaces we inhabit—are environmental and charged with affective qualities.

> Feelings befall us; they emerge from situations, persons, and objects which have their expressive features and which attract or repel us. This affective space is essentially felt through the medium of the body which widens, tightens, weakens, trembles, shakes, etc. in correspondence to the affects and atmospheres that we experience.
>
> *(np)*

I would add that this dynamic includes the felt or lived body, that it is not limited to the merely physical body. It is here, at the level of felt body, that Fuchs locates the sense of being alive, of being a self-aware, animate thing. It is the pre-reflective, and what he calls the "unnoticed background of all intentional feeling, perceiving, or acting" (2013). It is at the threshold of experience.

Ontological Status

> Atmospheres are indeterminate, above all, in regard to their ontological status. One does not quite know whether to attribute them to the objects or environments from which they emanate or to the subjects who experience them. One also does not quite know where they are. They seem to fill the space with a *Gefühlston* (feeling-tone), like a haze, as it were.
>
> *(Böhme, 2017, p. 14)*

Indeed. That is the controversy currently reverberating in contemporary gestalt therapy. Do we attribute quasi-things like atmospheres to something outside of oneself (the perceiver) or some process inside oneself? If it is something inside oneself, then in terms of clinical work the sense of an atmosphere is more of the therapist ascribing values to the patient and interpreting his or her meeting with the patient. The origin of the quasi-thing called atmosphere in such a case is intrapsychic and belongs to the countertransference of the therapist. Furthermore, it requires that the therapist relate to the patient as an inanimate thing to which he or she ascribes characteristics. That, to me, is an unacceptable understanding of atmospheres, and it would be unacceptable to most gestalt therapists. Given all that people are saying about the role of atmospheres in a field perspective in gestalt, it cannot be that therapists treat patients as inanimate things and simply attribute values to them from the encounter.

We have long since rejected one-person psychologies, and now we are even moving beyond the two-person, co-created experience to a more contextual, field perspective (Francesetti, 2019a, 2019b).

But if atmospheres are not simply the interpretation of the therapist upon the occasion of meeting with the client, do they exist entirely on their own and hang in spaces like mists? What are they? Where do they come from, and how do they affect us?

Atmospheres belong simultaneously to the perceived and the perceiver, between subject and object. The atmosphere is like an aura that emanates from an object, be that a work of art, a landscape, or building with its space, which comes upon the subject and is breathed in by the subject. As such, one "absorbs it into one's own bodily disposition. What is sensed is an indeterminate, spatially diffused quality of feeling" (Böhme, 2017, p. 18).

Böhme was thinking in terms of the architecture of lived space, and he believed that Schmitz attributed too much autonomy to atmospheres, because Schmitz conceived of them as floating freely, having nothing to do with things and not being produced by them. As such they would have little relevance to the enduring life themes patients bring to therapy (the patient being an animate "thing"). Böhme further regarded Schmitz's view of atmospheres to be strong on the aesthetics of reception but weak on the aesthetics of production; thus, it is not useful as a way of thinking about how atmospheres form in phenomenal fields, nor of their relationship to the qualities of things.

Contagion or Empathy?

Atmospheres concern affective space, but they are contrasted to empathy, a major concept when dealing with affect, in that they are more related to emotional contagion. They are given as one's own emotion, not the perceived emotion of another or others (which is what happens when one empathizes with another). Thus, there is a calling involved in the perception of an atmosphere, for one knows

The Organism-Environment Field **89**

the call in one's own experience of it (Chrétien, 2004). In perceiving an atmosphere, one knows the atmosphere as one's own emotion.

> A feature of emotional contagion "is that you literally catch the emotion in question. . . . It is transferred to you. It becomes your own emotion and is lived through first-personally by you. In emotional contagion, the feeling you are infected by is consequently not phenomenally given as foreign, but as one's own."
>
> *(Zahavi, 2015)*

So, atmospheres give themselves and call to those in their midst. Those perceiving the atmosphere receive the call and experience the atmospheric affect as their own

Perceived Rather Than Co-Constructed

Atmospheres are also not "we-experiences," (Zahavi, 2015) and so defy the common idiom of a co-created situation. Atmospheres are perceived but not static; so, they can be built upon and can evolve, but they are not co-constructed between two people (i.e. the therapist and the client) to begin with. That is, they do not originate simply as a product of the meeting between therapist and client.

Other kinds of affective experiences are sometimes called atmospheres, but they are attributions rather than perceptions. That is, they are emotional responses to inanimate things. They are not, thus, *given* but indeed created.

The Objective and Subjective Genitives in Atmospherics

Here it must be recognized that it is possible to stage or design atmospheres, and people working in theater, architecture, and social geography have been writing about the principles and ramifications of doing so (Edensor & Sumartojo, 2015; Bille, Bjerregaard, & Sørensen, 2015; Böhme, 2017). Thoughtful psychotherapists put effort into creating a physical surround—the aesthetic tone that will support the patient by virtue of them simply entering the waiting room or therapist's office and noticing the choices someone has made for interior design. Thus, in some cases an atmosphere is a space that has been filled with the emotional "charge" of the people who have inhabited it—the atmosphere emanates from the animate (living) things in that space. In other cases the atmosphere results from the catalyst of an inanimate (non-living) thing in a physical space. A person is exposed to the look and feel of that space and ascribes emotion to it. The atmosphere generated in such a case would have been designed, choreographed, provoked through the purposeful use of aesthetic qualities.

Animate things should be considered as it were in the subjective genitive whereas inanimate things take an objective genitive (see Table 8.2). With a subjective genitive the action arises from the thing (the affect perceived has been given by the

90 The Pneumenal Field in Gestalt Therapy

TABLE 8.1 Subjective and Objective Genitive of Atmospheres

Subjective Genitive	Affect from animate things infiltrates space and is perceived directly
Objective Genitive	Inanimate things catalyze affect which is created and attributed indirectly

thing), but with an objective genitive the action resides or comes to rest upon the thing (affect has been attributed to the thing). In the first case we sense qualities and features coming from something, and they overtake us in their givenness. In the second we attribute qualities to things that come before us. The staging or designing of atmospheres involves indirect affect through the process of an objective genitive.

For further illustration I want to use the analogy of a phenomenon of the physical body in order to illustrate the atmospherics of the felt body. When a medical provider introduces fluids or medications intravenously, they insert a needle into a vein in order to do it. The fluids or medication, then, affect the body more rapidly than if taken orally. However, if the needle is not inserted accurately, then the fluids leak out into the surrounding tissues, and that is called an *infiltration*. The fluids infiltrate the surrounding tissues, spreading to the most receptive first. Typical synonyms for this process are words like slip into, get into, invade, penetrate, enter; permeate, pervade, seep into/through, soak into. This, then, is what occurs when affect infiltrates lived space, not just physical space, in the form of atmospheres. That is true whether the atmosphere is perceived, given in the subjective genitive, or evoked, created as an objective genitive.

The clinical work of gestalt therapy is more the perception of direct affect. Of course, we can both catch what the patient brings into the room and we can watch the patient and attribute features to them. We can do both, but in terms of atmospheres there are two different kinds of processes going on, and we need to be able to distinguish which we, as therapists, are doing. When we treat the patient as a non-living, inanimate thing, we are attributing features to them, but when we respond to them as a living thing, we perceive what they bring into the room and, in terms of emotional response, experience it as our own.

Griffero (2018b) described the circularity of atmospherics in presence when he said, "we certainly felt-bodily perceive the atmospheric presence (and thus the feedback) of our outside, of the world, as if it were a gaze towards us and our presence were, as a consequence, our being looked at by them" (p. 68). We endure the calling of the infiltrating atmosphere as our own affective experience. The client simply comes into shared space and his or her life infiltrates the clinical situation.

Griffero identified three kinds of atmospheres relevant to these atmospherics, and Table 8.2 depicts them in relationship to etiologies and applications that I have added.

TABLE 8.2 Types of Atmospheres

Type	Description	Etiology	Application
Prototypic	Ontologically other, external, and unintentional	Subjective genitive	Psychotherapy
Derivative	Ontological other, external, but intentionally produced and always arising from the interpretation of the subject	Objective genitive	Architecture, interior design
Spurious	In relatedness; subjective and even projective	Unclear, ephemeral	Unclear

Developed from Griffero (2018a)

Clinical Atmospherics

Francesetti (2019b, n.p.) described this atmospheric as "the way we originally, vaguely, and globally perceive the situation . . ." which he further described as being prior to figure formation. The atmosphere is something that exists and is perceived (its significance to the perceiver is what becomes interpreted). Francesetti further stated, "It is something I perceive somewhere in the air, without being able to attribute it to myself or to the other. . . . In that hiatus without language, the word almost-entity or quasi-thing comes to the rescue, indicating an atmospheric that has yet to precipitate into a subject or into an object" (ibid.). Thus, it is of both perceived and perceiver.

This is surely post-representational language. Furthermore, it does not reduce to physical influences, as if the atmosphere were nothing more than an aerosol sprayed into the room and whose microelements could be measured by chemical analysis. Rather, atmospheres are meaningful perceptions of the lived body. They are detected *by* the lived body, and the lived body is decidedly not the physical body (although obviously it is related to the physical body). Again, this is not simply the subject perceiving another subject and attributing emotional features to that person. This is a subject suspecting, imagining, and wondering. This is a space filled with emotion and a phenomenon that resists clear antecedents. Further, as Francesetti has noted, this is pre-verbal (without language). It is not linguistically thematized; it is intuited, even if only crudely so.

Clinically both the therapist and the client suspect atmospheres. Can you imagine what the client must sense coming into a room where the therapist has already seen people bleeding emotionally, antagonistically resistant, traumatized and frenzied and then opened up by the therapist to explore such pathology? It is not simply that the therapist must attune to the atmosphere the client is bringing in, because what the client brings in, which is equally a mix of experiences, meets

92 The Pneumenal Field in Gestalt Therapy

the atmosphere already in the room. It's like mixing colors on a pallet. Both client and therapist do not simply co-construct out of the meeting of two sets of figures of interest; they navigate one another's phenomenal fields, which are intuitively sensed in the forms of atmospheres.

Atmospheres Are Spiritual

On July 18, 2019 *The Washington Post* reported that the House Chaplain had opened a session of the House of Representatives by casting out various spirits: the spirit of discouragement, the spirit of pettiness, and the spirit of sadness. The article noted that this was in response to particularly rancorous events preceding in the days before; "The high-test congressional atmosphere—coupled with venomous rhetoric, baleful brawling and general malignancy—prompted House Chaplain Fr. Patrick Conroy to deliver an opening prayer for the ages to the House session last Thursday."

The Chaplain attempted to alter the atmosphere by addressing its contributing elements, all of which were affective or pathic in nature. He understood them to be spirits.

Now, one can certainly conceive of a spirit as a kind of ghost, a spiritual being, and thus demonic or angelic. But an inductive study of the concept of spirit through the entire Old Testament would reveal that spirit is most often associated with the inner life of the person. In fact, a different Hebrew word is most often used for the concept of a ghost. Thus, spirit includes volitions, purposes, yearnings, desires, beliefs, emotions, and decisions. In German it is the word *geist* and understood by some to mean "mind." Spirit, however, is the overall bent of the human being.

The Holy Spirit is a literal personification of God's character, intentions, values, and as it were yearnings. So, when the Bible says that God will give us the desires of our hearts, one possible understanding is to accept that He does so by giving His own Spirit. When the Holy Spirit indwells a Christian, he or she becomes a new creature by virtue of a whole new set of spiritual dynamics exerting influence in his or her life (and there ensues the relentless tension between the older spiritual values and the new that Paul wrote about in Romans 7:14–25).

The concept of atmosphere is akin to the Biblical understanding of spirit. It is an influential presence, "similar to the demonic and 'numinous' powers (Otto, 1923/1958). As a specific subjective experience, a) inextricably linked to felt body (Leib) processes and b) characterized. . . ." by a quality "inaccessible to a naturalistic-epistemic perspective . . ." (Griffero, 2014a, p. 29). Indeed, Griffero (2014b) saw a clear analogy between atmospheres and the spiritual, drawing a corollary between the ineffable and pre-verbal of the atmospheric and the *mysterium tremendum/mysterium fascinans* inherent to the idea of the holy (Otto, 1923/1958).

Griffero also wrote of an atmosphere as more of a *spatial* state than a private *psychic* state. He claimed that we do not imagine or construct an atmosphere "to suit our needs in the moment. Rather, we perceive it because it is actually there" (2014a). Yet, we perceive it in a post-representational fashion captured by Riedel (2015) when she wrote

> Ensuing from the fragmentation of human existence into rational thought and emotional experience that has come to its peak in modern thought, the atmosphere just as the numinous and the musical is commonly located beyond the explicable, thus making it categorically resistant to intellectual apprehension.
>
> *(pp. 85–86)*

Riedel examined the use of music in Closed Brethren Congregations in Germany and found that although they emphasized the words and de-emphasized the music in their singing, the same songs, with the same words and the same approach to the music, would one day inspire but another day leave cold. It was the atmosphere that changed and made the difference. Another way of saying that is to realize it was the spiritual quality of the room on one day as opposed to the next, and some would say that it was the moving of the Holy Spirit in specific that makes the difference in such cases.

With this (the advent of quasi-things such as atmospheres and the link between atmospheres as affective phenomena and spirit, understood as qualities of affect, volition, and belief inherent to the person), we have moved into the realm of enchantment and the spiritual (see the next chapter for more on this). In addition, as soon as someone moves to such things as atmospheres being intrinsic to a field theory they cannot deny that spirituality is intrinsic to gestalt therapy. Griffero links the atmosphere to the lived body and thus the lifeworld. Spirituality is intrinsic to human life. The atmosphere may be something perceived, but then it is perceived by another means.[4] And to say that it is perceived begs the question of what, precisely, "it" is that is perceived. Of course, that is the issue.

The Organism-Environment Field

The organism-environment field is the anthropology of the initial theoretical integration that formed early gestalt therapy theory. It is exquisitely suited for comprehending how people operate with regards to atmospheric/spiritual spaces. These O-E entities, or fields, are ontologically of the environment and so inherently affected by it. They are also phenomenal fields. They are affected by the world, and they affect the world around them. Their values, purposes, yearnings, aspirations, beliefs, emotions, and decisions of the will contribute to the spirituality of interpersonal space, are extended, and are sensed through shared environments by others in shared spaces. Thus, worship is not simply a matter of cranking

94 The Pneumenal Field in Gestalt Therapy

up religious music and singing "worship" choruses. As Riedel observed, without a sufficient spirit of worship (i.e. devotion, humility, adoration, awe, sense of the numinous, and the presence of the sacred) the music, full of sound doctrine and volume, will fall flat. It won't move people. In terms of designing atmospheres, people must be affected by a spirit of worship in order *to* worship. If the music is more affected by a spirit of craftmanship, performance, or entertainment than a spirit of worship, it will go nowhere.

Synthesis

Some strands of philosophy overflow one another. Marion says phenomena give themselves, leading to their showing. Figal (2010) says they are *Gegenständlichkeit* (they stand over and against). But they cannot do that unless they are other, ontically other (Levinas's transcendent Other is Marion's saturated phenomenon). Meanwhile, the philosophers expounding quasi-things/atmospheres describe them as real (not constituted or "projected"), thus opening windows upon epistemologies of critical realism.

Some things are bounded objects to which we ascribe characteristics, but other things present themselves and the characteristics are given; they proceed from the thing and are perceived. There are various kinds of atmospheres, and in some writing they are the static features of a given space, with its architecture, surfaces, colors, etc., and people come into those spaces and generate a feeling; they "do a riff" off the static space and ascribe an affect to it. That would be a reflection of the spirit of the person ascribing value rather than a spiritual tone existing in the given space. But that is not the kind of atmosphere we are talking about when we discuss atmospheres in the context of field theory in psychotherapy. In that case we are talking about the affective tone of the space as a function of the affective status of the people who inhabit it (or have just inhabited it). The spirits of the people in that space fill the space, they exceed the physical bounds of their bodies and are a function of their lived bodies' influence on the field. Then, the atmosphere is real, and is *Gegenständlichkeit*. It gives itself and the people who encounter it exercise phenomenological voice in attempting to understand it (in other words, with self-interest they interpret what they encounter, and that is the chiasm of Merleau-Ponty). I say they exercise voice because Marion's saturated phenomenon has been criticized as too passive (people simply receiving what is given), but constitution or projection is too active (people simply creating their perceptive experiences), and so here is where the need to correctly understand Goodman's middle becomes valuable, but it's a middle *voice* (not mode). Understanding voice correctly here is a great help that coincides with hermeneutics. Hermeneutics *is* in the middle voice between givenness and constitution.

Having said that, I end this chapter with a reflection on Descartes.

The dualistic ontology proposed by Descartes included *res extensa* (an extended thing, and so related to Descartes' ideas on space) and *res cogitans* (a thinking

The Organism-Environment Field **95**

thing). One occupied physical space and so came with materiality in what could be called Cartesian space, the other did not, was immaterial and experiential, and is associated with non-Cartesian space.

Atmospheres are of non-Cartesian space. They are not extended materially. When contemplated in connection with field theory in gestalt therapy they link a field perspective to the life world.

Accordingly, we cannot escape a duality (Julmi, 2017). How else could it possibly be? One can contemplate either a physical body or a lived body while having both, but one cannot escape either and still be considered to have a life; one is *res extensa* (in terms of Cartesian physics), and the other is not. The other has no materiality. It is not extended. So, what is it? Phenomenal space? Yes. And that requires *at least* a property dualism. At least. One body and two perspectives? No. A perspective is itself phenomenal. Without accepting a dualism, people will inevitably reduce one to the other, either through reductive physicalism (the mind is the brain working) or idealism (we are all God dreaming).

The way I resolve this with regard to people is to propose one living thing (call it an organism if you want, a human being) with material and immaterial properties. I call the immaterial "spirit," based on an inductive study of the word in the Old Testament in which I discovered that spirit (*ruach*) is most commonly associated with the inner aspects of a person, what the Bible also calls "heart," but that include values, affect, beliefs, strivings, yearnings, etc. (Brownell, 2015).[5] I think our problem has been that we privilege the material when all along there has been in various people's thinking and experience the realization that we have to account for both modes of life (material and immaterial). They appear everywhere across cultures and in literature. Instead of starting with the basic substance being materiality and then wondering how we get such things as mind or self out of that, one can start with life (which cannot be reduced to either alone). Descartes went to the dichotomy between thinking and non-thinking instead of between living and non-living (animate and inanimate). As such, he left us "with the pure subject conceived as a *res cogitans*, as a thinking thing, and no longer with the human being, the living, reasoning and material being who essentially acts in and on the world" (Edgar, 2016, n.p.). In an ontology of things it's easier to see, and in such an ontology one can also more easily understand quasi-things. An atmosphere that is perceived as opposed to simply designed (constructed, imagined, projected, etc.) seems to have a life of its own, but cannot exist apart from the living things from which it emanates. It is between subject and object, between animate and inanimate.

Notes

1. Therapists, of course, need to conceptualize cases and arrive at diagnoses, but these things do signal an interruption to the flow of psychotherapy.
2. Thus, the relevance of hermeneutics for phenomenology also becomes clear.

96 The Pneumenal Field in Gestalt Therapy

3. About Körper and Leib, and about "Descartes's error," while probably not a resolution that would satisfy everyone, I don't think Descartes was totally wrong. We see dualities all over the place in life. I just think he did not go back far enough in establishing the substance of things. He stopped one step short. This is ironic to me, since he was a believer. When I started understanding that there is an ontology of things (which leads to an understanding of quasi-things), I took my lead from Genesis and the story of the creation of human beings (living things). God created a physical body, but it was not a living thing (and when death occurs it ceases to be a living thing and is just a corpse, an inanimate thing). Then he blew into it the breath of life, and it became a living thing. So, to me, the real substance is life, and there are various kinds of living things. Then, what follows, what Descartes focused on, is the duality of properties of this living (human) thing. It has the property of materiality and that of immateriality, or body and spirit. Further, the spiritual property of the living thing exceeds the material thing and extends beyond the surface boundary of the skin. If you do that, maintain one substance with two properties, the mind-brain problem disappears, because either is just one aspect of the whole interacting according to its property and affecting the phenomenality of the entire organism. So, Descartes's error was postulating the dual properties as substances and missing their etiology in the one, whole substantial and living thing. The lived body is the spiritual property in action. And, yes, it's related to the physical body, but more to the point, it is identified with the living thing. It is the living thing who says, "I cut myself" when slicing through a finger with some kind of blade. It is the living thing who says, "I have lost myself and don't know what to do with myself" when suffering from depression. The "self" in "myself" finds its antecedent in both a physical body and a lived body respectively.
4. One option being what I described in my chapter ("Touch of Another Kind: Contact with God and Spiritual Self") in Jean-Marie Robine's book on self.
5. There is another word for spiritual being like a ghost or a demon.

Resources

Aristotle. (2004). *De Anima*. London, UK: Penguin, Random House.

Bille, M., Bjerregaard, P., & Sørensen, T. (2015). Staging atmospheres: Materiality, culture, and the texture of the in-between. *Emotion, Space and Society, 15*, 31–38.

Bloom, D. (2019a). Neither from the "inside" looking "out" nor from the "outside" looking "in." In G. Francesetti & T. Griffero (Eds.), *Psychopathology and atmospheres, neither inside nor outside* (pp. 178–190). Newcastle upon Tyne, UK: Cambridge Scholars Publishing.

Bloom, D. (2019b). From sentience to sapience: The awareness-consciousness continuum and the lifeworld. *Gestalt Review, 23*(1), 18–43.

Böhme, G. (Ed.). (2017). *Atmospheric architectures: The aesthetics of felt spaces*. A. C. Engels-Schwarzpaul (Trans.). London, UK and New York, NY: Bloomsbury Academic, Bloomsbury Publishing Plc.

Buser, M. (2014). Thinking through non-representational and affective atmospheres in planning theory and practice. *Planning Theory, 13*(3), 227–243.

Brownell, P. (2015). *Spiritual competency in psychotherapy*. New York, NY: Springer Publishing.

Chrétien, J.-L. (2004). *The call and the response*. New York, NY: Fordham University Press.

Clark, A., & Chalmers, D. (1998). The extended mind. *Analysis, 58*, 10–23.

Edensor, T., & Sumartojo, S. (2015). Designing atmospheres: Introduction to special issue. *Visual Communication, 14*(3), 251–265.

Edgar, O. (2016). *Things seen and unseen: The logic of incarnation in Merleau-Ponty's metaphysics of flesh*. Eugene, OR: Wipf and Stock Publishers.

Figal, G. (2010). *Objectivity: The hermeneutical and philosophy*. New York, NY: State University of New York Press.

Francesetti, G. (2019a). The field perspective in clinical practice: Towards a theory of therapeutic phronēsis. In P. Brownell (Ed.), *Handbook for theory, research, and practice in gestalt therapy* (2nd ed., pp. xx–xx). Newcastle upon Tyne, UK: Cambridge Scholars Publishing.

Francesetti, G. (2019b). A clinical exploration of atmospheres: Towards a field-based clinical practice. In G. Francesetti & T. Griffero (Eds.), *Atmospheres and psychopathology* (pp. 35–68). Newcastle upon Tyne, UK: Cambridge Scholars Publishing.

Fuchs, T. (2013). The phenomenology of affectivity. In K. W. M. Fulford, M. Davies, R. G. T. Gipps, G. Graham, J. Z. Sadler, G. Stanghellini, & T. Thornton (Eds.), *The Oxford handbook of philosophy and psychiatry (online)*, np. doi:10.1093/oxfordhb/9780199579563.013.0038

Griffero, T. (2018a). Something more: Atmospheres and pathic aesthetics. In T. Griffero & G. Moretti (Eds.), *Atmosphere/atmospheres: Testing a new paradigm*. Milano: Mimesis International.

Griffero, T. (2018b). Come rain or come shine . . . The (neo)phenomenological will-to-presentness. *Sensibilia, Studi di estetica, anno XLVI, IV serie, 2*, 57–73. doi:10.7413/182586 46053

Griffero, T. (2017). *Quasi-things: The paradigm of atmospheres*. S. De Sanctis (Trans.). New York, NY: State University of New York Press.

Griffero, T. (2014a). Atmospheres and lived space. *Studia Phænomenologica, XIV*, 29–51.

Griffero, T. (2014b). Who's afraid of atmospheres (and of their authority)? *Lebensweld, 4*(1), 193–213.

Julmi, C. (2017). The concept of atmosphere in management and organization studies. *Organizational Aesthetics, 6*(1), 4–30. Retrieved from http://digitalcommons.wpi.edu/oa/vol6/iss1/2

Levinas, E. (1999). *Alterity and transcendence*. New York, NY: Columbia University Press.

Lewis, C. S. (1947/2002). Miracles. In *The complete C.S. Lewis* (pp. 301–462). New York, NY: Harper One, Harper Collins.

MacKinlay, S. (2010). *Interpreting excess*. New York, NY: Fordham University Press.

Marion, J.-L. (2002). *Being given: Toward a phenomenology of givenness*. Stanford, CA: Stanford University Press.

Otto, R. (1923/1958). *The idea of the holy: An inquiry into the non-rational factor in the idea of the divine and its relation to the rational*. Oxford, UK: Oxford University Press.

Riedel, F. (2019). Atmosphere. In J. Slaby & C. von Scheve (Eds.), *Affective societies: Key concepts* (pp. 85–95). New York, NY: Routledge.

Riedel, F. (2015). Music as atmosphere: Lines of becoming in congregational worship. *Lebenswelt, 6*, 80–111.

Robine, J.-M. (2016). *Self: A polyphony of contemporary gestalt therapists*. St. Romaine la Vivée: l'exprimerie.

Robinson, M. (2015). Givenness. In M. Robinson (Ed.), *The givenness of things* (pp. 73–91). New York, NY: Picador, Macmillan Publishing Group.

Rowlands, M. (2010). *The new science of the mind: From extended mind to embodied phenomenology*. Cambridge, MA: MIT Press.

Titus, C. S., Vitz, P. C., Nordling, W. J., & DMU Group. (forthcoming). Theological, philosophical, and psychological premises for a Catholic Christian meta-model of the person. In P. C. Vitz, W. J. Nordling, & C. S. Titus (Eds.), *A Catholic Christian meta-model of the person: Integration with psychology and mental health practice* (n.p.). Washington, DC: Divine Mercy University.

Washington Post, Politics Section for July 18, 2019, Washington, DC. Retrieved July 25, from www.youtube.com/watch?v=6xQcnP3-pwo

Wollants, G. (2012). *Gestalt therapy: Therapy of the situation*. Thousand Oaks, CA: Sage Publications.

Zahavi, D. (2015). You, me, and we: The sharing of emotional experiences. *Journal of Consciousness Studies, 22*(1–2), 84–101.

9

ENCHANTMENT AND THE PNEUMENAL

She dances in crystalline light
Spin twisting, curve curvaling,
A pixie, illumined in night.
Out elf-hame, free and enchantaling.
She dances there,
Or just a vision of?
Maybe perhaps.
Insightaling.

In 1975 Bruno Bettelheim published a book about the uses of enchantment, about the value of fairy tales. It won the National Book Award and the National Book Critics Circle Award. John Updike said that it was a charming book about enchantment, but what does that mean? Never mind that Bettelheim came under suspicion of plagiarism in the writing of that book. It has remained a good product for its publishers and was renewed in 2010. People still wonder about the uses of enchantment.

Bettelheim proposed that fairy tales communicate the struggle between good and evil, the drama of values played out in fantasy, but values that are appropriate for the ordinary human being. He contrasted fairy tales with myths (both fanciful narratives) by saying:

> Myths project an ideal personality acting on the basis of superego demands, while fairy tales depict an ego integration which allows for appropriate satisfaction of id desires. This difference accounts for the contrast between the pervasive pessimism of myths and the essential optimism of fairy tales.
>
> *(Bettelheim, 1975, p. 41)*

So, he did not really wonder about enchantment as such but of moralizing in fantasy according to a classical Freudian ontology. He noted that with myth, for instance, the point was not whether the narrative depicted the miraculous but that it was *described* as doing so. He analyzed the narratives *as narrative fantasies*.

Children, however, do not analyze. They do not create theoretical models and argue the merits of one abstraction over another. They play, and their play is enchanted. "Children explore, experience, and engage the world around them through play. How often have we watched a young child battling some ferocious monster and conquering this big beast, using all their superhero powers and ninja moves?" (Mallenthin, 2018, p. 1)

One day one summer when I was about ten years old my brothers and I were running around inside the house driving our mother crazy. She said, "Go outside and play."

We decided to play army in the pasture that went down the hill behind our house. We took shovels and built fox holes. We imagined fighting off an attacking mass of enemy soldiers, getting shot (and miraculously being healed enough to get up and fight some more). We built shallow trenches from one fox hole to the next, and we crawled along inside them, gradually but surely covering ourselves in dirt. It was so exciting! We were there for hours, but the time went by rapidly, because we were completely engrossed in the fantasy of our play. For us it was real. We were not simply playing "make-believe." We were *in* the fantasy, fighting off the enemy, dodging explosions, and throwing back unexploded hand grenades until the light faded and our parents called us in for dinner.

Children do not simply pretend, always carrying with them the realization that there is a separate reality that is not imagined, and thus being half in the fantasy and half out of it. When playing, they are so captured that the imaginal becomes a stand-alone reality all its own, and the veracity of it is in the absorption, the fascination.

This, I believe, is what Jesus was getting at when He said that the adults of His day needed to come to him with the simple faith of a child. People need to become enchanted by Christ. The difficulty is that we live in what Charles Taylor (2007/2018) described as a secular age that is disenchanted.[1]

The "Crisis" of Disenchantment in Psychology and Psychotherapy

In 1917 Max Weber said that the world had become disenchanted through "the loss of the overarching meanings, animistic connections, magical expectations, and spiritual explanations . . ." (Saler, 2006, p. 695). He was describing the same processes at work that prompted Edmund Husserl to warn of the "crisis" of the naturalistic attitude in science. The world had become hyper-empirical, viewing a split between subject and object.

An example of such objectifying in current psychology was given by Brent Slife, professor emeritus at Brigham Young University, during a presentation at the Psychology and the Other conference one year and then turned into writing with the help of colleagues for a discussion of the philosophy of science in research. Slife, Möller, and Chun (2019) wrote about the presence of a God who makes a difference in everyday life, but a God who is an excluded other in psychology. They observed that in the science of psychology in general there is a polarity between what is regarded to be subjective and that which is regarded to be objective and that belief in God is regarded to be subjective.

Belief in God as an objective given shifted between 1500 and 2000 (Taylor, 2007/2018) into a subjective, if not anachronistic concept. In the effort to eliminate all subjectivity from contaminating the empirical value of research, then, the psychologist separates aspects of his or her own values, beliefs, and aspirations from the research design and its application, thus constituting God as the rejected "other." However, Slife et al. point out that eliminating the subjective is ultimately impossible because researcher effects leak into the work at several levels. The same could be said for any approach to psychotherapy in which one assumes a "professional" stance and attempts to keep all self-disclosures—personal, subjective elements—out of the room. It is impossible. It is best, in both research and psychotherapy, to acknowledge and account for them.

Thus, the spiritual beliefs, commitments, worldviews, and religious experience of both therapist and client are relevant and aspects of the life world for each. It is the naturalistic attitude that demands only the objective, measurable, uncontaminated variable be the focus of research.

Husserl viewed this skewed approach to be a crisis (Moran, 2012). He had been writing in contrast to the rise of positivism.[2] The logical positivists of the Vienna School offered a scientific picture of life to replace what they considered to be a naïve, natural, and pre-scientific perspective (Moran, 2013). Writing about Husserl's *Crisis of the European Sciences*, Moran observed that Husserl saw Galileo as the archetype of scientism, of mathematizing the experience of nature.

Husserl contrasted physical things as aspects of our perceptual encounter in the world with the mathematical model of them found in physics (Moran, ibid.). He proposed in *Ideas I*, "to put aside our conception of the physical thing as found in physics in order to focus on the manner in which the thing is given in perceptual experience and the specific kind of 'transcendence' which the object has relative to the experience . . ." (Moran, ibid., p. 77, Kindle version).

In the *Logical Investigations* Husserl had criticized the philosophical position found in Descartes and Locke that regarded perception to be an indirect apprehending of a thing through representation rather than a direct grasping of the perceived object itself (Moran, ibid.).[3] This direct grasping is something Merleau-Ponty later developed in *The Visible and the Invisible* (1968) through his concept of a chiasm, or a crossing (X) of the perceiving subject, thus subjective experience,

102 The Pneumenal Field in Gestalt Therapy

with the world that actually exists. I have described this as bumping into a wall in the dark night and receiving a painful knot on the head.

Merleau-Ponty put it another way in referring to the relative experience in touch between sleek and rough.

Imagine you have a cheese grater. Run your fingers over the chisels in the middle of it. They tug at the skin, scratching it. Now run your fingers over the smooth metal of the frame around its edges. They feel flat and polished. The experience is a product of both the person with the finger and the object with its two different surfaces. It is not simply a represented, constructed experience, a sole product of the subject. The material thing itself exerted an influence in the total experience. It gave itself to the phenomenon of touch. The place where features of the object meet perceiving subject is what Merleau-Ponty called the "chiasm."

It is the same thing for a perceiving subject in contact with an actually existing God, a God who makes a difference. God's presence *makes* the difference, and it can be perceived through touch of another kind.

Merleau-Ponty wrote,

> an experience is always contiguous upon an experience, that our perceptions, our judgements, our whole knowledge of the world can be changed, crossed out, Husserl says, but not nullified, that, under the doubt that strikes them appear other perceptions, other judgements more true, because we are within Being and there is something. . .
>
> *(ibid., p. 128)*

Indeed, there *is* something. The ephemeral, the inscrutable, the ineffable may be mysterious. They may elude physical measure or sensation. But the objects that communicate such experience give themselves because "there is something."

Who is to say that God cannot underly what seems mysterious at first take?

In the split between the experienced object and the scientific object there is often a privileging of the scientific as true and the experienced "perception," which is made relative to the perspective of the perceiver, is seen as perhaps a true experience but an experience separated from the object as it is. In gestalt therapy, though, we need contact with the thing itself or else we just have pseudo-contact. In Christianity we need contact with God or else we just have a dry and constricting religion. Further, no mathematical, scientific measurement of the other person or the environment will achieve interpersonal contact, and God is spirit, a whole dimension of experience in contrast to the naturalistic attitude in much of science and life.

The naturalistic attitude constrains the possibility that something unexplainable, something mysterious, something ineffable, might actually be at hand and present to experience. Thus, when we come to the issue of quasi-things, such as atmospheres, gestalt therapists might be inclined, oddly, to backtrack on our Husserlian heritage and to embrace Descartes, asserting that the atmosphere is a

Enchantment and the Pneumenal **103**

representation, a construction, or a perspective on the meeting between therapist and client.[4] They would not then affirm that the atmosphere is a thing that is experienced and actually there. In the same way, a naturalistic attitude would not permit the presence of the Holy Spirit in a counseling session because one cannot weigh it, see it, taste it, or measure it, even though the presence of God could be an aspect of the experience of the client, therapist, or both. Actually, it would not be uncommon for gestalt therapists in general to sidestep the issue of a possible divine presence in therapy due to the privileging of the disenchanted, naturalistic perspective, and that is inconsistent with the phenomenological base in gestalt therapy theory, because, for example, the lived body is immaterial, immeasurable, and imperceptible to the senses, even though it is the home of our meaningful and experiential lives.

The Lived Body, Life World, and the Pneumenal

Husserl wrote to situate science within the life world. The natural attitude (not naturalistic attitude) is that every-day, common way of seeing the world in which embodied people live; it is the currency of one's life world. Such a view is inescapably related to one's socio-cultural context, one's field, and it often includes the uncanny sense of being in touch with something that seems supernatural. That is because it is the object as experienced that becomes figural and not the scientific object, nor even the philosophical object (after it has gone through the thickening of critical scrutiny).

The life world and the lived body are intertwined and of one cloth.

> The lifeworld is the natural world—in the attitude of natural life. . . . Everything objective about the lifeworld is subjective givenness, our possession (Habe), mine, the other's, and everyone's together . . . what is lived is lived experience of the surrounding world, and that holds also for what is seen and thought.
>
> *(Ideen II, p. 385; Hua IV, 375)*

Lived experience of the surrounding world indeed. Since we are all embodied in the natural world, and we all have a mundane, common experience in it (don't read confluent experience), that lived experience *is* the lived body. The lived body is the phenomenological correlate of the physical body. But you cannot weigh it. You cannot see it. You cannot taste it. It just is. Only the phenomenologically illiterate or the skeptically disenchanted claim that one's sense of being in the world (the lived body) is reprehensibly mystical and unacceptable.

The *Körper* and the *Leib*—the physical body (what Merleau-Ponty called the sensible) and the lived body (what he called the sentient)—intertwine in perceptual experience. Merleau-Ponty's "flesh," a technical term for him, is neither simply physical nor mental, but something between that captures aspects of each. It is an intertwining that brings together physical body and lived body:

> perception is crucial for the formation of a paradigm for viewing the relation of the human person with the world around him: for, in perception, the domain of causes, of physical events, is connected to the domain of reasons, or mental events; things are connected to thoughts.
>
> *(Edgar, 2016)*

Does that sound familiar? He was playing with the *res cogito* and the *res extensa*. It seems we keep doing that. We don't like Descartes' substance dualism, but we cannot escape him entirely. Living things have properties held in tandem by which they touch and are touched, by which they think about touching, value the intimacy of touch, and fill both their nostrils and their horizons with the fragrance of tangible life.

Spiritual things, the things of the pneumenal field, are unseen. You cannot see *them*, but you can see what they do, the effect they have. You can experience them. Jesus likened them to the wind.[5]

On the high desert of Southern Idaho the wind often blows at a steady 20 mph. I can feel it against my skin. I can see how it bends the trees I've planted and makes the leaves twist and vibrate. Over time I can see the effect of the wind on tree growth as it slows growth in the length of branches and makes them thicken up. It also turns the direction of tree growth to conform to the vectors of the wind. I can't see the wind, but I know it's there, because I can sense it in other ways, and I can see what it does, its effects. My experience of the wind and the trees is a metaphor for my experience of the pneumenal, the spiritual aspects of my lived body and life world.

Immanence and Transcendence Redux

Taylor, in his description of a secular age (2007/2018), worked the binary of immanence and transcendence, pointing out that when the "something" beyond (that which transcends) is abandoned in favor of the immediate and proximate aligned with human life in the here and now (the immanent), then the conditions for dialogue have shifted. For him the secular is characterized by a naturalism that narrows the focus. He asserted that with the current age a self-sufficient humanism emerged in which human flourishing in this life became the aspiration that captures the imagination and energizes striving.

J.R.R. Tolkien asserted that the fantasy of faerie stories, by which he pointed to art rather than magic, suspends the skepticism of naturalism and escorts the reader into a secondary world in which one is caught up as if such a place were actual.[6] It is a type of wonder, but it is a wonder of full immersion (Curry, 2012).

Enchantment and the Pneumenal **105**

The "Enlightenment emphasis on reason and science at the expense of other ways of apprehending and being in the world" (Saler, ibid.) established the fundamental stance that provides the contrast to such faerie stories. What are some other ways of apprehending and being in the world? Intuition, a basic element in phenomenological systems is one. With it something simply comes to a person. The aesthetic criterion, the felt sense in experience, is another. Marion's saturated phenomenon, or what Christians might call revelation, is another. Chretien's call and response is still another.

What, then, is enchantment? What is going on when the immanent frame is shattered by something that transcends pure reason and empiricism? Enchantment refers to the allure of fascination, the charm in beauty. It can mean bliss or ecstasy itself. It also refers to wizardry and magic, or the supernatural. I am using it here as Taylor used it, to refer to spirits, demons, angels, God, saints to whom one prays, and a spiritual realm. It is certainly the full immersion of childlike play, but in Christianity it is also pneumenal. By what criteria might the stance of gestalt therapy claim that it is otherwise?

The Pneumenal Is a Sphere of Enchantment

> Ψυχικὸς δὲ ἄνθρωπος οὐ δέχεται τὰ τοῦ πνεύματος τοῦ θεοῦ, μωρία γὰρ αὐτῷ ἐστίν, καὶ οὐ δύναται γνῶναι, ὅτι πνευματικῶς ἀνακρίνεται· ὁ δὲ πνευματικὸς ἀνακρίνει τὰ πάντα, αὐτὸς δὲ ὑπ' οὐδενὸς ἀνακρίνεται.,[7] (SBL Greek New Testament)[8]
>
> (But a natural man does not accept the things of the Spirit of God, for they are foolishness to him; and he cannot understand them, because they are spiritually appraised. But he who is spiritual appraises all things, yet he himself is appraised by no one.)

The pneumenal field is enchanted. That means it is filled with the possibilities of spiritual beings one cannot see and dramas being played out at a level beyond the mundane and about which one is commonly unaware. In Christianity the enchanted, pneumenal field includes experience of the sacred.

> Religious believers and mystics assert with certainty that our interior awareness of the absolute, the transcendent, the spiritual, and the sacred comes from a divine source because this interior awareness is of something other, something higher, something not controllable by us.[9]

It is that, but it is also a numinous mystery that is at once irresistibly fascinating and attractive while provoking fear, awe, and terrible respect (Otto, 1958).

Paul of Tarsus called such things πνευματικὸς (*pneumatikos*/spiritual). He said that a spiritual person is able to ἀνακρίνω (*anakrino*/examine, investigate, or question) them. However, he also said that a disenchanted person, a skeptic, a natural person, cannot.

Apart from enchantment the pneumenal field simply becomes ψυχικός (*psychikos*/natural, psychological). A person operating in a pneumenal field, for instance, having dulled him or herself to the potentialities of enchantment, having turned from them and hardened themselves against the sacred, is left with nothing more than mundane experience, interpretations that leave God out of consideration, and explanations or models that a priori ignore spiritual influences.

Let's put this into phenomenological terms. Paul said that a person in a merely psychological attitude cannot *receive* the things of the spirit of God. Since no phenomenon can be received unless it is first given, then within a phenomenological frame we might understand that a mere psychological, naturalized phenomenology somehow blocks what is given, the spiritual things of God that are available in an otherwise sacred pneumenal field. In gestalt terms we could say that the person with such an attitude interrupts contact with God. The Bible describes it as hardening so as to resist the voice of God, the call of God.

In Christianity the enchantment that turns a mere psychologized spirituality into a window on the ineffable is an enchantment infused with verity. It is not enough to be fully immersed and taken with one's appreciation, say of beauty, the play of a childlike moment, or the blush of one's emotions, the urgency of one's values and desires, or the impact of one's decisions. All those are certainly of a pneumenal field because they come from the spiritual property of a living human thing, but in order for the pneumenal to not simply be psychological one must entertain the numinous, the ineffable, the mystery, the narratives of the Bible as being true.

> The extraordinary facts and actions of Christ, his companions, those mysterious women who served him, are known to us only through the texts of Scripture. But Scripture is true only if these deeds and actions, despite their extraordinary character, really happened.
>
> *(Henry, 2003, p. 8)*

Notes

1. Even in literature describing a post-secular perspective much of it is academic, sterile, void of the enchantment that suggests the actuality of supernatural processes beyond our current understanding and that can produce awe.
2. Husserl's term for that was "naturalistic" science, which he contrasted with humanistic science.
3. In gestalt therapy, subject and object are brought together through contacting.
4. Atmospheres "are not accessible to a representative-oculardistal perception but to a deambulatory and synesthetic one. And that they set upon us as quasi-things that, regardless of their constituent vagueness—which can be stigmatized only by those who idealise the naturalistic pathos of certainty—radiate effects that are largely shared . . ." (Griffero, 2013, p. 2).
5. John 3:1–8.

6. "On Fairy Stories" was originally a talk Tolkien delivered for the Andrew Lang Lecture Series at the University of St. Andrews in Scotland, but was later published as an essay.
7. 1. Corinthians 2: 14 & 15.
8. 1. Corinthians 2:14–15 New American Standard Bible.
9. From the Magis Center, downloaded September 27, 2019 from https://magiscenter.com/gods-presence-to-our-consciousness-the-numinous-experience-intuition-of-the-sacred-and-conscience/.

References

Bettelheim, B. (1975/2010). *The uses of enchantment: The meaning and importance of fairy tales.* New York, NY: Vintage Books, Random House.

Curry, P. (2012). Enchantment and modernity. *PAN: Philosophy Activism Nature, 9,* 76–89.

Edgar, O. (2016). *Things seen and unseen: The logic of incarnation in Merleau-Ponty's metaphysics of flesh.* Eugene, OR: Cascade Books.

Griffero, T. (2013). The atmospheric "skin" of the city. Ambiances [En ligne], Enjeux - Arguments - Positions, mis en ligne le 20 novembre 2013, consulté le 12 novembre 2013. Retrieved from http://ambiances.revues.org/399

Henry, M. (2003). *I am the truth: Toward a philosophy of Christianity.* S. Emanuel (Trans.). Stanford, CA: Stanford University Press.

Mallenthin, C. (2018). *Play therapy: Engaging and powerful techniques for the treatment of childhood disorders.* Eau Claire, WI: PESI Publishing & Media.

Merleau-Ponty, M. (1968). *The visible and the invisible.* Evanston, IL: Northwestern University Press.

Moran, D. (2012). *Husserl's crisis of the European sciences and transcendental phenomenology: An introduction.* Cambridge, UK: Cambridge University Press.

Moran, D. (2013). From the natural attitude to the life-world. In L. Embree & T. Nenon (Eds.), *Husserl's Ideen. Contributions to phenomenology* (Vol. 66, pp. 105–124). Dordrecht: Springer.

Otto, R. (1958). *The idea of the holy* (2nd ed.). Oxford, UK: Oxford University Press.

Saler, M. (2006). Modernity and enchantment: A historiographic review. *The American Historical Review, 3*(3), 692–716.

Slife, B., Möller, E., & Chun, S. (2019). The excluded other in psychological research: Diary of a probing theist. In P. Brownell (Ed.), *Handbook for theory, research, and practice in gestalt therapy* (2nd ed., pp. 65–87). Newcastle upon Tyne, UK: Cambridge Scholars Publishing.

Taylor, C. (2007/2018). *A secular age.* Cambridge, MA: The Belknap Press of Harvard University Press.

Story Two

A CHANGE IN ATMOSPHERE

Some pushed at those in front of them as if they wanted to escape. Others seemed confused.

The Vatican is a city, but it's unique. There are streets and buildings of course. The buildings are most often more like monuments, exhibits in a huge museum of religious history. Yet, it's not just historical, because the religion in question is actively being observed.

We came to Rome to participate in The Roots of Gestalt Therapy conference in 2007. They were meeting daily in a five-star hotel at the edges of the historical district. I was presenting "The Acting Man," a description of Karol Józef Wojtyla's phenomenological philosophy. Wojtyla, who later became Pope John Paul II, asserted that people reveal themselves through what they do, how they act. He used to convene meetings with phenomenological philosophers when he became Pope. That's how he acted.

We were in Rome. I marveled at it and wanted to experience the history of the place. I wanted to have an experience commensurate with the place where Peter and Paul had come to minister and die.

We were staying at the Casa Santa Sofia, a monastery run by Catechist Sisters of St. Anne—originally for the pilgrims coming to the Vatican from Ukraine. The monastery was drab in places, simple. Our room was on the fourth floor and its windows opened onto the back alley of two apartment buildings. The room was quite plain.

In the Piazza della Madonna dei Monti, the courtyard outside the monastery, there was a fountain, and children played "football," what Americans call soccer. Sometimes a band performed with wind and brass instruments. Somebody banged a bass drum.

A Change in Atmosphere **109**

Standing in the Via dei Serpenti next to the piazza we could look down that street and see the Coliseum, which was an easy walk from the fountain. However, the conference and the Vatican were in the other direction.

Each day, walking to the conference, we passed ancient ruins on either side of the Via dei Fori Imperiali. These were active archeological digs. One day we decided to visit the Vatican.

We walked along the Via dei Fori Imperiali past the Altare dell Patria to Trajan's Column and the Piazza Venezia where we picked up the Via del Plebiscito, making a turn in the general direction of the Vatican.

I was of two minds. I am Protestant and not Catholic. The whole place was stamped with the Catholic church. But it was also the history of the church in general. "Who," I pondered, "are Protestants but the descendants of Luther, a man who wanted to reform the Catholic church, not leave it?"

We came to a group of people. On the sidewalk a man was drawing with chalk, and a number had gathered to watch. He was depicting the last supper, with Jesus in the middle and disciples on either side. It was a copy of medieval styled art.

The table was set with food that could not have been present in Palestine and was not recorded in the Bible. A pop-top can of Coca-Cola sat within reach of Christ, but Judas was grasping it. Jesus looked toward him with a tender expression.

People put coins in a large hat turned upside down, but the man was not watching. He was too focused on what he was doing.

Three nuns stood in silence watching his work. They were dressed entirely in white. They wore no makeup. They were simple but serene. They watched the man as if there were nothing else that needed to be done.

I wondered what they were thinking. Was it sacrilege to change the scene of the last supper? Did they think the artist was a cynic? They did not seem offended.

Gradually other people stopped next to the nuns. They joined them in silence.

Eventually we started walking again, because our goal was to see the holy places of Catholicism that have stood for so many years.

We picked up the Corso Vitorio Emanuele II and crossed the Tiber River at the Ponte Vittorio Emanuele II, a well-traveled bridge, noting the Castel Sant'Angelo to the right. Then we turned slightly to the left and picked up the Via della Conciliazione. That is when we saw the Basilica di San Pietro at the far side of the Piazza San Pietro. Shortly thereafter we arrived at the Vatican.

The square of the Piazza is like a giant keyhole with the Basilica at the top. We entered at the bottom. Around each side, curving in two arcs are colonnades. Bernini, the architect who built them, asserted that those two arcs stood for the outstretched arms of St. Peter's Basilica, embracing the world. They were built in 1660 and were made with four rows of gray, white, and golden travertine, totaling two hundred and eighty-four Doric columns and eighty-eight pilasters. The columns are sixty-six feet high and five feet wide. On top of them Bernini and his students created one hundred and forty statues of popes, martyrs, and other figures from Christendom. They peer into the square, where as many as four hundred thousand people can assemble during celebrations like Easter.

In the center of the square stands the Egyptian obelisk, which was created in 2500 BC. It was transported to Rome, and Caligula put it in his circus, which was later called the circus of Nero. A Roman circus was like a modern track or open-air stadium. Nero's circus was used for chariot races but also for the execution of Christians. The apostle Peter was crucified, and the apostle Paul was beheaded in that Circus. St. Peter's was later erected on that site. Pope Sixtus V had the obelisk moved to a central point in the square. It was sanctified through a formal exorcism of pagan spiritual influences. So, the place of St. Peter's is not just rich in history, architecture and art; it is also a place of sanctity.

One hundred and thirty-five Swiss guards are stationed at various positions around the Vatican. They protect all entrance and exit points. Each one wears a blue beret or metal helmet and a brightly colored uniform of blue, red, and yellow stripes in the style of the Renaissance—a combination of the Della Rove and Medici family banners. They stand with a halberd or Swiss Voulge, which is like a spear with an axe-like blade at the top, while also wearing a dress sword.

As we entered the square I paused. The size of the place would have overwhelmed me if it were not for the stands where people were selling religious trinkets. We could not really avoid them. They were on either side of the key. There were booths that were congested with rings, statuettes, and refrigerator magnets depicting Jesus, the cross, and the Madonna. There were rosaries with various colors. Shot glasses with St. Peter's square shown on the outside sat next to crucifixes. More ornate shot glasses had gold rims. Medallions hung from the sides of these booths. Some had images of Pope John Paul II.

We walked up to one of the booths and the people who ran it took to us immediately. They offered one thing after another in rapid succession. I wondered if we ought to get something to bring back with us from our trip. We both looked over the various trinkets. I picked up a stack of postcards, but I realized I was taking my own photographs. I did not need them. I put them back down. I didn't need a rosary. I began to feel an urgency, as if I needed to come away from that booth having purchased something. The owners seemed to collude and to inspire commerce. They picked up one item after another and thrust it in my face. "This? How about *this?!*" They spoke in Italian, and when I told them I did not speak Italian, they shifted to broken English. They offered a shot glass. They smiled. When they saw me interested in the various versions of Christ on a cross, they offered miniatures of the last supper. They were trying to make my religious pilgrimage profitable and to also make a profit in the process.

I began to feel tired. The booth was brightly colored, and the trinkets were visually compelling. Yet, they drained me. For all their glaring, feigned significance, they left me feeling used.

I looked at Linda. We moved on.

We visited St. Peter's Basilica inside, and we checked the line for the Sistine Chapel, but it was too long. We decided to see the tombs of the Popes, and we got into the line for that. It snaked along beside one colonnade. It moved slowly, steadily. I realized I was weary from walking to get to the Vatican, then strolling around the square and looking inside the Basilica. I did not think the tombs of the Popes was going to be very stimulating, but we had the time, and I didn't think we would ever be going to Rome again. We decided to stay with it.

Linda was quiet. We did not talk. The energy seemed to have gone out of us. She tried to sit in places as the line moved forward. The air was warm and still.

The line consisted of hundreds of rows of people standing six abreast and moving a few steps forward every few minutes. We were all headed for the Grottoes below St. Peter's.

A young woman leaned against a man about two rows in front of us. He comforted her by stroking her hair, but he was staring away, down the rows of columns, past the people behind us.

We moved forward in a series of staggered adagios, posing one moment at a time among the marble like still-life personages. Eventually I could see the line ahead turn and begin descending. I told Linda. We gained a little energy, but I wondered what I could possibly see there that would be meaningful. It was, after all, a bunch of dead people I did not know under cold, hard slabs.

We finished the stairs and turned a corner, entering the vestibule. From there the line formed a horseshoe around the central nave. Ahead loomed a corridor with alcoves and niches to the right and the nave itself with tombs and sarcophagi to the left. Yellow light reflected off the old marble. While the walls were a consistent tint, some tombs and sarcophagi were quite aged and dull. Some wore the stain of centuries. Rounded, broad archways occurred at stages in the wide hallway. It all had a dull, custard look.

When we came to John Paul I's sarcophagus to the left of us, I noticed it looked different. It seemed new and shiny with contrasting horizontal, gray veins of Greek marble. At the front stood two angels, one at each corner, and they were lighter in color. They looked new and more well-defined in their stone features. Their wings were unfolded and their arms crossed over their chests. It was as if they stood guard over the Pope's body.

On the right was the tomb of Marcellus II, stained and worn from age. It came from the 16th century. Moving forward once again on our left was Benedict XV. His sarcophagus was made of Cipolleno marble with a contrasting, bronze sculpture on top showing the pope reclining, with his head resting on two pillows.

Then came Innocent IX on the right, followed by the tomb of Queen Christina of Sweden. Between Marcellus II and Innocent IX I felt a change in the situation. It wasn't a scent or a sound. There was music playing, sacred and soothing music, but something more than music had entered the Grottoes.

Up ahead I could see people bunching up and falling out of line to the left. Something was happening. I noticed there were about a dozen people gathering there. One young woman, dark hair falling to her shoulders with a silk Italian scarf over her head, pulled away from the line and joined them. She turned around to face the right side of the nave, the opposite side of the line, crossed herself, and

112 The Pneumenal Field in Gestalt Therapy

then dropped to her knees. She held her hands in front. Tears ran down her cheeks. Her eyes turned upward. Her lips moved as she formed words I could not hear.

I noticed an older man standing behind her. His face was contorted into a serious state. He turned his head from side to side, watching the line and then looking back toward the opposite side of the nave.

We moved closer to all that. Then I began to hear the mournful crying from people either in the line or from those who had dropped out. I could not tell. It seemed to be growing nearby and around us. I could feel my heart beating more rapidly. Whatever was happening it had gotten into me.

I scanned the place intently. What was all this about?

As we moved forward once again, I could see to the right. It was the tomb of John Paul II, the man I had come to Rome to talk about. Linda and I dropped out of the line when we came to be across from his resting place, joining the young woman on her knees and the older, intense man, and all the others who chose to do the same. I felt unsettled.

Across and over the heads of the people in the line I could see the alcove where John Paul II was buried. To either side of it stood a Swiss guard, but these two did not seem normal. They each held a Voulge slanted menacingly across the chest. I felt I could only glance at them a bit at a time. I did not want to be discovered watching them.

The one on the right of the alcove, standing between Queen Christina and John Paul II, held his head still, but his eyes surveyed everyone. He looked daunting and unapproachable. He seemed to be responsible for the area immediately in front of John Paul II and back down the line from where we had come. The other guard scanned the area to our left, where the line kept moving and turned a corner in front of St. Peter's tomb to head on back out of the Grottoes. His Voulge turned across his chest in the opposite direction.

The side of his face seemed burnished. He was radiant. He was not just muscular; he was powerful. He suddenly turned his head in my direction and looked straight at me. His eyes twinkled. A faint smile formed at the corners of his mouth. Then he turned back to the area he was guarding.

I looked quickly toward Linda and the others to see if they had seen what I had seen. No one moved. I felt hollow, profoundly hollow, as if I had not eaten for several days. I felt cold. I wanted to sit or kneel, somehow to get off my feet. I was not tired but very weak.

Linda crossed herself and fell to her knees.

What was happening?!

This man I had come to speak about seemed to be looming up in front of me. I recalled what I knew of his life. He had run his race. He resisted the Nazis during World War II and organized a youth group. He resisted the communists in Poland during the Cold War and supported the miners against the established government. He ascended to the Papacy and led the Catholic church for many years. He was a philosopher priest. He traveled the world as an ambassador for the church. He was loved. He was known. Two months after he died they started the process of making him a saint and the same year we were there a child was healed at his tomb, the very place we were standing.

The magnitude of a life given as a living sacrifice overwhelmed me. And there his body lay, guarded by two angels.

The place around his tomb had become transformed. There was no visible mist, no spiritual cloud hanging in the air, but the feel of the place infused people as they walked through it. Even those who kept walking, who did not drop out, were tearful. I could see them wiping at their eyes and looking around semi-agitated. Some pushed at those in front of them as if they wanted to escape. Others seemed confused.

Eventually, we got back into line and moved along until we left the Grottoes and emerged into the sunlight on the far side of the Basilica. There was a Swiss guardsman standing there, but he never looked at us.

PART 3

The Experience of Contact With God

10

A BASIC ORIENTATION TO PHENOMENOLOGY

What's it like inside a jar?
That depends on kind by far.
What's it like to be a bee?
A wasp or just a bumblebee?
What's it like to never chew?
Well, does it just occur to you
That everything depends upon
The base the question sits upon?

Gestalt therapy is an experiential approach, and so is Christianity. Gestalt therapy is also a phenomenological approach. The same could be said about Christianity, because the Bible was written from the perspective of human, subjective experience. It situates human beings within a long-term and developing relationship with a divine being, a creator who is at once transcendent and immanent. It depicts the history of human contact with God over time, and that is what turns theology, theorizing and abstracting about such things as the nature of God into life.

Husserl (Husserl & Carr, 1970) pondered the relationship between reasoning and experiencing. Reason alone does not determine what is, the *ontos*. Experience alone does not determine what is, because it cannot transcend one's finite ways of knowing. However, reason helps one understand what is relevant and meaningful about what one experiences, and experience contributes to our understanding of what is. Phenomenology is the philosophical investigation of meaningful subjective experience.

In this chapter I want to provide some basic phenomenological tenets as a way of understanding the post-secular[1] possibilities in gestalt therapy. With the coupling of religion in global conflicts, contradicting the secularist belief in the fading of the relevance of religion, the increase of religious perspectives in public issues, and the increase in immigration of peoples from religiously vigorous cultures, philosophers and sociologists have admitted the advent of a post-secular trend in western cultures (Dew, 2019; Habermas, 2010; Moberg, Granholm, & Nynäs, 2012; Staudigl & Alvis, 2016).

I am not, however, merely talking about societies, trends in academic or philosophical studies, discussions in the public square, or the effects of the migration of religious people in various parts of the world. I am concerned with the experience of a present God who makes a difference to individuals who are inextricably entwined in relationships and embedded in environmental contexts of various kinds.

Husserl turned Kant around. While Kant claimed that we clothe all sensation in cognizing so that we do not see things as they are but as we are, Husserl's cry was "to the things themselves" (Duns, 2016). In a similar way the critique on theism is that we create a god in our own image, but the response is, "To the transcendent, yet immanent God Himself."

Consider the following basic elements of phenomenology as a way of seeing what I mean: lived body, intentionality, attitudes, horizon, and life world. These are some of the essential philosophical building blocks of gestalt practice, they are all of one cloth, and they are basic to the experiential knowledge of God.

Experience and the Lived Body

Thomas Fuchs (2019) wrote, "Embodiment means the human experience of both having and being a body . . ." (n.p.). It is the experience of being a living thing. God formed a physical body, but it was not a living thing until He blew the breath of life into it. Then it became a living body that would immediately become a lived body. The lived body is not merely a living, physical body; it is *the experience of being a living body* and of interacting in the world. And yet it is even more than that; it is the experience of being a person, a living human being.

Once a living thing begins to move and act it generates a phenomenal field. "The phenomenal field is thus centered in the lived body, which functions as the background of all experience, and as the medium of one's relations to the world" (Fuchs, ibid., n.p.). We cannot see the lived experience (*Erlebnis*), nor the feeling of life (*Lebensgefühl*) inherent to the lived body (Nelson, 2015), but we can see what these things produce, what a person does because of them. It is the same with the things of the spirit (wind); as I've already said, we cannot see the wind, but we can see its effect on the things in this world that we can see. We cannot see a person's feelings, beliefs, values, commitments, intentions, figures of interest, faith in God, devotion, or sense of calling, but we can see what he or she does because of them.

Some may consider the lived body to be unacceptably "mystical" because it escapes a reductive physicalism—you can't see it or measure it and yet people

118 The Experience of Contact With God

suggest its presence. Like all the immaterial properties of a living thing, though, the experience of self, the ability to say, "I am," "I feel," or "I think," is obvious, and these are properties of the lived body. People exist in the matrix of their emotions and thoughts coupled with their physical sensations. It is also not as simple as believing that everything correlates positively *to* the physical body.

Consider the phenomenon of gender dysphoria. In gender dysphoria the experience of the person is opposite or counter to the physical body. The biological sex, and the initial gender assignment, may be male, with male genitalia; however, the person develops the sense of being at odds with that assignment, and often feels uncomfortable with her physical body, considering it to be "not me." Thus, the dysphoria is the experience of the lived body contradicting the physical body.

The sense of contact with God is also a function of the lived body. I have described it as a proprioception of the spirit (Brownell, 2016). "How might a person experience contact with God? It is a kind of touching; it is an impression . . ." (ibid., p. 359). It is a proprioceptive sensing, but it is not exclusively a function of the physical body. That is, the etiology of this experience is not found in physical touch; it is touch of another kind, sourced in the lived body, but with often corresponding physical outcomes or sequelae.

Follow this logic: If something is present in the ontical field, and a living thing comes into contact with it, that something will be encountered by the whole organism comprising that living thing, not just some of the aspects or some of the "parts" of that organism. It will be experienced by the entire living thing. That includes the lived body—the spiritual properties of the whole organism. Conversely, if something is encountered at the spiritual level, it will affect the physical level as well.

Contact is a whole-person experience. One can consider contact as simply material, starting with the physical body but having emotional and cognitive implications, but one can also consider contact as a function of the lived body, at the spiritual level, a phenomenal occurrence that develops into physical sensations. The living thing brings both these properties or dimensions into play, and it is impossible to say which is preeminent. They are fully integrated.

Jesus said that God is spirit and those who worship Him must do so in spirit and in truth. Now that Jesus is no longer physically present, no one can experience contact with God outside of the lived body. Neither can they empirically prove that such contact occurred. No one can prove that the lived body truly exists. Similarly, no one can prove that pre-reflective contact in the psychological attitude of the pneumenal field has occurred through sensing an atmosphere, nor that a pre-reflective contact in the spiritual attitude of the pneumenal field has occurred through contact with God. Neither can anyone prove that these things have not taken place. A person has to examine the phenomena and consider these means of explicating what it is like to be in this world as a living thing to decide what they will believe.

Intentionality and the Aboutness of Experience

Intentionality points to the focus of one's experience, the figure of one's interest (Brownell, 2010); "each act of consciousness is a consciousness of something, that is, intentional, or directed toward something" (Smith, 2018, n.p.).

Intentionality is the nature, the quality, the aboutness of one's experience, and it is simultaneously the linkage to related issues and past, formative experiences. Conscious minds have both intentional and phenomenal properties. A mental state that is intentional is directed toward some object (it is about something). A mental state that is phenomenal feels a particular way (Menary, 2009). The focal point of one's experience is called the intentional object.

Upon reflection one might understand that intentional states are also phenomenal. That is, the experience of being intentional, directed toward some kind of object, *is an experience.*

In gestalt therapy the model of health is the fluid identification and satisfaction of figures of interest; another way of saying that is that a healthy person easily forms intentional objects and pursues them or that a healthy person easily follows his or her experience through awareness.

In Christianity awareness includes spiritual sensitivity. This can be understood as responsiveness to the Holy Spirit, but it can also be understood as discernment, in which one can consider critically the spiritual influences present to a given situation. Writing to a group of Christians, the apostle John put it like this: "Beloved, do not believe every spirit, but test the spirits to see whether they are from God, because many false prophets have gone out into the world." (1 John 4:1)

There are many psychological theories about what we feel and what we think, what we believe and what we do. They can be persuasive, and as such they affect a person spiritually, even though they do so at the psychological level of the pneumenal field. Likewise, there are many theories about matters of the Christian faith and how one might live based on that faith. Simply because one calls him or herself a Christian does not mean they really know God, nor that they know what they are talking about.

Yet, there is more to this. One must have the sense of self, one must be intentionally aware in order have self-experience. Having a strong sense of self is also linked to having a strong conscience. It is the weak conscience that requires rules from the outside, external authorities, to prop up the weak sense of self. The strong conscience understands the grace of God and the freedom that is in Christ so that, as Paul says, all things become legal and the person can choose that which is most profitable.

Still further, one must *have* a sense of self before one can set self aside to follow God or serve someone else. So, Christ's admonition to deny oneself and take up one's cross to follow Him must be understood as a call to the intentionality of sacrifice and servanthood, not as a call to the obliteration of self, which would actually be impossible for a living thing. All human beings are intentional. Even

120 The Experience of Contact With God

someone who has lost his or her mind is having an experience, the experience of insanity. Even someone who is in dementia is having an experience, and the aboutness of their experience is confusion.

Attitude as a Sphere of Experiential Interest

It is one's attitude that gives direction to one's intentionality—one's experience. There are many possible attitudes, and they are governed by the sphere of a person's interests. If one is a carpenter, then at any given moment he or she might be interested and focused upon nails, hammers, or shingles and walk right past books, computers, or hairspray. Then one could say that that person was in the carpentry attitude or the craftsman attitude.

Most relevant to gestalt therapy is the personalistic attitude. It is the attitude in which we live and relate to other people as persons. It is *inter-personal*. So, as therapists this is the attitude in which we make contact with clients. We can also function in a theoretical attitude when we think about our theory, how we do things and why we do them in the way that we do, but if we find ourselves theorizing with clients, chances are we have left them behind. We can also function in a vocational attitude and take care of the technicalities that health care professionals must do.

It is much the same in Christianity. We experience contact with God and with other people following Jesus in faith communities called churches. If we interact with them solely around theology or argue about points of doctrine, then we are in the theoretical attitude and leaving the personal relationship momentarily behind. If pastors build programs of ministry and attempt to make things happen "in the ministry," then they are operating in a professional attitude, as professional Christians (people who make a living by leading or teaching in the church). I learned early on, however, that the ministry is people and not programs; so, it is something that relies on people in contact with one another functioning in the personalistic attitude.

Yet, there is an even more important kind of attitude in Christianity. One might call it various things. It could be called a reverential attitude, as when a person feels worshipful. It could be called a humble attitude, as when one realizes he or she is a creature made by God. I will call it the spiritual attitude and contrast it to the psychological attitude, both possible in a pneumenal field. The spiritual attitude is that sphere of interest in which a person is cognizant of the enchantment of the pneumenal field and oriented positively toward the potential of contact with God. In the spiritual attitude one is cognizant of the sacred.

Imagination, Awareness, and Possibility in the Personal Horizon

"The 'horizon' is constituted by those aspects of a thing that are not given in perception but rather are possibilities which can be given in further acts of perception or reflection" (Moran, 2006, pp. 161–162).

A Basic Orientation to Phenomenology **121**

The horizon is all that a person can imagine. It's the realm of the possible. The physical horizon is as far as one can see, and the phenomenological horizon is as far as one's intuition might permit him or her to "see," which is to say fully perceive.

For instance, when we perceive an object, we receive it as given from a physical place, a specific vantage point, and we establish a perceptual perspective in relationship to it. Being situated, we see one of its sides, but not the others. However, the others are co-given in the horizon (Smith, downloaded November 2, 2019 from www.iep.utm.edu/phenom/#SH4c). We intuitively understand, as a matter of further phenomenological perception, that there are other sides, and we also comprehend the object has having an inside. This horizon, this kind of perception, is not simply physical. Its etiology is found in the lived body; the thing is perceived as a whole in one's experience, one's sense of being in the world. As such it is not mystical; it is perceptual and a function of contact in a physical world that induces a "fleshing out" of the life world.

If something is not in a person's horizon, it never occurs to them; it's beyond. It's not as simple as saying that it's been considered and rejected. It's never been seriously considered.

Imagination is a word that can be used for the intuitional perception in one's horizon, and both Christians and gestalt therapists deal with it on a regular basis. The therapist observes the client talking but not engaging with his or her eyes. They look around the room, darting from one part of it to another, but meeting the eyes of the therapist only in passing, while moving to another object. The therapist physically observes darting eyes and a lack of visual engagement; the therapist imagines the client is nervous. The Christian invites into his house a visitor at the door who wants to tell him about salvation in Jesus Christ. The Christian tries to inform the guest that he already knows the Lord, but the guest skips over every attempt and moves on to provide his speech about how a person might get saved. The Christian imagines the guest cares more about making his speech than getting to know him.

Life World and Phenomenal Field

The life world, according to Husserl, is the basis for meaning and purpose (Moran, 2012). It "is the world of the pre-given, familiar, present, available, surrounding world, including both 'nature' and 'culture' (however they may be defined), that envelops us and is always there as taken for granted." It is the world of our common experience. It is our κοινωνία (*koinonia*—partnership, contact, community) with all of life that is constantly in flux, going on, of which we are parts and partakers. The life world, then, is not simply another term for field, because "field" would be too vague. It is not, for instance, the actual physical environment, nor the ontical field (which is all that exists, has influence, but is independent of our thoughts about it). It is, however, one's phenomenal field since it is the domain of one's experience. The life world, or phenomenal field, is the domain in which intentionality, attitude, and horizon come together to situate the lived body within a world of experience going on—the phenomenal field.

Putting It All Together

In the commonality of life, which is to say in the natural attitude, while advancing in life and contacting the world, "we move in a current of ever new experiences, judgments, valuations, decisions" (Husserl, 1970, n.p.) and we point the focus of our awareness and concern at the things in this world. In such a manner we are not customarily taken with the process, the way in which we live, but with the content of our living. None of the elements in such content, which is to say not one of the intentional objects, is isolated. The intentionality involved implies an expanding horizon of valid possibilities.[2] One's past experience influences one's current phenomenal field; it lingers through linkages to current intentional objects. These intentional connections are not static and dead. They come to mind with various degrees of potency and can be tapped in order to elevate them to the center of attention. Thus, the horizon is not a fixed, rigid structure such as a vast tile floor. It is a malleable, heaving, oscillating membrane bringing together attitude and life world in one, cohesive lived body. It is the proving ground of faith, existential risk, and the abode of hope.

Because the natural attitude is the basic ground that supports any subsequent development, such as the psychological attitude or the spiritual attitude, both can be understood in light of the above. They both operate as subsets of the natural attitude.

In the psychological attitude one's life world, one's experience of living in the world, is governed by the corresponding psychological horizon. Thus, Perls, Hefferline, and Goodman's (1951) assertion that one can trust that the field will supply the means in various situations can be understood in an entirely secular way. As such it would be akin to Merleau-Ponty's (1968) use of the term "perceptual faith," by which he referred to the simple belief that what one was seeing, hearing, tasting, or touching was there and corresponded to what was seen, or heard. He called it "the certitude I have of being connected up with the world by my look ..." (ibid., p. 28). While the psychological attitude and horizon allow a pneumenal field and life experience that includes emotions, beliefs, values, convictions, and so forth (all legitimate elements of a pneumenal field), they do not permit the validity of Christian spiritual experience.

In the spiritual attitude one's life world, one's experience of living in the world, is governed by the corresponding spiritual horizon.[3] The faith in that kind of context could be called sacred, because the intentionality involved is focused on the things of God and the faith itself is described as the assurance of *things* hoped for, the conviction of things not seen.[4] This does not mean that there is no perception involved, that the faith is a blind, baseless leap in the dark and a hope against

A Basic Orientation to Phenomenology **123**

hope. Rather, there is a sense of contacting, of κοινωνία with divinity, which is an experience and includes the perception of a proprioceptive shift (the touch of another kind) to which I have referred previously (Brownell, 2016). So, there is a kind of corresponding certitude of being connected up with God through one's inner "look." Thus, the spiritual attitude and horizon would include all the elements of the psychological attitude and horizon, but also such things as the sense of the presence of God, the experience of contact with God, joy (something C.S. Lewis asserted gripped him during his conversion from atheism; Lewis, 1955), and שָׁלוֹם (*shalom*) or peace (which in Hebrew points to harmony, wholeness, completeness).

In the gospel of John, the fourteenth chapter, after Jesus makes the classic statement, "I am the way, and the truth, and the life; no one comes to the Father but through Me,"[5] the apostle Philip said, "Lord, show us the father . . ." And Jesus responded, "Have I been so long with you, and *yet* you have not come to know Me, Philip? He who has seen Me has seen the Father . . ."

Imagine the dissonance arising in Philip's mind. Christ's divinity had not been a common and consistent understanding among the disciples before the resurrection. Philip wanted to be shown the father; he had a sense of incompleteness about that and was not at peace. Yet, later, after the advent of the Holy Spirit and the Spirit's indwelling of believers, Philip became quite certain what those words meant. He stopped striving and found rest, shalom in the knowledge of God.

This is what happened with me as well. Before putting my trust in Jesus and believing what the Bible said about God, I was constantly trying to figure out which religion or spiritual system could be trusted. I read the *Upanishads* and the *Bhagavad Gita*. I read *Siddhartha* (Hesse, 1951). I read secular tracts like *The True Believer* (Hoffer, 1951) or *The Glass Bead Game/Magister Ludi* (Hesse, 1949) that came with the aura of supposed truth. I had people trying to tell me about Christianity. My roommate while in the Navy had studied for the priesthood and was attempting to integrate Catholicism and Buddhism. We lived in the San Francisco Bay area during the summer of love. The place was a smorgasbord of spirituality, philosophy, and activism. I was not at peace. I was unsettled. I was what Paul told his protégé Timothy to watch out for, people "always learning and never able to come to the knowledge of the truth."[6] But that all changed when God made Himself known to me.

The experience of living in this world as a Christian is a matter of the lived body. We experience great ecstasy and feel swept up in worship, in admiration, in amazement at the person and works of God. And we also experience the other side. We may not bump into physical walls, but we routinely encounter doubt, skepticism, rejection, and contempt. Paul said that we are to be most pitied if our belief, our message, our story about Jesus is not true. But that is what many people believe (that Christians are lame, limping pathetically through life leaning on the crutch of a futile faith in God), and when we meet them, we also meet their belief structures and their disdain. That may not be running into a physical wall, but it

124 The Experience of Contact With God

feels like getting hit in the face because one can feel rejection and contempt when it's aimed between one's eyes.

Notes

1. I use this term, post-secular, in the sense of a paradigm that exceeds and supplants the secular. However, I do not mean by using it that I accept all the assertions of post-secularism, such as its stance on the issue of truth.
2. Husserl calls it an "infinite horizon," but of course it is not without limits at any given time, thus I prefer the term "expanding."
3. Here I am thinking of Christian spirituality, which might be obvious given the nature of this book. Others can work out the specifics with application to other religious-spiritual systems.
4. Hebrews 11:1.
5. John 14:6.
6. 2.Timothy 3:7.

References

Brownell, P. (2010). Intentional spirituality. In J. H. Ellens (Ed.), *Personal Spirituality: Vol. 1. The healing power of spirituality* (pp. 19–40). Santa Barbara, CA: ABC-CLIO.

Brownell, P. (2016). Touch of another kind: Contact with God and spiritual self. In J.-M. Robine (Ed.), *Self: A polyphony of contemporary gestalt therapists* (pp. 351–370). St. Romain la Vervée, France: L'experimerie.

Dew, R. (2019). Beyond secular borders: Habermas's communicative ethic and the need for post-secular understanding. *Critical Horizons*, np. doi:10.1080/14409917.2019.1616483

Duns, R. G. (2016). Beneath the shadow of the cross: A Rahnerian rejoinder to Jean-Luc Marion. *Philosophy & Theology, 28*(2), 351–372.

Fuchs, T. (2019). The interactive phenomenal field and the life space: A sketch of an ecological concept of psychotherapy. *Psychopathology, 52*(2), 67–74.

Habermas, J. (2010). *An awareness of what is missing: Faith and reason in a post-secular age.* Cambridge, UK: Polity Press.

Hesse, H. (1949). *The glass bead game/Magister Ludi.* New York, NY: Holt, Rinehart & Winston.

Hesse, H. (1951). *Siddhartha.* New York, NY: New Directions Publishing.

Hoffer, E. (1951). *The true believer.* New York, NY: HarperCollins.

Husserl, E., & Carr, D. (Trans.). (1970). *The crisis of European sciences and transcendental phenomenology: An introduction to phenomenological philosophy.* Evanston, IL: Northwestern University Press.

Lewis, C. S. (1955). *Surprised by joy: The shape of my early life.* New York, NY: Harvest, Harcourt, Inc.

Menary, R. (2009). Intentionality and consciousness. In W. P. Banks (Ed.), *Encyclopedia of consciousness* (Vol. 1, pp. 417–729). Oxford: Elsevier.

Merleau-Ponty, M. (1968). *The visible and the invisible.* Evanston, IL: Northwestern University Press.

Moberg, M., Granholm, K., & Nynäs, P. (2012). Trajectories of post-secular complexity: An introduction. In P. Nynäs, M. Lassander, & T. Utriainen (Eds.), *Post-secular society* (pp. 1–26). New York, NY: Routledge.

Moran, D. (2006). *Introduction to phenomenology*. New York, NY: Routledge, Taylor & Francis Group.

Moran, D. (2012). *Husserl's crisis of the European sciences and transcendental phenomenology: An introduction*. Cambridge, UK: Cambridge University Press.

Nelson, E. (2015). Life and world. In J. Malpas & H.-H. Gander (Eds.), *The Routledge companion to hermeneutics* (pp. 378–389). New York, NY: Routledge.

Perls, F., Hefferline, R., & Goodman, P. (1951). *Gestalt therapy: Excitement and growth in the human personality*. New York, NY: The Julian Press.

Smith, D. W. (2018). Phenomenology. In E. N. Zalta (Ed.), *The Stanford encyclopedia of philosophy* (n.p.). Retrieved October 20, 2019, from https://plato.stanford.edu/entries/phenomenology; https://plato.stanford.edu/archives/sum2018/entries/phenomenology

Smith, J. (downloaded 2019). Phenomenology. In *The internet encyclopedia of philosophy: A peer-reviewed academic resource* (n.p.). Retrieved from www.iep.utm.edu/phenom/#SH4c

Staudigl, M., & Alvis, J. (2016). Phenomenology and the post-secular turn: Reconsidering the "return of the religious." *International Journal of Philosophical Studies*, *24*(5), 589–599.

11

A PHENOMENOLOGY OF SPIRITUAL LIFE

There is the thing.
There is the thing-to-me.
The nature of the thing
Constrains
The thing-to-me.
Without the thing,
There would be no
thing-to-me.
Without the thing-to-me,
There would be no
Thing-for-me.

The thing is, I believe in God. God *is* the thing. I am a living thing and so is God, but I am also a finite thing, and that's where the similarity ends.

God is infinite. His love, His patience, His wisdom, His power—these things have no limit. He pursued me. Chased me down in a relentless, inevitable courtship until, exhausted, spent from the struggle, I said, "Okay then! If you are real, make yourself known to me."

Every terrible day at Sunday school in churches when I was a child shouted at me. "What are you doing?!" I didn't care. This was going to be the end of something. Either this God people were telling me about, hounding me about, this God I had also been yearning for, wondering, "Who is God?" was either going to respond, or I was done with it—the whole "God thing."

I did not expect what I was about to experience. I could not have imagined it. The only frame of reference I had was sitting in small classes at church with children I did not know, with the teacher talking, and with the sense that I did not

A Phenomenology of Spiritual Life **127**

belong and the panic of not being able to escape. I could not listen; so, I did not get instructions for what we were supposed to do. I hung back and watched others. I did not speak. If asked a question, I said, "I don't know." I was checked out.

Years later when I checked back in, I made a deal. It makes me laugh to think of it. I was in my room in a house in the Oakland hills talking to a God I was not sure even existed, telling Him that on my part I would read the New Testament, but on His part He should make Himself known to me. He took me up on the deal. When I started reading the New Testament it made perfect sense. It never had before. Not only was it intelligible, it was also compelling. Over the following weeks I read through and pondered the entire New Testament. Along the way, when I got to the gospel of John, my big question ("who is God?") was answered.

In the beginning was the Word. The Word was with God and the Word was God. Jesus is the living word of God. Jesus *is* God. That astounded me. I suddenly got it. When I arrived in my reading at the letter of Paul to the Christians in Philippi, my astonishment was compounded.

Jesus, not regarding equality with God a thing to be grasped tightly at all cost, although he existed as God, He emptied Himself and took on the form of a human being. Being found as a human being, He humbled Himself, even to the point of death on a cross. Doubly astounded.

And when I got to the letter to the Hebrews it was confirmed again.

Jesus is the radiance of the divinity found in the godhead. He is the exact imprint of divinity among people. He gives human form to an immaterial, spiritual existence; he is the shape of God in the soft clay of our world.

The Experience of Living Spiritually

A phenomenology of spiritual life is a description of the experiences involved in living spiritually. As I've said previously, the pneumenal field (complete with horizons, intentionalities, and various sub-sets of the life world, each called a world of its own) operates along two basic attitudes: the psychological and the spiritual. Understanding the differences between these two attitudes is important for a gestalt therapist, because they set up two difference kinds of experiences and two different sets of resources. It is a matter of spiritual competency to understand this point and then to respond accordingly with clients.

Since there are manifold spiritual experiences, I will provide a limited view, a brief phenomenology of spiritual life, through contrasting examples.

Example One: The Appreciation of Nature

This is the awe and wonder that people have when they get into the mountains. It's the grandeur sensed while watching the sun set on the thin line that separates water from sky at the edge, where land and sea divide. It's the awe one feels gazing up into the starry sky and feeling the vastness of our galaxy. It is also the

128 The Experience of Contact With God

amazement people feel when they look into the microscopic, interdependent systems in nature, such as the way the blood-brain barrier works or the development of an action potential along myelinated sheaths in the central nervous system.

TABLE 11.1 Psychological and Spiritual Attitudes in the Appreciation of Nature

Psychological Attitude	Spiritual Attitude
In this approach nature functions like an idol; it points to itself. Appreciation, affection for, devotion to nature, the earth itself. A contemporary spiritual manifestation is in Wicca societies and their practices that worship earthy forms and creatures, but it can also simply be an aesthetic love of the beauty in nature that moves one by its appearance, producing a reverence for the environment.	In this approach nature functions as an icon; it points beyond itself. As an icon it catches the attention because of its beauty, but it is not an end in itself. Nature, as creation, points beyond itself to a creator, and so the person is elevated to thinking about God, to wonder at His infinite creativity, skill as a master artisan, respect for His power and love for His creation out of love for He Himself.

Example Two: The Approach to Scripture

Scripture is a term denoting the authoritative writings of various religions that describe rituals and points of theology and practice. For Christians scripture is the Bible. It is given, embodied in various literary genres—cherished narratives, stories of the history of God's interactions with people over time, and in arguments related to the origins and reasons for faith.

TABLE 11.2 Psychological and Spiritual Attitudes in the Approach to Scripture

Psychological Attitude	Spiritual Attitude
People have devoted entire scholarly careers to the study of the Bible, its formation, and/or its textual history. These kinds of people approach the scriptures as an intellectual discipline but not as a reason for personal belief; they are like cultural anthropologists whose discipline is academic and professional.	The Bible is regarded to be inspired, sacred, and a major revelation of God. Through the Bible people can encounter a God who is alive, transcendent yet immanent, and active in making Himself known. The approach is reverent and characterized by a thirst for the knowledge of God. It is relevant to personal and existential belief.

Example Three: Response to the Other-Worldly and Ineffable

Some ideas seem too great to be captured by words and some experiences seem to transcend this world; their existants exceed our abilities to fully comprehend. Yet, we glimpse them, as if brushing up against them, and we can imagine them,

A Phenomenology of Spiritual Life **129**

even though our imaginations are inadequate and do not exhaust them. It is a pathetic imaginal, doomed to defect, and we instinctively sense that. Still, there is the experience.

TABLE 11.3 Psychological and Spiritual Attitudes in the Response to the Other-Worldly and Ineffable

Psychological Attitude	Spiritual Attitude
The approach is through curiosity, often with dissonance. There is appreciation for mystery, but the mysteries are regarded as of the immanent domain, and they are investigated through naturalism.	The approach is curiosity, often with dissonance. There is appreciation for mystery, but the mysteries are often regarded to be of the transcendent domain, and they are investigated with an appreciation for the supernatural.

Example Four: Tragedy, Affliction, and Pathos

Tragedy, affliction, and pathos—that which moves us concerning the human condition—affects our sense of justice, equity, and fairness. These things lead to ethical judgments and even questions about the existence of God. How could an all-powerful and loving God allow evil? This example is typified in the videos of people jumping from the smoking Twin Towers on 911 because they knew they were going to die and they had to choose between burning or falling. When bad things happen to innocent people who are doing their best, we call that tragedy. When people bear up under affliction, we call that courage. When people step in front of the gunfire to save their children, we call that self-sacrifice. Both the

TABLE 11.4 Psychological and Spiritual Attitudes in Tragedy, Affliction, and Pathos

Psychological Attitude	Spiritual Attitude
People are drawn to consider what there is about human beings that they can exhibit the most noble and the most savage. The answers in the psychological attitude would be found in anthropology, psychology, sociology, or in research that focuses on biosocial and environmental antecedents to behavior. But still, people celebrate the human capacity to rise to a moment.	Human beings are created in the image of God, and we retain that image. However, we are also marred, undermined by our own self-centeredness and brutality. This approach recognizes human shortcomings and the experience is one of pathos, regret, confession, repentance, but also of celebration whenever the best about people shows itself. We see the worst and the best in people through the works of the flesh and the fruit of the spirit and the ongoing processes of sanctification.

secular pilgrimage sites of the Memorial Hall to the Victims of the Nanjing Massacre in Nanjing, China and the Gettysburg National Military Park and Cemetery in Gettysburg, Pennsylvania (Newman, 2017) draw people in a reverential, captivating hush. The anguish of real people touches the heart, and it is a spiritual phenomenon.

The first two examples cover two types of revelation, general and special. Nature is a general revelation and scripture is a special revelation; both relate to the issue of saturated phenomena, which will be dealt with more in chapter thirteen. The third example introduces the issue of mystery (also chapter thirteen), and the fourth example the issue of human striving (chapters fourteen and fifteen). These do not exhaust categories of spiritual experience, but they form at least one kind of foundation with which to consider a phenomenology of spirituality.

A truly adequate development of a phenomenology of Christian spirituality would take a whole book all by itself. There is not the room here to do anything but point in directions. For both pastoral workers and gestalt therapists people need to realize that the Christian person resides in this world and so has all the problems and experiences anyone would, any person living whether or not they believed in Jesus. However, the Christian also has a whole set of challenges related to their identity in Christ.

In Christ I am not just "he" or "she." I am "His." I belong to Jesus. I am not my own. I have been bought with a price and the life I live I live by faith in the one who died for me. That changes everything. It compounds and complicates living in this world (as if it were not complicated enough already).

Gestalt therapists working with Christians would benefit from considering the phenomenality of spiritual life. For Christians the process does not always run in the psychological attitude. They would not recognize a phenomenology of religious life (Heidegger, 2010) based in the psychological attitude. So, it's not as simple as tracking cognitive or affective functions and placing process within a theory of pathology or therapeutic practice that bypasses the intentionalities and horizons commensurate with the spiritual attitude. In the spiritual attitude the pneumenal field is particularly "God-inclusive." A gestalt therapist can listen to a client talk about spiritual things, but they will inevitably try to comprehend what is being said in accord with their perspective—the psychological attitude, unless they have acquired the Holy Spirit and have access to a spiritual attitude.

So, the phenomenology of Christian spirituality comes down to what it is like to *be* a Christian.

Christian Phenomenology of Spiritual Life: A Typical Scenario

There is the excitement of initial enlightenment. This is the realization of the validity of Christ. This is the understanding that what the Bible says, and what people proclaim about Jesus, is true, and the person believes it. Joe believed it.

A Phenomenology of Spiritual Life **131**

The world seemed brighter, like a new car, like the fresh morning on a new day. The leaves were more emerald green than olive drab. The light was crisp. He took a shower because he wanted to fit in.

He considered what it meant that the old had passed away and that he had become a new creature, for that is what Paul wrote to the Christians in Corinth: "Therefore if anyone is in Christ, *he is* a new creature; the old things passed away; behold, new things have come."[1] He felt free of his past and happy for it. He felt at peace with himself for the first time. He felt grounded more solidly than ever before. He could not stop smiling. He was happy.

He threw himself into the study of the Bible. He went back to church and sat in on discussion groups with people he'd never met before, but with whom he suddenly felt a kinship. He found himself rising spontaneously to his feet when worship music played. His chest warmed and tears formed when he sang the lyrics. He loved God.

Had he lost his mind and been brainwashed? No. No, *that* was the deception, that there is a brainwashing that has happened for anyone who believes in Jesus. Call yourself a disciple of Christ, a Jesus follower, weep at the cross, and other people look at you like you're strange. He was okay with that. There was a knowing, the kind of knowing that approaches certainty, and it scrubbed the deception out of his mind. He decided to go with this new faith rather than second guess himself. There was no turning back.

Weeks went by. He established the routines of this new life. He learned tenets of theology. He solidified his stand, but he began to struggle with some old habits, and he began to notice with more scrutiny things about himself that never mattered before. He did not like the way he used foul language. He became grieved about the way he seemed to put himself and his accomplishments into almost every conversation. What was going on? For a new creature, he seemed to be exhibiting a lot of the old one. He pondered what Paul wrote to the Christians in Rome about this subject:

> For what I am doing, I do not understand; for I am not practicing what I would like to do, but I am doing the very thing I hate. But if I do the very thing I do not want to do, I agree with the Law, confessing that the Law is good. So now, no longer am I the one doing it, but sin which dwells in me. For I know that nothing good dwells in me, that is, in my flesh; for the willing is present in me, but the doing of the good is not. For the good that I want, I do not do, but I practice the very evil that I do not want. But if I am doing the very thing I do not want, I am no longer the one doing it, but sin which dwells in me.[2]

It did not feel good. The more he tried to clean up his mouth, the worse it seemed to get. Every time he swore he condemned himself. Every time he condemned himself he confessed to God and said he'd try harder. Every time he tried harder, he failed. He felt miserable. He felt guilty. His vision narrowed. He turned in on himself and avoided people. He stopped going to church, because he felt like a hypocrite. He could not sing the songs about being a new creature, because he failed so badly. He felt like an old creature. He found himself lamenting to God that he was not a good Christian, and one day the thought came to him, "What is that?"

What is a good Christian? He found himself talking back to himself, but was it himself he was addressing? The question had been his thought, but it had not come from him. Was this God?

As days passed, he noticed that he scoffed at the Christian books that offered seven principles for living "the overflowing life." He thought, "It's just not that simple." He could not go back to his old life, because he found it to be even more futile and deadening than before, but he was disgusted by the dysfunction in the church, and the church was supposed to be Christ's vehicle in the world. Didn't Jesus say that he would build his church and the gates of hell would not prevail against it? He wondered if this was what Jesus had in mind. He found he was not the only hypocrite, not the only one using old coping strategies inside the church. He was disgusted at the spiritualizing, the adding of veneers of godly sounding platitudes over everyday failure and self-serving effort. Where was the simple admonition to stop striving and know God? Where was the knowledge of God? The world was blind to God and God's people were dysfunctional. It was all a mess.

He sat down one day in the hot sun and said, "I give up. This is all broken—*all of it!*" Then a thought came given "What do you think I came for?"

Notes

1. 2. Corinthians 5:17.
2. Romans 7:15–20.

References

Heidegger, M. (2010). *The phenomenology of religious life*. M. Fritsch & J. Gosetti-Ferencei (Trans.). Bloomington, IN: Indiana University Press.

Newman, R. (2017). When the secular is sacred: The Memorial Hall to the Victims of the Nanjing Massacre and the Gettysburg National Military Park as pilgrimage sites. In M. Rectenwald, R. Almeida, & G. Levine (Eds.), *Global secularisms in a post-secular age* (pp. 261–270). Boston, MA: Walter de Gruyter Inc.

12

EAVESDROPPING ON RELATIONSHIPS WITH GOD

There in my eyes, before me.
Sitting.
Now in my ears, within me.
Talking.
So, in between us both
Trusting.
Moved by the life in my presence
Passing.

Marie Hoffman asserted that from "a Christian perspective, patients are not only recognized in their complexities and struggles, but they are also recognized as bearing God's indelible image within them . . . and having a meaningful destiny before them, a destiny in which the therapist has a role to play" (Hoffman, 2011, p. 2). That is what this chapter concerns, and it's a reminder of what all this therapy stuff is really about.

I started working with people in mental health contexts in 1967. I've done it as a Navy corpsman, as line staff in a psychiatric hospital, in a children's residential treatment center, in an adolescent residential treatment center and therapeutic school, and then as a mental health therapist in a co-occurring disorders psychiatric hospital. I've been a pastor using pastoral, nouthetic counseling. I've also done outpatient psychotherapy since 1995 as a gestalt therapist. That's been over fifty years of working with people.

There are those who come to treatment because someone else made them. One has to work with them, and it's rewarding when they shift and start engaging even though they never really wanted to. There are those who never shift.

134 The Experience of Contact With God

I've also been a patient in psychotherapy. I've sat with cognitive-behavioral therapists and Biblical counselors. I've worked with gestalt therapists. There is a saying that the therapist can take the client only as far as the therapist him or herself has gone. That sounds like there is a set journey, like a board game, and we can only take someone else as many spaces on the board as we've been able to go, but the steps are not all the same for everybody. The steps are all different for everyone.

So, what does that saying mean? There is a facing of one's self in therapy. Although the issues certainly differ, the process of facing them for one person resembles the process for another. So, one kind of going only so far involves the willingness to face oneself and deal with one's issues. Therapists who avoid doing that cannot take their clients very far, because the anxiety feels too dangerous. Then, there are the issues themselves, and therapists need to know what theirs happen to be so that they don't mistake them for the client's issues. When the client must deal with similar things as the therapist has had to deal with, and the therapist has "gone there," then the therapist knows what it's about at an experiential level, and they can come alongside the client to support them as they face difficulty and pain without working out their own "stuff" on the client's time.

This is not just about attuning to someone. This is not applying unconditional, positive regard. This is not telling oneself mechanically, "Oh! This is where I provide support" or "This is where I use technique 64-B."

There is no mechanical cookbook that will tell the therapist how much time to baste the client at a given temperature before adding spice. Neither can you do this kind of work as a paint-by-numbers therapist. A theory of doing therapy will help, but it's the person of the therapist and the quality of their contact with the client that makes for great advances. When contact happens, we meet people.

When we meet people, we have the opportunity to witness how they conduct their lives. The ones who work hard in therapy have impressed me as courageous and relentless in their desire for growth. I have admired them. I have observed many things about people, and that includes the unique paths they have in relating to God. I learn from them. Everyone is unique.

Here I would like to draw a contrast between gestalt therapy and Biblical counseling, keeping in mind the difference I've been noting between the psychological attitude and the spiritual attitude. It is possible to use both these approaches in either attitude. Understand what I am saying. It is possible to be a gestalt therapist and use gestalt therapy in the psychological attitude and in the spiritual attitude. It is possible to be a Biblical or nouthetic counselor and to use such in both the psychological attitude and the spiritual attitude. I know that it seems odd or impossible to practice Biblical or nouthetic counseling in the psychological attitude, but it isn't.

I have sat with Biblical counselors who listened to me for a few minutes and then started telling me verses in the Bible that applied to my problems and things that I should do based on those verses in order to solve my problems. That was doing Biblical counseling in the psychological attitude. It was a positivistic,

Eavesdropping on Relationships With God **135**

stimulus–response, cause-and-effect use of the Bible as leverage to quick and easy change. There *is no quick and easy change*. Biblical counseling in the spiritual attitude uses much more listening than telling, because the counselor understands that people meet God in diverse ways and God's agenda with each one varies. There is a humility involved that respects the patient's relationship with God. There is an eavesdropping on the client's experience with God.

I have sat with gestalt therapists who seemed to be working some angle, some procedure by which they were trying to get me to be more aware. Aware of what? Notice my butt in the chair. Pay attention to my breathing. Look around the room and see what is happening around me. Okay. Then what? It is the oddest thing to feel like we are heading for some goal only to realize that the therapist has no clue what it is. And we never do seem to get there! That is gestalt therapy in the psychological attitude. Frankly, even the more sophisticated forms of gestalt process are theory driven. I sometimes wonder which gestalt writer the therapist is thinking of while I'm sitting with them.

Is it possible for gestalt therapists to work in the spiritual attitude? Would a gestalt therapist have to *be* a Christian in order to work in the spiritual attitude with a Christian client? It is a provocative question that I have gone round and round on with my colleagues.

A therapist can take the client only as far as the therapist has gone. If the therapist does not know Jesus experientially, has not given him or herself to believe in Him, to trust Him, then how can they understand what the client means when they say that everything changed for them when that happened? If the client hates himself for his sin, can the gestalt therapist keep from objectifying the client?

I believe the gestalt therapist who does not know the Lord cannot fully understand the client who does. However, I believe that the gestalt therapist who will allow the spiritual experience of the client to stand on its own, to allow the veracity of it as it presents itself, as it is given, that this gestalt therapist has a chance to eavesdrop on the client's relationship with God.

Carol

Carol was a mid-twenties woman who had grown up in a religious cult. She was trying to sort out what was cultic and an aberration from what was true Christianity, because although she had been strangled by the legalism of the cult, she felt intuitively that God is real, and as such He was important to her. So, the work was about guilt, false guilt, introjects, polarities, and about the sadness of having had her life so influenced as a child by a rule-bound economy.

Fred

Fred was a believer in Jesus. He had been for some time. He did not remember when he was not. However, he did not regard himself to be a "good Christian,"

136 The Experience of Contact With God

because he had cheated on his wife and he knew he was a liar. He told me he didn't want to make his spirituality an aspect of our therapy, but I noticed he repeatedly brought up how judged he felt by his friends in the church. He resented that.

Delores

Delores became a Christian by responding to the invitation of friends on her campus at college to attend evangelistic outreach meetings. She quickly embraced Christianity, and she determined to read the whole Bible. She started in the Old Testament. When she read about God ordering the Jewish people to wipe out entire villages of men, women, and children and to burn everything in those villages, she stopped. She could not abide a God who would be so cruel. It did not fit with the message that God is love. Instead of letting Christianity go, however, she became bitter and angry and went to war with Christians on her campus. She picketed their meetings and sought to disrupt them whenever she could. It got her into trouble, and she came for "anger management."

Bud

Bud was a Christian man who came precisely because he knew I was a Christian. He did not want to go to any pastor, because he was very ashamed of his addiction to pornography. He had tried over and over to stop going to the internet pornographic sites. The work was around his damaged self-image and his belief in God's grace, even in the face of repeated failure. So, we spent time exploring the limits of grace as they applied to him and his repetition compulsion, what the Bible calls slavery.

Eavesdropping on Relationships With God

I have children. I believe God gave them to me. That is what the Bible says. Children are a gift from the Lord. I looked at each one of them as on loan and not belonging to me. Yet, I had the chance to influence them. And then I had to let them leave. They each think for themselves. They each make decisions about God on their own. I do not get to determine how that goes. And I love them.

It is the same with clients. They are given to us, and they make their own choices. We do not get to determine what they will do. I know that we know that. Gestalt therapy largely has not bought into the medical model in which clinicians do things to people to make them get better. We do not do clinical things to clients to make them change. The medical model is a deception in mental health and personal growth. It is a reduction of a much more complicated process. Consider what is happening in psychotherapy. None of the techniques and interventions

Eavesdropping on Relationships With God   **137**

typically described take place between a human being and a kiosk or robot. It is all interpersonal. Relational. One person to another—even if the relationship is a bad one. Either that or it is extra-therapeutic and just life going on all around us.

The issue of change will be taken up further in chapter fifteen, but it's enough here to point to Paul's statement to the Christians in Corinth that regardless of what people do, it is God who supplies growth.[1]

With both children and clients we have the opportunity to observe another's life, to be with another person as they navigate life. It is a rich privilege. Our clients are certainly not our children, but there is a similarity in that we have influence, and we get to observe what they will do with it. We do not determine the direction nor the pace of any change. The best we can do is be there, be present. The best we can get is to eavesdrop on change when it happens, and that includes, if we are fortunate, the ways in which God works with another person. This is the way it is for both Christians working to disciple another believer and to help them grow in their knowledge of God and for therapists working to serve the social and mental health needs of their clients.

My wife and I run a faith-based recovery house. This morning we had breakfast with someone involved with it. It is her birthday. We took her out. Over coffee she told me of some incidents in her life, traumatic assaults, heartbreaking disappointments, and frustrating turns of "bad luck." She made some poor choices along the way. She experienced loss.

She had been involved with a cult, a false religious system, for most of her youth, and she was firmly entrenched in it. When it came time for her to break free of the slavery of addiction, she found herself in a faith-based program across town from us. That is where she put her trust in Jesus and fully leaned on Him. She started to deconstruct the cultic teaching of her youth. She sees a therapist. She goes to groups. She works her recovery program. She works with us to help others.

The reason I mention her is because the hope she now has is like nothing I've seen in many years of doing psychotherapy. It is a hope I've seen before in people who come to know Jesus in a personal way. This morning I asked her, with all that she has lost, if she has the presence of the Holy Spirit, and her whole face lit up.

"Oh *yes!!*" she exclaimed.

All is not loss. She has gained, and that is the sense she now has. There is something upon which to build—her trust in God. This kind of relationship has been the foundation, the support, that many other people have used to make gains, but it is something entirely between themselves and God. There is nothing another person can do to cause it. Other people can have influence, and God certainly uses them to bring about His purposes, but the growth comes from God Himself.

This morning at breakfast I had the chance to eavesdrop on our colleague's relationship with God. I could see it made all the difference to her and drove the momentum in her recovery and personal growth.

Note

1. 1. Corinthians 3: 6–7.

Resource

Hoffman, M. (2011). *Toward mutual recognition: Relational psychoanalysis and the Christian narrative*. New York, NY: Routledge, Taylor & Francis Group.

Story Three

THE LONGED-FOR PEACE

She was young again. She had her life ahead of her without any mistakes . . .

There might as well have been canons firing, explosions tearing through the house, and sonic booms thundering in her ears. It felt like there was.

Her eyes could not focus for the shock of the force when he hit her. Then he shoved her against the wall, took her face in his large, coarse hands, and squeezed her lips into a forced pucker.

"Give us a kiss, Babe," he mocked. But then he pushed her face away and complained, "Oh hell! You got blood all over my hand."

She dared not look him in the eye. She didn't want to provoke him, but more than that she just didn't want to see him at all. She slid down the wall and sat on the floor. Her heart was racing. Would he leave now?

"I think you do it on purpose. You test me."

She said nothing.

"Did you do it on purpose?"

"No," she said.

"You know I love you," he declared.

His voice softened. "You know I love you."

He stood over her and said, "You know. You *know* you need to tell me where you are at all times."

He reached down and lifted her up off the floor. "Why did you make me angry?"

She tensed at his touch.

"Now don't do that. You know I love you."

"Yes, I know," she said.

140 The Experience of Contact with God

He went on. "You're supposed to text me and let me know where you are. That's all you have to do."

"I know," she said. "You're right," she said.

This is how it went. That is how it would go. She could not please him, and he would blame her and get angry.

She wished it were not so. She longed for peace.

One day it was overcast, and he phoned and told her he would be gone on business. He'd see her in a couple days.

She threw some clothes in a bag and grabbed a coat. She got into her car and started driving. She headed across the Bay Bridge, picked up highway 280 and then turned south to highway 17. She took that over the mountains to Santa Cruz and then picked up the coast highway and drove through Monterey past Carmel Highlands going south.

The Little Sur river starts in the mountains above and east of Big Sur. It winds through the mountains heading north and west, joined by creeks, until it reaches the ocean at Little Sur River beach. There is an inlet there with a large rock and dune. On one side is the ocean; on the other side is a lagoon. The river runs into it and disappears.

The highway makes a deliberate switchback at that place. She stopped there and sat in the car. She took a breath and sighed. The stress broke a bit. She bowed in front of the steering wheel, put her face in both hands, and moaned. She could not go back.

The sun began to set.

Finally, she started the car and drove a little further in the growing darkness. She found a campground that had some cabins. Someone had forfeited their reservation and she snatched it up. She decided to stay for several days and paid for them all.

No one knew where she was, and that felt good.

She looked around inside the cabin. It had wood paneling throughout. There was a kitchen of sorts and a bathroom. It had a loft with a king-sized bed. The living room had a couch. There was a wood burning stove.

She put some wood in the stove and lit it. She curled up with a blanket on the couch and stared into the flames, and that is where she fell asleep.

In the morning the fog moved in. It was chilly, and she put on her coat and a hat and went outside. She walked down to the beach, and when she got there she sat on a log and looked out to sea. She could not see very far. She watched waves roll in and stop on the shore.

Little birds ran where the thin surf was absorbed by the sand. Pelicans and gulls flew overhead. She was thankful to be alone.

"Is this the peace you wanted?" a thought came given.

"Feels right," she answered.

Later that day a couple arrived at the cabin. They were the people who had missed the deadline on their reservation. They arrived two days late on a five-day reservation.

The Longed-For Peace **141**

She had paid for the entire difference when she arrived the day before.

"I'm Valerie," she told them.

The other woman said, "I'm Jake and he's Ashley. Some folks keep turning that around and calling me Ashley and him Jake." She seemed nervous. She looked worried and a bit tired.

Obviously, there was a problem.

Ashley said, "We got our dates mixed up."

Jake said, "He's being nice. What happened is that *I* got the dates mixed up." She quickly looked his way. "I insisted I knew when we were supposed to be here and made a big deal about it."

Ashley shook his head. He said, "That doesn't matter."

Valerie said, "Well, I've paid for four days, and I got here yesterday."

There was a moment of silence. Then Jake turned to Ashley and leaned into his arms. She started weeping and said, "I'm so sorry." He stroked her hair and nuzzled against the top of her head.

"It's okay," he said gently.

The first impulse was to hate Jake for playing the weak, needy female. But it didn't seem like manipulation. She seemed genuinely sorry, and Valerie felt jealous. "Who can be that vulnerable?" she wondered.

She warmed to them. The thought came to her to just leave, but she hesitated. She said, "Well. If you pay me for the rest of the time, I'll leave and give you the place back."

She could feel the sadness immediately. It was like a death; her need for solitude and a place to figure things out burned inside. She felt panic rise. She still could not go back, but where could she go? She needed more time alone. She wanted to be alone now more than ever.

Another moment passed. They all stood in the living room in an awkward silence. Finally, Ashley said, "If you don't mind sleeping on the couch and giving us some privacy, we could all stay. I'll pay you half of what you've already paid."

Valerie thought about it.

Ashley added, "And we'll go get some food for all of us."

Valerie hesitated. Then she said, "And some wine?"

"Sure!" said Jake.

Valerie agreed. "But," she said, "I need time alone too. That's why I came here. I don't need the cabin to be alone. I can do that outside. I just need a place to sleep. And I'm not in a space for a lot of conversation."

The rest of the day they went their own ways. Valerie went back to the beach. The fog lifted. She took her shoes off and walked in the water, but it was achingly cold.

She found herself staring. She could find no solutions. She lost her thoughts. She became mesmerized. She couldn't focus. She considered the appearance of the rocks, the trees, the surf, the birds, but nothing stuck. Each one dissolved and drifted away. She considered her time of life, the person of her boyfriend, all the relationships before him, her job, her friends, the place where she lived. It was a series of disconnected snapshots.

142 The Experience of Contact with God

That night she fell asleep on the couch frustrated and troubled.

The next morning it started raining. Jake and Ashley started fixing breakfast.

Valerie took some coffee out on the porch and sat in the wooden rocker that was there. She pulled a blanket up around her. "This will do," she thought.

Inside she could hear Ashley's voice rise. "You got sliced ham instead of bacon?" She expected to hear him get angry.

"Oh well," he said. "I'm making scrambled eggs; can you slice some cheese?"

They seemed to be working well together. No bombs going off.

She sipped her coffee, snuggled down inside the blanket and watched the rain.

"What do you want?" a thought came given.

"That's a good question," she said.

"Him?"

She considered her boyfriend. "The nice him," she said.

"Impossible."

"I know," she said.

The rain grew heavy and danced with itself in layers of thick drops that shimmied in the slight breeze. Valerie could feel the moisture blow across her face.

"If I haven't got him, though, then I don't have anybody," she said.

"No one?"

"Who else?" she asked.

Nothing came given after that.

"Who else?" she repeated.

"Who are you talking to?" said Jake. She was standing at the door. "Breakfast is ready," she said.

Inside they all sat at the table. "This girl's talking to herself," said Jake. Ashley looked at Valerie.

Valerie said, "What can I say?" After a moment she admitted, "My boyfriend hit me, and I had to get away. That's why I'm here."

No one said anything. They ate in silence for a while, but then Jake said, "Been there."

Ashley shook his head and looked at Valerie. "Sorry," he said.

Valerie said, "Probably too much information."

"No, honey," said Jake. "Not too much."

"I've been trying to sort things out, but I can't keep a focus. I just keep watching the waves and now it's the rain."

"Zoning," said Jake.

"Yes."

"That's one way to get away. But then you have to come back."

"I know! And that is what worries me. What am I going to do?"

"What do you want?" asked Jake.

Valerie smiled. "Was that *you* talking to me earlier?"

Jake looked puzzled.

The Longed-For Peace **143**

"Never mind," said Valerie. "What do I want?" she continued. "Good question. Well, I guess I want a man more like Ashley here."

Jake said, "Well, you can't have him!"

Ashley blushed.

Valerie admitted to them that she liked watching them together and that she wished she could be as vulnerable with someone as she'd seen Jake be with Ashley. Valerie remembered her father and how she used to cuddle up with him when she was little. But he died when she was twelve.

"I miss my dad," she admitted.

"Let me guess, "said Ashley. "Boyfriend not like dad?"

"No. My dad never hit my mother."

"Mm," said Ashley.

"My father was strong. He didn't need my mother to check in with him all the time."

"And the boyfriend?" asked Jake.

Valerie wrinkled up her face. "I thought he was strong. He seemed like he knew what he wanted. He looked good."

Jake laughed. "They always *look* good!"

"Hey," complained Ashley.

Valerie laughed, but sadness overtook her. Tears formed in her eyes, and she got up from the table and went back outside. Jake motioned for Ashley to remain, but she followed Valerie out onto the porch and sat in the other chair.

The rain was still falling.

"It sucks."

"Yes, it does."

The wind started blowing harder, and Jake felt a chill. So, Valerie scooted the rocker over next to Jake's chair. She spread the large comforter-styled blanket across the both of them and leaned her head against Jake's shoulder. Jake leaned back and cuddled up to her. They watched the rain together.

"Why can't men be more like women?" asked Valerie.

"Well, we don't really want that. Do we?" Jake responded.

They both laughed.

Sometimes a person can hardly know what to think. Some things don't come to mind, and others just seem impossible. The world gets small. But still there is the need to do something; change it. Make it better. Make things work.

That night she lit another fire and spread out with her blanket on the couch. She could hear Jake and Ashley upstairs in the bed. Oddly, it all felt like family. She was young again. She had her life ahead of her without any mistakes again.

"Is this what you wanted?" a thought came given.

"Yes," she said. "I wanted to start over. To hope again. To make my life work."

"Can you make that happen?"

"No. But maybe. Maybe it could happen."

"Go to sleep little girl."

144 The Experience of Contact with God

She felt herself letting go. Somehow it seemed things would work themselves out. She felt peaceful. Happy. Safe.

"Daddy, was that you?" she asked.

A thought came given. "I've got this."

PART 4

Risk and Trust

13

THE INEFFABLE AND
THE ENIGMATIC

> When gazing out from way down
> Here upon the vast universe,
> But even simply watching
> Clouds drift in the blowing wind
> As snow begins to fall,
> I think how small we are,
> How little we know, and
> How much we make of that.

The enigma machine in World War II was an encryption device by which communications by Germany could be made obscure and unintelligible to their enemies. So, without it, or without breaking its mechanisms, Germany's communiques were *enigmatic.*

An enigma is a puzzle, a mystery. As such one knows that it is a puzzle, but one cannot perhaps solve the puzzle. A person can detect a mystery, and not be able to fathom it, but the person knows it as a mystery. This is different from the ineffable. In speaking of the ineffable, Abraham Heschel (1951/1079) said, "when trying to hold an interview with reality face to face, without the aid of either words or concepts, we realize that what is intelligible to our mind is but a thin surface of the profoundly undisclosed . . ." (p. 5).

Paul, in writing to the Christians in Corinth said, "we speak God's wisdom in a mystery, the hidden *wisdom* which God predestined before the ages to our glory; *the wisdom* which none of the rulers of this age has understood; for if they had understood it they would not have crucified the Lord of glory."[1]

The difference between a mystery and the ineffable is the difference between the wisdom of God and the nature of God Himself. It's not that human beings never had the concept of a god. There have been many fabrications, constructions of what a god would be like. However, the God of the Jews, who is the God of the Christians, exceeds them all. The Jewish people to this day will not utter the name of God, and they will not even spell out the word "God" because no words can capture the greatness of God. A mystery is a puzzle, but we don't even have an adequate word for God. Thus, the ineffable may be enigmatic and mysterious, but it is even more.

The ineffable is not just "a synonym for the unknown or the nondescript; its essence is not in its being an enigma, in its being hidden behind the curtain" (Heschel, 1951, p. 21, kindle version). Abraham Heschel repeatedly pointed to such things as the vastness of the universe to give example to something difficult to describe. He likened it to being "stunned by that which is but cannot be put into words" (ibid., p. 3). "The world in its grandeur," he claimed, "is full of a spiritual radiance, for which we have neither name nor concept." (ibid., p. 21).

Justin Martyr is regarded to be the foremost apologist for the Christian faith in the second century. He regarded God to be nameless, inexpressible and this is partly because we cannot see God.

The nature of God transcends human ability to comprehend. God is inscrutable. That means He is incapable of being scrutinized. Does this mean we cannot know anything about God? Is talk of God simply absurd? Nonsense? I would not say so.

We can know things about God from what He has made, but that only allows us a little—more like a suspicion than a comprehension. We can know things about God from what He has given in Scripture; it is a revelation of Himself, His purposes, and His desire for relationship with people. So, we can know things about God from what He has said, but also from what He has done (and what He does). Every time God dips into human history people get a glimpse of Him from His relations, from the way God interacts with people.

God does intercede in human history. He alters our *personal* histories, and He does so on the individual, group, and societal levels. Some of those interventions have been written down and referred to in Scripture, but there are daily relations with God all over the world going on. They could be reported, but they are not authoritative for everyone. Still, for the individuals in question, they are illuminating. They answer a question: "What is God like for me?" What God is like for me is not authoritative for anyone else. It is specific to my relationship with Him.

Without giving details, I have prayed some desperate prayers in my life, and God has answered. It has *never* been as simple as asking for a fruit basket and then having one show up on my doorstep. Miraculously. It has always involved a major change in the trajectory of my life that came with some kind of great loss that also set me free or provided restoration, personal reconciliation, or new and wonderful opportunities, and the answer to prayer came with the realization that *that* is what it was. So, what do I know about God from these things? I know that for me God is responsive; He cares about me and is involved in my life. I know that He is not

148 Risk and Trust

simple; when God works, it touches many aspects of my life and involves complex issues and relationships with other people. God does not work down one linear vector at a time; He is the Great Multi-tasker.

God Is Amenable to Being Known

That which God has made He has made so that it can be investigated. Just as there is a narrow band of planets that can support life as we know it, there is a way in the universe that some say was bound to support sentient and sapient life. In other words, the creation was made to be discovered. Just so, the creator of the universe made it all so that it would point to Him and draw people in their curiosities toward Him.

More than that, though, God desires a give and take, a dialogue, with human beings. God says through the prophet Isaiah, "'Come now, and let us reason together,' says the LORD, 'Though your sins are as scarlet, they will be as white as snow; though they are red like crimson, they will be like wool.'"[2]

Martin Buber (1952) claimed that God is not indifferent to being known. One might say, "So God wants to be known, but how can we know a thing, even a living thing, that is inscrutable and ineffable?"

Kant's Generalization of the Ineffability of God

I want to make an observation here. I'm not claiming a linear thread of cause-and-effect between the theological concept of inscrutability and Kant's phenomenology, but there is a remarkable corollary to be seen.

Bavinck (1951/1977) traced the development of the inscrutability of God from the age of Justin Martyr to philosophical developments in Emmanuel Kant. Justin Martyr was a second century apologist for Christianity who claimed that one cannot name God, that God is inexpressible. The assertion was that God in His essence was not comprehendible. Athanasius of Alexandria, noted theologian of the fourth century, claimed God is exalted above human thought and Eusebius, fourth-century Christian historian, agreed. This was the basic position of the church for centuries. Fast forward to the Enlightenment and the latter part of the eighteenth century and to a Prussian philosopher named Immanuel Kant. Kant claimed the what we know is limited to our sensibilities in experience and that we cannot get to the things themselves, the world that exists outside of our subjectivity, because all we can know is our idea, our representation of it. Kant, and those following him, claimed that we cannot know things as they are.

So, in both theology and philosophy, up until Husserl, there was a disconnect between experiencing subjects and the objects of experience. It was made explicit in Descartes's distinction between extended things and thinking things. Husserl offered a different perspective when he asserted, "to the things themselves," and Merleau-Ponty changed it up again by proposing contact with things outside of

The Ineffable and the Enigmatic **149**

our subjectivity, but interpreted contact with the things themselves and a resultant lived body of personal experience with its personally meaningful life world. The world of experience is not representational but actual.

There is a similarity between the philosophical position on knowability of objects and the concept of the knowability of God. "Just as phenomenality over-flows (rather than simply conforming to) the capacities of the subject, so too is God revealed in a way that cannot be anticipated or adequately comprehended by any a priori horizon established by the would-be addressee" (Robinette, 2007, p. 90).

It is possible to have direct knowledge of things themselves, but that knowledge is incomplete, not absolute. Further, it is always from a personal perspective; thus, it is an interpreted knowledge, and the knowledge of God is similar.

- Both take a factical, situated, historical hermeneutic to support interpretation.
- Both limit knowing, which is to say the knowledge is not an absolute, exhaustive knowledge.
- Both require contact—a touch—to generate a relational experience.
- Both require a givenness that overwhelms mundane intuition.
- Both become meaningful through an interpretation of such contact.

The still small voice of contact, communication with God, is itself ineffable. Words do not capture the nature of what is happening when God communicates directly to human beings. The person learns to accept by faith hearing something from God. The phenomenality of it, the experience of it, is surprising, because it comes unexpectedly, as it is impossible to schedule God and slot Him into an appointment on one of our calendars. It is puzzling, like a mystery, but again more than that. It is experienced as one's thought, yet not from one's self. It is "a thought came given." It comes from beyond, but where is that? How is that? It leaves one wondering, when doubt asserts a second possibility: perhaps it's all one's own doing—a kind of wishful thinking. But then one comes back around, plays it over again to inspect it, and that's when the words of description fall short of explanation, and one realizes no description is good enough. It's not just mysterious; it's ineffable.

The revelation of God is ineffable. Marion has described it as "saturated," by which he means overwhelming intuition, and intuition is not simple logic. Each saturated phenomenon is not conditioned by a horizon or reduceable to an ego (Mackinlay, 2010). It can be understood as having the following characteristics:

- It is given, but more to the point, it gives itself
- It exceeds the horizon
- It decenters a person's intentionalities
- It eclipses intuition
- It overwhelms thematizing

This is also what revelation is and does.

Dialogue, Relationship, and Saturation

Both gestalt therapy and spiritual guidance or discipleship depend on revelation. No one would know God unless He revealed Himself. No one knows another human being, their subjective experience—their phenomenality—or their personal spirituality unless that person self discloses—unless that person reveals him or herself.

Gestalt therapists warmed to the ethical imperatives resident in the face of the transcendent other which were elucidated by Emmanuel Levinas (1999). The other person, be that client or follower of Christ, is beyond our ways of knowing. We can imagine, diagnose, and otherwise thematize the other, creating a story we tell ourselves about them, but we cannot know what it is like to *be* them unless they show us. Their alterity confounds us.

Gestalt therapists work to increase awareness. It is not the only thing they do, but it is one important thing they do. What is it like to be the client at any given moment in session? What is it like to be the therapist? How do they manage the balance between support and contacting in the meeting between them? One might say that the purpose of this process of awareness building is that the two people might find themselves in the situation.

Revelation is not a static poster—a picture or statue of God that never moves. Certainly, the given word of God, the Bible, might seem static, but it is the teaching, the revealing work of the Holy Spirit that makes that Bible come alive so as to self-disclose God to someone within the constantly evolving nature of history and society.

It is the same between people. There is no static body of information that a therapist can gather during interview that will capture the client. No matter how many facts one writes down about the client, no matter how much "data" one collects, none of it makes any sense apart from the self-disclosing, the revealing presence of the client. Unless you know that person, the facts about them seem irrelevant, dead. And there is no knowing the other outside of a relationship, a relationship that depends on personal experience. One must know the other experientially, and not just know facts and bits of information about them. The two people in question must meet; there must be contact.

Thus, the importance of revelation within relationship. In relationship there is room for surprise, because contact is an experiential realization of difference. One does not simply deduce things about the client, as it is impossible to be surprised by one's own deductions, and deductions apart from self-disclosure leaves one with a useful fiction, but not contact, not experiential knowing.

In contact one is given the client, and that givenness comes as a saturated phenomenon. Even the resistant client is given as such. Thus, practically speaking, the therapist might turn on his or her senses when coming into the presence of the client but wait on the sense of the client to emerge. One may offer one's own presence as an invitation to meet, and one may realize that the call of the other is in the experience of one's silent, waiting self. Further, the therapist may allow an atmosphere to guide, realizing that the leading edge of givenness may be a quasi-thing, a mood.

When the other in contacting is God, we can call that religious experience or revelation (Horner, 2016). Not all religious experience is revelatory or authoritative, but revelation is meant to be dynamic, difference-making, and experiential. We call the given Word of God, the Bible, God's revelation, and so it is, but if it is not received as God continually revealing Himself, then it has become static, and the effect is not contactful. Consciousness "radically determines phenomenality by imposing upon it the actuality of presence, the absoluteness of intuition, and the test of lived experience (Horner, 2007, p. 6). The experience of God's presence is a saturated phenomenon commensurate with contacting. It is something people understand who have been in physical space inhabited by the Spirit of God. It is something people understand who have been affected by the revelatory, enlightening work of the Holy Spirit in opening up the Word of God to one's consciousness, igniting a meeting with God Himself.

Such meetings are dialogical in nature. Although different, the people in question become non-independent as soon as they find themselves in the same situation. Finding themselves thus, they provide one another a conduit for their mutual presence. Giving themselves through presence, each develops the potential to emerge as a saturated phenomenon for the other, which is revelatory.

A pastoral or nouthetic counselor cannot achieve this if they come to meet someone with a list of Bible verses to paste over the skin of the other. I am not claiming that, as a lot, this is what Biblical counselors do—no more than secular counselors who utilize a positivistic and formulaic approach to dosing their clients with interventions. Bible verses disconnected from relationship are static. When human relationship contextualizes them, they become iconic, pointing to the relationship with God through the Holy Spirit, and ultimately they become revelatory.

Would it occur to a gestalt therapist to use scripture? Would it occur to a Biblical counselor to use relationship? Without relationship and experiential knowledge, without revelation and expansion of one's horizon, thematizing and formula Christianity suffocate in the ineffability of God for one and the alterity of the other person for another.

Notes

1. 1. Corinthians 2:7–8.
2. Isaiah 1:18.

References

Bavinck, H. (1951/1977). *The doctrine of God.* Edinburgh, UK and Carlisle, PA: Eerdman's Publishing Company, Banner of Truth Trust.
Buber, M. (1952). *Eclipse of God: Studies in the relationship between religion and philosophy.* New York, NY: Humanity Books.

152 Risk and Trust

Heschel, A. (1951/1979). *Man is not alone: A philosophy of religion.* New York, NY: Farrar, Straus, & Giroux.

Horner, R. (2007). The insistent and unbearable excess: On experience (and God) in Marion's phenomenology. *ARC: The Journal of the Faculty of Religious Studies,* McGill University, *35*, np.

Horner, R. (2016, April 14–16). *The challenge of God plenary address.* "A phenomenology of revelation: Contemporary encounters with Saint Ignatius of Loyola." Continental Philosophy and the Catholic Intellectual Heritage Conference, Hank Center for the Catholic Intellectual Heritage, Loyola University, Chicago.

Levinas, E. (1999). *Alterity and transcendence.* New York, NY: Columbia University Press.

Mackinlay, S. (2010). *Interpreting excess: Jean-Luc Marion, saturated phenomena, and hermeneutics.* New York, NY: Fordham University Press.

Robinette, B. (2007). A gift to theology? Jean-Luc Marion's 'saturated phenomenon' in Christological perspective. *The Heythrop Journal, 48,* 86–108.

14

RISK AND TRUST

How in the world is it possible?
To follow a person I cannot see?
The world says he does not exist.
The world claims the whole project
Is fantasy and ignorant, wishful thinking.
Like a children's fairy tale.
They laugh at the gospel.

They do not know.
I did not know.
What it's like
To live by faith.
To walk behind God's Spirit.

I offer succinctly one quote from a noted phenomenological philosopher about faith, one assertion by a gestalt therapist concerning the role of faith in our lives and in respect of field theory in gestalt therapy, two sections from the New Testament that combined provide a balanced, Biblical definition of faith, and a couple of comments about faith from Paul of Tarsus, the apostle to the gentiles. All involve risk and trust.

The writer to the Hebrew Christians said, "Now faith is the assurance of things hoped for, the conviction of things not seen" (Hebrews 11:1). James, the brother of Jesus, wrote,

> faith, if it has no works, is dead, being by itself. But someone may well say, 'You have faith and I have works; show me your faith without the

works, and I will show you my faith by my works.' You believe that God is one. You do well; the demons also believe, and shudder. But are you willing to recognize, you foolish fellow, that faith without works is useless?

(James 2: 17–20)

Merleau-Ponty, French phenomenological philosopher said, "the certitude I have of being connected up with the world by my look already promises me a pseudo-world of phantasms if I let it wander. . . . It is therefore the greatest degree of belief that our vision goes to the things themselves" (Merleau-Ponty, 1968, p. 28). The writers of the classic statement of early gestalt therapy wrote, "faith is knowing, beyond awareness, that if one takes a step there will be ground underfoot; one gives oneself unhesitatingly to the act, one has faith that the background will produce the means" (Perls, Hefferline, & Goodman, 1951, p. 343). Finally, Paul of Tarsus, the apostle to the gentiles, observed that "in hope we have been saved, but hope that is seen is not hope; for who hopes for what he already sees? But if we hope for what we do not see, with perseverance we wait eagerly for it" (Romans 8:24–25). For we walk by faith, not by sight (2 Corinthians 5:7).

Where there is no risk there is certitude; however, there is no certitude in this world (Taylor, 1992). We live, all of us, by faith, and the faith stance requires trust. Merleau-Ponty said that by faith we trust our senses, and they bring us to the things in this world themselves. We trust that is so. He risked going cross currents with many people in philosophy to say that. Kant had asserted that we cannot *get* to the things themselves, and he still held a fair amount of influence. If Kant was right, then we all live in the certitude of our own representations and risk nothing.

Kierkegaard asserted that, against all logic and even ethical decorum, authentic trust in God produces a kind of hope that is existentially risky, because it exposes one's authentic self and comes with a behavioral imperative. A person reveals him or herself through works of faith, the things they do based on what they believe (Wojtyla, 1979). To retreat, to defer and obscure one's spirituality—one's convictions, values, beliefs, concerns, emotions, and relationship to God—is to demonstrate bad faith (Brownell, 2008).

Experiential Learning

Experiential learning is based on faith, upon stepping into novel situations and testing one's theories. The experiment in gestalt therapy relies on what Perls et al. (1951) called faith—one gives oneself to the act trusting that the means will be provided.

The experiment in gestalt therapy is a move to action in order to provide more experience from which one might learn. In an experiment, "the client experiences themselves in a new, exciting, but often also fearful and shameful way. This kind of experience evolves while in the accepting and supportive presence of the other, thus opening a new way of being in the world . . ." (Roubal, 2019, p. 225).

In Christianity when one comes to believe in Christ and the light goes on about life because of the influence of the Holy Spirit, everything seems new and exciting. It seems as if the revolution has taken place and a new heaven and earth have already come, but of course, that is not reality. A revolution *has* taken place, but what is new is the person. There is a new creature there who still carries around the remnants of the old, and the world chugs right along in its previous direction.

Eventually, after one has learned key tenets of theology and the practices of the particular church group with which one has identified, there is a plateau. Routines set in. One begins rehearsing ideas that were once novel. Principles and tenets of theology and the values and policies of the church are repeated to one another in study groups. Social norms dictated by religious opinion leaders influence patterns of behavior, and experimenting under those conditions is risky, because it might seem off target to some.

The author of the letter to the Hebrew Christians advocated moving on from rudimentary aspects of salvation: "Therefore leaving the elementary teaching about the Christ, let us press on to maturity, not laying again a foundation of repentance from dead works and of faith toward God."[1] The ongoing process of sanctification is very risky, because not only does one have to face the opinions of other people, but also the new challenges brought to bear by the providence of God. God disciplines everyone who comes to Jesus, which is not to say penalizes them. The discipline of God is aimed at growth in capacity, character, faith, the knowledge of God, and wisdom. No one increases in any of those areas apart from struggle, often pain and loss, and the humbling of one's estimations.

To continue learning, to continue treading new ground is to eventually diverge, because everyone is different. God never created two people exactly the same; so, there *has to be difference, variety, diversity.* To follow one's unique path in life means following God into parts of the world and people cultures where cloistered Christians do not risk going. As one fellow Christian counselor once told me, "Phil, what happened to you? You used to be such a good guy." What he meant was that I no longer talked about things familiar to him, no longer in the way we used to speak with each other before I went back to school for my doctoral studies in clinical psychology and before I did my gestalt therapy training. I seemed to have gotten too far off track for him, and he is an example of the fact that there is always a risk of being judged a heretic. But to pull back, go along to get along, to never risk the unfamiliar is to take the opposite risk—stagnation.

The actual model of the way church is supposed to operate, described by Paul, includes tremendous diversity, novelty, and creativity.

> Now there are varieties of gifts, but the same Spirit. And there are varieties of ministries, and the same Lord. There are varieties of effects, but the same God who works all things in all persons. But to each one is given the manifestation of the Spirit for the common good. But one and the same Spirit works all these things, distributing to each one individually just as He wills.[2]

156 Risk and Trust

The Christian community is supposed to be a place where individuals can thrive, where support allows exploration and where depth of sanctification and individual gifting gives back so that relationships are quite mutual and nourishing (Brownell, 2010).

Impasse

In gestalt therapy the impasse is that point at which one feels he or she cannot go forward into novel territory but cannot go back to the old and likely stifling ways of life either. It is ambivalence and stuckness (Goulding, 2000; Hycner & Jacobs, 1995) and gestalt therapists look for that ambivalence and build awareness around it, chiseling away through clarifying the client's intentionalities (what the ambivalence is about and related to).

The impasse often revolves around binaries of various kinds: perception of competent vs incompetent therapist, safe vs unsafe, familiar vs unfamiliar, good vs bad. In Christianity growth is also often stymied by the perception of binaries: Christian vs non-Christian, believer vs non-believer, right vs wrong, orthodox vs unorthodox, truth vs error, goodness vs evil. I am not saying all is relative and there is no such actual thing as goodness and evil. I am saying that often Christian people fear when there is no need to fear, because perfect love casts out fear, all has been decided, and the great cosmic act of redemption has been accomplished. We can afford to venture into the unknown, because there is *a lot we don't know*. There is a huge world to find out about. There are adventures of learning possible if we are courageous enough to risk exploration. The Holy Spirit will guide into all truth, constantly accompany us, convict of sin when and where that is needed, and continue to lead us, never leaving us alone. God is for us; who or what could possibly be against us?

The impasse itself is a polarity, but its dynamic is not a content. The impasse does not come with its own intentionality; it's not about being stuck unless the therapy makes that clear. The links of the stuckness are often related to the residue of experience.

In the dynamic of addiction, for instance, "an approach-avoidance cycle develops in which a person approaches the using because of the pleasure it brings, but avoids it also because of the destruction it brings. Thus, an ambivalence develops, and in gestalt terminology that means an impasse has been reached . . ." (Brownell, 2012, p. 33). The client is then stuck between two ends of a polarity.

And that is the same for Christian growth as well.

A therapist working with a Christian might detect anxiety, depression, tension, stress, or guilt, and the tendency would be to try to deconstruct the meaning making that leads the person to feel like that. A gestalt therapist might investigate what those feelings are about as well or what there is in the meeting between them that resonates with those feelings. Sometimes the ambivalence, the polarity, resides in the realm of the Christian's religious, spiritual, theological life world. It may be a clash between authentic self-expression and perceived standards of Christian community, which may in themselves be imagined rather than actual. Sometimes the work, were it to take a natural trajectory, might flow into the hermeneutics of the pneumenal field. That is when doing gestalt therapy would look and feel pastoral.

I wonder sometimes if gestalt therapists are prepared to go there with their clients. For that matter, I wonder if most any psychotherapist would be able to do that.

Notes

1. Hebrews 6:1.
2. 1. Corinthians 12: 4–7 and 11.

References

Brownell, P. (2008). Faith: An existential, phenomenological, and biblical integration. In J. H. Ellens (Ed.), *Medical and Therapeutic Events: Vol. 2. Miracles: God, science and psychology in the paranormal* (pp. 213–234). Westport, CT: Praeger.

Brownell, P. (2010). The healing potential of religious community. In J. H. Ellens (Ed.), *Religion: Vol. 2. The healing power of spirituality: How faith helps humans thrive* (pp. 1–22). Santa Barbara, CA: Praeger, ABC-CLIO.

Brownell, P. (2012). *Gestalt therapy for addictive and self-medicating behaviors.* New York, NY: Springer Publishing Company.

Goulding, R. (2000). Transactional analysis and gestalt therapy. In E. Nevis (Ed.), *Gestalt therapy: Perspectives and applications* (pp. 129–145). Cambridge, MA: GestaltPress.

Hycner, R., & Jacobs, L. (1995). *The healing relationship in gestalt therapy: A dialogic/self psychology approach.* Highland, NY: The Gestalt Journal Press.

Merleau-Ponty, M. (1968). *The visible and the invisible.* Evanston, IL: Northwestern University Press.

Perls, F., Hefferline, R., & Goodman, P. (1951). *Gestalt therapy: Excitement and growth in the human personality.* London, UK: Souvenir Press.

Roubal, J. (2019). An experimental approach: Follow by leading. In P. Brownell (Ed.), *Handbook for theory, research, and practice in gestalt therapy* (2nd ed., pp. 220–267). Newcastle upon Tyne, UK: Cambridge Scholars Publishing.

Taylor, D. (1992). *The myth of certainty: The reflective Christian & the risk of commitment.* Downers Grove, IL: InterVarsity Press.

Wojtyla, K. (1979). *The acting person: Analecta Husserliana the yearbook of phenomenological research* (Vol. 10). Dordrecht, Holland: D. Reidel Publishing Company.

Story Four
OBVIOUSLY NOT OBVIOUS

*He wasn't searching for a spiritual leader. Truth is not a concept.
Truth is not a fact; truth is a person.*

Jacob was gay. He had realized he was gay before he knew what "gay" was. He knew that he was different. He liked sitting with girls fixing each other's hair, trying on make-up. Maybe he had a little gender blurring as well. At any rate, it did not go over well with his father. His older brothers made fun of him. Oddly, he didn't care what his brothers thought, because he regarded them to be crude, but that was before he knew what "crude" was. When he reached puberty, the boys started paying attention to the girls, but it wasn't to try on makeup, and that was not a scent he could smell.

Jacob also grew up in a religious family. They all went to church every Sunday, and from an early age he had learned about how Jesus died to take away the sins of the world and that people appropriated that gift through believing it was true and putting the weight of their lives down fully upon it. He did that as best he could when he was about five years old, and then he did it again when he was about twelve years old. He made deliberate decisions to trust. He chose a path. When he was sixteen, he began to wonder if he still believed as he had. Some troubling considerations started intruding on that simple story.

If God was loving, why did He let bad things happen? Maybe God wasn't as powerful as he'd been told. He wanted to kiss a boy, but he was told God would hate that. He wanted a boy to kiss him, not any boy. He had an eye for one in particular.

By the time he turned twenty-two he had already kissed a boy, and then some. He was conflicted. He wanted to resolve the conflict between his growing

Obviously Not Obvious **159**

identity as a gay man and his Christian beliefs. These did not seem to belong together. It was more than discouraging; it was depressing.

He went first to a priest who was the chaplain at the university he was attending. The priest wanted him to confess his sins. He told the priest about his most recent sexual encounters, but it didn't seem to be the point. Had he confessed? Had he sinned? He began to wonder what sin was.

He went next to a Protestant pastor at a local church in the city. The pastor listened to him for about fifteen minutes and then pulled out his Bible and started reading scripture verses to him about how homosexuality was abhorrent to God. The pastor said, "You can't be a homosexual and a Christian."

No? What is a Christian?

Next he found a Christian counselor. That man started to do the same thing the pastor had done, and when he saw Jacob shut down, he said, "Look. I know someone who helps people get free of this sin. He can heal you of homosexuality so that you can lead a normal life."

That did not prove to be valuable either.

Next, Jacob found a cognitive-behavioral therapist who questioned Jacob's belief system and suggested his faulty religious hypotheses were complicating his life. He needed to see the error in them. Jacob could do an experiment. The therapist suggested that he interview thirty clergy from the city and ask them "If God is love, why is there so much hatred in Christianity?" So, Jacob did that and returned to the therapist.

The therapist said, "What did you find out?"

Jacob said, "Some told me that some things are beyond our understanding. Some said that God is love but he gave us free will, so the hatred comes from sinful people. Some said they did not know. Some said they were too busy to fuss with abstract questions."

The therapist said, "And I bet that if you went on asking until every pastor, priest, rabbi, imam, and other kind of religious leader in this town had been interviewed, you'd get so many different and conflicting answers that it would be like mud."

Jacob considered that statement. He then asked, "So? What is the point?"

"Just that it's a faulty hypothesis to believe there actually is a right answer."

"Oh," said Jacob. The therapist seemed to have an agenda. He had proven his point, but it wasn't Jacob's point. The experiment changed nothing, because he believed that Jesus was the God-man who sacrificed his life so that Jacob could have eternal life. He liked that part of the Bible where Jesus is talking to his Father and says, "This is eternal life, that they may know You, the only true God, and Jesus Christ whom You have sent." He counted himself in the group Jesus was talking about, even though he felt confused.

It seemed the therapist did not understand. It was like the therapist was looking at a different picture or seeing the same picture but seeing it color blind. There was no life in his approach.

160 Risk and Trust

So, Jacob looked for a different kind of therapist. He had tried a Biblical counselor, and he had tried a cognitive-behavioral therapist. He searched online for psychotherapists and found someone who called herself a gestalt psychotherapist. That sounded exotic enough that he was curious, and he decided to give that person a try.

He asked the gestalt therapist if she believed in God, and she said, "I will answer that, but first I would like to know why you ask."

Jacob said, "Because I don't want you to try to convince me that I'm wrong if I tell you that I *do* believe in God."

"Oh," she said. She assured him that she did not want to change him, but she would like to get to know him.

Then she said, "You and I are different. What you believe is important. What I believe is important. One of us doesn't have to cancel out the other."

"So, you *don't* believe in God?"

"I do not know about God. I have not figured that one out. And I notice when I say that, you shift around in your seat."

"Right. I don't know if it's worth being here."

"I don't know either. Would you like to find out?"

Jacob smiled. "Only way to find out is to stick around."

She smiled as well.

Jacob felt more at ease with her. He at least felt met. Because of that he self-disclosed more than he had with anyone else, and they met several times.

The therapist said that as people grow up they accept as given what they see and hear.

"So, you mean I just accepted what my parents said about God?" He began to feel like he was back with the cognitive-behavioral therapist. But it seemed she was on to something. It seemed very simple—and obvious. He felt foolish.

He also realized that it wasn't just his parents that he had been accepting. He accepted what the church said about being gay. He accepted what the gay people said about the church. He began to wonder and question, and he wrestled trying to resolve what seemed to be unresolvable.

"God is love. How could God be against me loving someone?"

"God is love. How could the church people be walking with God if they were filled with hate for gay people?"

"God is love. What the heck does that even mean!?"

Jacob made a practice of reading the Bible. He did not tell his gay friends of this practice. When he read the Bible, he found himself thinking, putting together more of the puzzle of God. When he tried to articulate that puzzle, though, when he tried to describe what was becoming more and more true for him, he stumbled over himself and failed to find adequate words to describe it. That was frustrating.

As he read the gospels, he discovered a custom. Jesus routinely got away from everyone to be alone and pray. Jacob was attracted to that idea, but he felt discouraged because he struggled with prayer. What was the right way to pray? He had

Obviously Not Obvious   161

no formula. Frustrated or not, however, he decided to try the solitude that Jesus revealed.

The more he contemplated this decision, the more the moment loomed large. This was going to be it. He decided to stay gone and alone until he got things straight with God. How could he be a Christian and be gay at the same time? But how could he *not?!*

He threw warm clothes and water into the back seat of his car. He took his Bible. He turned his phone off and put that in the glove compartment. He started driving east and south out of town. He had no plan but to drive until he found a place that seemed right to stop. It had to offer solitude. It had to give him time.

He found the interstate out of Boise, turned east and north at highway 20 and then south just after Fairfield, headed toward Gooding. He stopped at the turn off for Little City of Rocks and parked at an undeveloped area shy of a creek. It was ten in the morning.

Jacob put a jacket, his Bible, and some water in a small backpack and started out from the car. He crossed the creek and followed a thin trail across flat land and sage brush. He headed for the big rocks where the creek came out. He reached a fence that looked like people routinely ignored it, so he did the same. He found himself among large formations of rock created by ancient ash fall and lava. They were in strange configurations; some were like groups of giants silently watching. Some were like huge mushrooms. Some felt as if they must fall over, but they did not.

Jacob followed the creek through the rocks that populated a shallow ravine. He looked for a place to get off the little trail, somewhere he could sit without being seen. He found a space between two large towers and left the trail. Soon he was out of sight of the creek and he found a simple place to sit. He sighed. "Arrived."

He looked around. The place was beautiful. He thought about the forces of nature that would have created it over time. So much, it seemed, exceeded him. His place in the world seemed small and short. He felt insignificant. Who was he to expect God to respond? He felt foolish and considered leaving.

"But no," he said. He said it out loud. "I'm going to deal with this even if I'm all alone and nothing comes of it. I will not give up."

He tried to pray. He called to God. He asked God all the questions he'd been wondering. He came with his frustrations. He came with his wounded emotions. He told God how alone and rejected he felt, both by the church because he was gay and by the gay community because he was a Christian. There was no answer. He felt companionless among the stone. Did God reject him as well?

This went on for several hours.

The sun reached its zenith. It started descending on the day. There were no clouds, and a breeze blew through the ravine. The shadows all shifted.

He was truly alone. The place was utterly still. Is it possible for silence and solitude to keep one's company?

162 Risk and Trust

He knew he was gay. He knew he believed in Jesus. He had never met someone who put those two together. "Am I truly Christian?"

He picked up his Bible and read in the gospel of Matthew. He came to the eighth chapter, toward the end of it. He read where Jesus said, "The foxes have holes and the birds of the air *have* nests, but the Son of Man has nowhere to lay His head." He felt he could understand that experience. Where did he belong? He did not feel comfortable anywhere.

Next, he opened to the fifty-third chapter of the book of the prophet Isaiah. "He was despised and forsaken of men, a man of sorrows and acquainted with grief; and like one from whom men hide their face. He was despised, and we did not esteem Him." He knew the prophet had been talking about Jesus, pointing to the Messiah. He also recognized the description in that chapter of a crucifixion. He considered the experience described as being despised and rejected. He felt that Jesus would understand him.

These thoughts percolated within him, and Jacob warmed to the person of Jesus. He found that he did not have an answer, a resolution to his conundrum—the apparent contradiction in a God of love and the rejection of a form of human affection. "I don't get it, Lord, but I want you. Please help me to know the truth of this."

He spent more time among the rocks, but his prayers did not ascend any higher than that. He read other scripture, but nothing superseded the attraction he felt to the man Jesus. He became roused and encouraged by him.

As the sun began to approach the horizon, the light dimmed. He picked up his things, put the backpack on, and started back.

After rejoining the trail that followed the creek through the ravine, he saw another person approaching. As he got closer, Jacob could see what he looked like.

The man was ragged in appearance. His hair was uncombed and knotted. He wore a long sleeved, woolen shirt open in the front. He had nothing under it. He wore baggy pants. But the thing that stood out for Jacob was that he carried a staff and he had patches and religious ornaments attached to his clothing. A Tallit, a Jewish prayer shawl, was draped over his shoulder.

They greeted each other on the trail, and Jacob was on his way around and beyond the man when the man called to him. "You must stay longer."

"What?"

"You must stay longer. You have not waited long enough on God."

Jacob felt unnerved, but wary of the man. He believed he had been there long enough.

The man said, "I am a prophet. I am a channel of the earth in this place. You must stay longer."

Jacob did not want to offend. He said, "So you are Jewish?"

The man said, "I am of all things, and this is a holy place. You would do well to stay longer."

Jacob said, "Well, it's getting dark, and I do have to get back."

Obviously Not Obvious **163**

The man asked, "Is that what God has said?"

Jacob knew it was not, but he did not trust the man. He did not give himself to what he said. He wanted to leave.

The man said, "Trust me. Walk with me, and I will show you a sacred place back over behind those rocks. There are petrographs from long ago, and it's a place where things come alive."

"Come alive?"

"My medals heat up and shine. The shawl slithers like a snake around my shoulders. And you can get answers for what you seek."

Why could Jacob not simply leave? Who cared if he offended the man. He felt intimidated, frightened.

"It will be good for you." The man took hold of Jacob by the arm and started walking. Jacob's arm suddenly felt cold. He pulled away and stopped. He said, "I don't think it will be good for me really. I want to leave."

"You should stay."

"No. I was on my way and had peace about that. I have no peace about staying here with you."

"Do you believe that I am a prophet?"

"I am a Christian," said Jacob.

"Oh," said the man. His voice sounded sarcastic. Jacob wondered if he were claiming too much. And there it was again. What is a Christian?

The man said, "A Christian follows the prophet Jesus, but there have been more prophets that have gone into the world. And I am one. You would do well to listen to me."

Suddenly, Jacob recalled reading the words "This is my son. Listen to him." But those words did not point to this ragged man. They were about Jesus. Jacob knew that. He recalled what Jesus had told the Roman governor, "I am the way, the truth, and the life." He sat himself down inside with those words, with that reality. He grounded himself in Jesus, and that felt solid.

Jacob said, "I am leaving." With that he turned away from the man and started walking along the creek in the direction of his car.

On the way back he kept repeating to himself, "I want Jesus." All else could fade away. He wasn't searching for a spiritual leader. Truth is not a concept. Truth is not a fact; truth is a person.

"Do I believe that you are a prophet?" he rehearsed. "I believe in Jesus, and now I will have to get on with that."

PART 5

Change, Salvation, and Growth

15
CHANGE IS CONSTANT

I used to live on Cresta Way.
I used to live on Lemon Street.
I used to live near Mississippi Bar.
I used to live on 32nd Street.
I used to live on Nostaw Drive.
I used to live in Fair Oaks.
I used to live in Portland.
I used to live in North Carolina.
I used to live in Bermuda, and then I moved to Idaho.
But now, I live above Shoshone Falls, and hear it roar in the night.

I used to be afraid of the night. I used to be a child,
but now I'm patient with complexity and other's ways,
and I try to put away childish things.

One might think that if change were constant, if things were constantly forming, evolving, emerging, then that constant differing would produce massive inequalities. Differences. But if change is so constant, then difference loses its potency. All things become equally different.

For decades gestalt therapists have adhered to a theory of change elucidated in 1970 by Arnold Beisser (Beisser, 1970). Beisser said, "change occurs when one becomes what he is, not when he tries to become what he is not" (p. 77). That dictum has been repeated over and over and is taught in gestalt therapy training programs around the world.

More recently, however, some have objected.

Change Is Constant **167**

The problem is not that it is just a one-person view of change. It is an intra-psychic, almost isolated, one-person view.

It's also puzzling. Wouldn't one already *be* whatever he or she was, even if that was a person trying to be something he or she was not?

How might a person discover what he or she actually is? How might one actualize the present and come out of a dream of the present to find oneself fully *in* the present? It all seems too convoluted.

Ironically, Beisser acknowledged field factors as motivation for figuring out a theory of change. Perls's theory of change was at that time becoming more acceptable because change was accelerating and people were having a hard time dealing with it. That is, the impact of the context, the environmental field, the ontical field, the situation, was influencing people to adapt.

Change Is Constant

Change will happen. People don't have to make it happen. The sense of stuckness is an illusion. People may attempt to live in a preferable, static moment in time, but that is impossible. People may think they are incapable of finding a new life, a new way of life, but it will find them. They may replicate, carry over a perspective, a fixed gestalt, but the circumstances in which they find themselves will move relentlessly along, changing the nature of the situation for any given person, and then ultimately affecting how they function, how they view themselves and their circumstances, how they feel, and what they do.

Gestalt therapists look for stuckness, and psychotherapists in general do, in fact, observe repeating patterns of behavior in their clients. So, it may seem that the patient does not change. However, nothing in the world, in the environmental surround, stays the same; and so stuckness, or repetitive patterns, abide against a background of increasingly difficult and demanding situational factors. Going to the comic book store, purchasing the latest superhero comic, and taking it home to read all evening, to the neglect of everyone else in the house, may have been quaint when one was twelve. At forty-five that behavior would be viewed as likely pathological. And the field factors, the interpersonal and social stressors, would weigh with profound consequence on that person. It would take increasing amounts of energy to ignore them. All things would not be the same.

Personal change takes place in a world that is constantly moving. The Bible describes the world as constantly in the process of "passing away."[1] The verb is in the passive, so the sense is that it is being led away, but whether it is actively or passively changing it is constantly doing so.

The universe is expanding. Galaxies farther from us are racing away at greater velocity than those closer to us. Everything is proceeding, distancing from everything else[2] in a mind-boggling array of swirling gases, decaying and emerging stars, dark matter, and black holes.

168 Change, Salvation, and Growth

Nothing stays the same. In regard to human beings the sense of constancy is illusory. Just look at something, and it changes.

We cannot really understand the infinite constancy of God when our lives start and stop and change along the way in myriad ways. God likened human life to the grass that comes up but withers in a day, and He asked how we could grasp a level of reality like the one at which He lives. The truth is that we cannot, but we can understand that everything in us and around us is in flux.

An example of this transitory existence is the concept of "contingent universals" (Bemme, 2019). Contingent universals are "concepts that are true and measurable until they stop working in the field, or until the parameters of 'what works' shift to a new iteration" (n.p.). In other words, they are true until they're not, and they are universal until they're contingent. Thus, something that carries the name of a constant (universal) is dependent on an ever-changing situation and is therefore *not constant*. Speaking globally, when the contingent universal of field conditions shifts, then the experience of people in that field changes.

The phenomenal field is contingent upon the ontical field. So, paying attention to field properties, something also referred to in outcomes research as "extra-therapeutic factors," could be useful. Those factors are not fixed, and they are the greatest influence on psychotherapy, even more so than the therapeutic relationship (Thomas, 2006; Leibert, 2011; Duncan, Miller, Wampold, & Hubble, 2010; Hoffman, 2012).

Personal change is contingent on these kinds of field dynamics. In 1997 Michael Lewis, a well-established child development researcher, concluded that attachment theory was not the dominant influence that people had been claiming. Lewis asserted that the current context is the greatest predictor of change and that change could be understood as adaptation (Lewis, 1997).

The Influence of Healthy Living on Change

Gestalt therapy's model of health is the flowing, natural identification and pursuit of figures of interest. Figures of interest are intentional objects. Thus, a healthy person is aware of what their experience is about, and they easily flow toward that which interests or has relevance. They don't tend to obscure themselves with confusing and distracting abstractions and intellectualizing, something gestalt people call egoism. They don't divert themselves out of anxiety into distractions, something gestalt people call deflection. They don't avoid contacting in order to play it safe; rather, they reach out in contact, engage with others and the world, and get what they want, pursue what interests them, resolve dissonance, and answer questions. When people do those kinds of things, they affect others and they move from one figure of interest to another. They grow, and they bring change. The field evolves.

Change Is Constant **169**

The Influence of Contact With God on Change

For a Christian immediate intimacy with God in itself becomes a change factor, a dynamic influence in the field. Paul of Tarsus, in 2 Corinthians 3:18, indicated that he and other believers were continually in the process of being changed by contemplating Jesus, who is the mirror image of God's immaterial nature. The apostle John affirmed this dynamic (that of change through the perception of Christ) when he wrote, "Beloved, now we are children of God, and it has not appeared as yet what we will be. We know that when He appears, we will be like Him, because we will see Him just as He is."[3]

In the context of Paul's statement there is another assertion. It is stated in one verse and restated in the subsequent verse:

> Now *the Lord is the Spirit*, and where the Spirit of the Lord is, *there* is liberty. But we all, with unveiled face, beholding as in a mirror the glory of the Lord, are being transformed into the same image from glory to glory, just as from *the Lord, the Spirit.*[4]

Why is this significant? Because it is through the work of the Holy Spirit that one perceives Jesus, that one *sees God*. Jesus told His disciples He would never leave them, that He would come to them; He promised the Holy Spirit would provide intimate contact, and that contact is transforming. So, here and now we continuously learn about God, but it's partial. According to the Bible when Christ returns, either for us individually or to the earth in the second coming, change will increase dramatically.

Immanence and Transcendence Revisited

There is obviously more to change than the paradoxical theory in gestalt therapy or the miraculous transformation that occurs in contact with God. A whole book could be given to such a two-fold subject. What is important here is to realize that there are different processes going on. The pastor can understand that someone in his or her church can still change by following human interests, and the gestalt therapist can understand that the impetus for change can be God given.

Also of importance is to appreciate the difference between an immanent and a transcendental frame with regards to change. In the first everything is immediate, of the world, even intrapsychic, contained "within" a natural, material, psychological, intrapersonal explanation. In the second primary change comes from outside the immanent frame, transcending it and providing an epiphanal, supernatural influence.

I suggest that, just as God is simultaneously the immanent but transcendent other, that elements of both immanence and transcendence are present in a

170 Change, Salvation, and Growth

relational model of change that is inherent to both gestalt therapy and Christian discipleship.

The Boston Change Process Study Group published a paper titled "Engagement and the Emergence of a Charged Other" (Bruschweiler-Stern et al., 2018). They claimed that people develop, that is, change or grow, through relationships of engagement in which three elements are present: (1) core positive affective investment (feeling special to someone), (2) priority (the other is on one's side and can be counted upon), and (3) continuity (the relationship is enduring and reliable). When all three factors come together, it creates heightened trust and gives rise to the emergence of a charged other. The charged other is a special person of positive value who catalyzes increased mental, affective, and social capacities for relationship.

These are also some of the elements, some of what it is like to "see" Jesus, to comprehend His person and work as it pertains personally to one's self. To see Jesus, in the sense of comprehending, is to instantly find Him present and focused on one's self. Staring in amazement at Jesus, one suddenly finds Him engaged, looking right back at you. He is the shepherd that goes the distance in seeking out and saving the lost and stranded sheep.

Core Positive Affective Investment

It is common to see a Christian turn the familiar statement "For God so loved the world that He gave His unique, one-of-a-kind son that whoever believes in Him might have eternal life . . ."[5] into "He died for me. If I were the only sinner in the world, He still would have died for me."

I have told this story before. I had grown up in a dysfunctional, alcoholic family and felt alienated from my parents. We were cordial. My mother had quit drinking when she asked Jesus to be her savior. But there was a residue of caution inside me still. I felt distant.

Through a set of circumstances, I found myself out of a job, virtually homeless, and with a disabled brother in tow—nowhere to go but back to live with our parents so that I could get back on my feet. We all lived in an RV trailer, and I slept on the back seat of truck. We were in the Columbia Gorge at an RV park east of Cascade Locks, Oregon. At night the stars were out. I would lay in the truck feeling miserable and gaze at the universe. What had happened to my life? How did it come to this—living again with my parents. Where were the purposes of God in that? I had given my whole life to God, gone to seminary, pastored churches. I had gone back to school and become a clinical psychologist. I had graduate degrees. I had experience in the ministry. I knew theology and had taught the Bible. Wasn't it supposed to have worked differently? I felt defective, as if I surely had been the weak link in the chain of providence. I was miserable. I really just wanted to call it quits and get out of here.

Change Is Constant **171**

One night I lay in the dark crying, and crying out to God. "Why?"

Then a thought came given. My parents were helping me. I felt they loved me. Then I realized that God loved me and that He had given them back to me as "mother" and "father." It was worth all the loss, confusion, and struggle. The oft-repeated saying that God loves us, that God loves *me*, became for me an experiential reality like it had never been before. In the midst of brokenness, God turned a mess around and brought about a reconciliation. God *did* have His eye on me, and God *was* active in my life. Because of that I could believe that it was all still going somewhere.

Priority

Paul experienced what it was like to have God set His affections on him. He wrote in response: "For I am convinced that neither death, nor life, nor angels, nor principalities, nor things present, nor things to come, nor powers, nor height, nor depth, nor any other created thing, will be able to separate us from the love of God, which is in Christ Jesus our Lord."[6]

An infinite being has an endless capacity to make each one of us a priority. It is not a zero-sum situation for him. He does not have to ignore one to make another a priority. If He says "wait," for instance, it's not because He's too busy with someone else more important at the moment.

Continuity

Jesus always remains committed to us. God in His nature and purposes does not change. He may be the prime mover of all change, but He himself is constant.

We change because we see Jesus as He is, and part of that is that we see His love, commitment, and perseverance with regard to us.

> He who began a good work in you will perfect it until the day of Christ Jesus.[7]

> But because Jesus lives forever, He has a permanent priesthood.
> Therefore He is able to save completely those who draw near to God through Him, since He always lives to intercede for them.[8]

> Who will bring any charge against God's elect? It is God who justifies.
> Who is there to condemn us? For Christ Jesus, who died,
> and more than that was raised to life, is at the right hand of God—
> and He is interceding for us. Who shall separate us from the love of
> Christ? Shall trouble or distress or persecution or famine or nakedness or
> danger or sword?[9]

172 Change, Salvation, and Growth

> The Spirit also helps our weakness; for we do not know how to pray as we should, but the Spirit Himself intercedes for *us* with groanings too deep for words;
> and He who searches the hearts knows what the mind of the Spirit is, because He intercedes for the saints according to *the will of* God.[10]

In the immanent frame of psychotherapy the therapist can be a charged other, and then the therapist can have a corrective influence on the patient with regards to the inadequacies of early attachment and the frustrations of other kinds of relationships. Yet, if one allows for a transcendent other, then it is possible that a divine Other can emerge in the pneumenal field as a supernaturally charged Other, and then change comes over a person in giving oneself entirely to *that* relationship, in seeing Him as He is, the one who loved us and gave Himself up for us. The one who constantly intercedes for us. The one who will never leave us. The one closer than any other.

Either-Or, Both-And

I sometimes think people find themselves stuck in a binary of "either-or." That is, change can take place in psychotherapy either this way or that, either with medication or psychotherapy, either with evidence-based interventions or within the scope of a comprehensive and cohesive theory.

In gestalt therapy it's not the cycle of experience; it's the continuum of contact. It's not awareness; it's relationship. It's not experiment or experiential work; it's dialogue. It's field. It's the latest twist on our theory that sets up the latest binary as we embrace a new piece of mind candy and reject the one that came before it.

Sometimes the choice seems to be between a Biblical or Christian approach and a secular or agnostic approach.

God is not limited to our binaries. He can use a completely godless, god-hating atheist to open up understanding. If He can speak to His people out of the mouth of a jackass,[11] he can certainly get done what is needed by a psychotherapist. Conversely, He can lead a person to see the inadequacies of their meaning-making processes, their stubborn and debilitating unforgiveness, and the grievous fear attached to the memory of abuse through Biblical counseling.

The farmer-therapist-pastor turns the soil and waters, but it is God who supplies the growth. Change is not either-or. Change is both-and.

Notes

1. 1. Corinthians 7:31 and 1 John 2:17.
2. Hubble's law and the expanding universe. Proceedings of the National Academy of Sciences of the United States of America, www.pnas.org/content/112/11/3173.
3. 1. John 3:2.
4. 2. Corinthians 3: 17 and 18.

5. John 3:16 and17; cf. John 17:3.
6. Romans 8: 38–39.
7. Philippians 1:6.
8. Hebrews 7:24–25.
9. Romans 8:33–34.
10. Romans 8: 26 and 27.
11. Numbers 22:21–39.

Resources

Beisser, A. (1970). The paradoxical theory of change. In J. Fagan & I. E. Shepherd (Eds.), *Gestalt therapy now: Theory techniques applications* (pp. 77–80). New York, NY: Harper & Row Publishers.

Bemme, D. (2019). Finding "what works": Theory of change, contingent universals, and virtuous failure in global mental health. *Culture, Medicine and Psychiatry*, published online. doi:10.1007/s11013-019-09637-6

Duncan, B., Miller, S., Wampold, B., & Hubble, M. (Eds.). (2010). *The heart and soul of change: Delivering what works in therapy* (2nd ed.). Washington, DC: American Psychological Association.

Hoffman, M. A. (2012). Individual counseling as an intervention. In E. M. Altmaier & J.-I. Hansen (Eds.), *The Oxford handbook of counseling psychology*. Oxford Handbooks Online. doi:10.1093/oxfordhb/9780195342314.013.0019

Leibert, T. (2011). The dimensions of common factors in counseling. *International Journal for the Advancement of Counseling, 33*, 127–138. doi:10.1007/s10447-011-9115-7

Lewis, M. (1997). *Altering fate: Why the past does not predict the future*. New York, NY: The Guilford Press.

Bruschweiler-Stern, N., Lyons-Ruth, K., Morgan, A. C., Nahum, J. P., Reis, B., & The "Boston Change Process Study Group" (2018). Engagement and the emergence of a charged other. *Contemporary Psychoanalysis, 54*(3), 540–559.

Thomas, M. (2006). The contributing factors of change in a therapeutic process. *Contemporary Family Therapy, 28*, 201–210.

16

GRACE, REGENERATION, AND SALVATION

A prayer of gratitude:
Without you, Lord,
I would have lived
A futile and shallow
Life.
Simply put.

John Calvin (1960) wrote, "Nearly all the wisdom we possess, that is to say, true and sound wisdom, consists of two parts: the knowledge of God and of ourselves" (p. 35).

There are two great theories inherent to gestalt therapy and Christianity. Of course, they stand on their own; neither one is dependent on the other, but together they create some interesting considerations. The two theories are gestalt therapy's theory of self and Christianity's theology of salvation. Having said that, one will find diverse understandings of both. The theory of self can be found in Perls, Hefferline, and Goodman's text (1951) and elaborated periodically from that point forward, with the latest as of this writing in an anthology of perspectives on the subject edited by Jean-Marie Robine (2016). The theology of salvation can be found in numerous texts outside of its description in scripture and has been elaborated for centuries.

What I present here is extremely simplified and incomplete. The purpose is not to be exhaustive for either of these subjects but to suggest ways in which an understanding of each can facilitate both spiritual growth and gestalt psychotherapy among Christians.

Brief Orientation to Gestalt Self-Theory

I want to take us back to something I said previously, namely that there are animate things and there are inanimate things. Some things are living and some are not. Consistent with such an ontology of things, Sylvia Crocker (1999), relying on Greek philosophy, stated "The actual *power of living*—the *psyche, soul, or anima*—is that which empowers those processes in organisms which constitute the very living actions themselves" (p. 166). Self, then, is the conscious awareness of that living. Further, Dan Bloom (2012) wrote, "The human being as *sensing* organism perceives and adjusts to its environment in phenomenal awareness. The human being as *knowing* person also adjusts to the world with consciousness" (Bloom, 2012, p. 79).

We can speak of the self as if it were a thing,[1] and then we might say, "It is a function of the field," or "It is a function of contacting" (Vázquez-Bandín, 2016, p. 24). But the self is the subjective owner of experience identified with grammatical voice. The self is not something a person possesses but something a person is (Staemmler, 2016). *It* is actually an *I* or a *me*. When one views the experience in the active voice, one says something like "I hit the ball." When one views the experience in the passive voice one says "The ball hit me." When one acts in the middle voice it is with clear reflexive self-interest. "I hit the ball myself," "I hit the ball to myself," or "I hit the ball for myself." The self is not an object. The self is a subject and personal. The self is the living thing, the person, acting or functioning in a world. So, the self is always situated and related to others and the environment. It is impossible to have an absolutely isolated self. Such a condition can only exist as a thought experiment.

In gestalt therapy there are three ways of viewing the action of the self: id function, ego function, and personality function. Gestalt therapy was originally cast as a revision of psychoanalysis; so, these terms are hold overs and suggestive of Freud's terms. It is not necessary to learn Freud in order to understand the gestalt theory of self.

Id Function

Id function is considered to be the organism's capacity for contact at a physical and sensory level that includes the sensory-motor ground of experience over time and physiological needs (Spagnuolo Lobb & Lichtenberg, 2005). It is an undefined, pre-reflective sense of a given situation. It is the diffuse surround. This is the level at which one first detects an atmosphere, and one might say, "*Something is going on*," but not know what or how and really not know how that concerns one's self (Mann, 2010; Brownell, 2010).

Ego Function

Ego function expresses the organism's capacity for contact in a different way. It is the way a person identifies or differentiates him or herself from aspects of the field (Spagnuolo Lobb & Lichtenberg, 2005). This is a move from the vague and diffuse to the clear and specific. This is where mere sensation becomes an intentional object—a well formed figure of interest or need. This is where the person might say, "This is me" or "This is not me," "I like it and I want it" or "I don't like it, and I don't want it." This is where people pay more attention, investigate, and view figures with critical thinking. With ego function a person makes choices.

Personality Function

Personality function expresses the capacity of the organism for contact on the basis of what one has become. More to the point, this is the person's definition of him or herself (Spagnuolo Lobb & Lichtenberg, 2005). It is the story one tells oneself about who they are based on the residue of experience, based on what they have lived through and their hindsight, their interpretation of those historical events. It is also the relic of adjustments along the way so that one's coping strategies in the face of difficult situations influence one's horizons and contribute to what a person believes is possible for them in the present. Thus, personality function influences relational patterns in an ongoing fashion.

Brief Orientation to Salvation

"Salvation" is a big word. It is a word like "love" or "field." It has a range of meanings and the context is usually needed in order to help one figure out what it means. At one level it means to be rescued or delivered from trouble, but is that all?

Salvation is one of the main concerns of religious people (in one form of it or another), and that certainly applies to people involved in the Christian religion. How might one "get saved?" What does it mean to *be* saved? Saved from what? Save *to* what?

In the Bible it can mean deliverance from almost any kind of evil or suffering that can come upon a person. As such it can refer to being saved in battle, delivered from trouble, rescued from enemies, death, or sin (Barabas, 1978).

The whole subject is too large to deal with comprehensively in this chapter. So, I want to describe in simple terms the means of salvation and its two forms.

Grace

> *For by grace you have been saved through faith;*
> *and that not of yourselves, it is the gift of God;*
> *not as a result of works, so that no one may boast.*

Grace, Regeneration, and Salvation **177**

For we are His workmanship, created in Christ Jesus for good works,
which God prepared beforehand so that we would walk in them.[2]

The Greek word χάρις (charis/grace) in classical Greek came from a root
(*char*) indicating "things which produce well-being" (Esser, 1976, p. 115). In the
Greek version of the Old Testament (LXX) it is used to translate the Hebrew
word *hen* and indicated "the stronger coming to the help of the weaker who
stands in need of help by reason of his circumstances or natural weakness"
(ibid., p. 116). The stronger in such cases is under no obligation to provide that
help, and a typical expression became "to find favor in someone's eyes." Thus,
Ruth found favor with Boaz,[3] Hannah with Eli,[4] and Esther with the king.[5]
When used to speak of God's favor it denotes an undeserved gift of God, as
when Noah is singled out from among all human beings (Genesis 6:8) to be
saved from the flood.

The New Testament uses the word *charis* 155 times. It is a common term in the
letters of Paul. One might say he emphasized it. It also appears in Peter's writing
and the letter to the Hebrew Christians. In the book of Acts it refers to the power
flowing from God that gave effectiveness to the apostles and their ministries. In
Paul's letters *charis* is the antithesis of law and the human effort that is required to
satisfy legal demands.

Paul said that by grace, by means of undeserved favor, we are saved. It is an act
of God, the stronger one, coming to help us—all of us weaker ones—because He
loves us and we are utterly lost without Him. None of it, from beginning to end,
is a contribution of our own. It is true that through faith we appropriate this gift,
but it is not our faith that prompts God to act in our behalf. Rather, God works,
and we believe. God works and the belief that He engenders in us picks up the
gift when we trust what God has said.

Regeneration

Salvation can be understood as regeneration. Regeneration is like a point rather
than a line. It occurs at a point. There may be a process getting to that point, but
the act of regeneration is like the action potential in a synapse. There is build up,
but at a point, the synapse is triggered, and there is a sudden shift.

There is a difference of opinion between the Calvinistic and Arminian wings
of the church as to the order of things regarding regeneration, and Strong nicely
captured both sides in one statement:

Regeneration, or the new birth, is the divine side of that change of heart
which, viewed from the human side, we call conversion.
It is God's turning the soul to himself,—conversion being the soul's turning itself to
God, of which God's turning it is both the accompaniment and cause.

(Strong, 1907/1976, p. 809)

178 Change, Salvation, and Growth

Is it that a person believes and God gives him new life, or is it that God gives him new life which enables him to believe (Erickson, 1985)? The point to me is the new life. Yes, the grace, the gift of new life, is appropriated through faith. It is as if a priceless gem rested upon a table and one was told it was his. Only if he believes that statement and acts on that belief would he reach out and pick it up. Faith, the action based on what one believes to be true, is the means, but the gift is a free gift. Faith is not grace, but faith takes hold of that for which one has been taken hold of by God.

Regeneration is also linked to justification, because the grace in regeneration requires a forensic shift to take place. Once law was given through the Jews, people stood condemned under it, for everyone breaks God's law at some point and in some way. We are guilty. The prophets in Israel were prosecuting attorneys bringing cases against God's people for their legal failures. It is Christ's atonement on the cross that makes our exoneration possible. Christ's death paid the legal penalty and upheld the righteousness of God in the face of grace and regeneration. God is both just and justifier. Justification is the point of the spear in regeneration. When one believes what the Bible says about Jesus, one picks up the priceless gem off the table; at a point one is justified and experiences new life. One is born again.

> *Now there was a man of the Pharisees, named Nicodemus, a ruler of the Jews;*
> *this man came to Jesus by night and said to Him, "Rabbi, we know that You*
> *have come from God as a teacher; for no one can do these signs*
> *that You do unless God is with him." Jesus answered and said to him,*
> *"Truly, truly, I say to you, unless one is born again he cannot see*
> *the kingdom of God." . . .*
>
> *Do not be amazed that I said to you, "You must be born again."*
> *The wind blows where it wishes and you hear the sound of it,*
> *but do not know where it comes from and where it is going;*
> *so is everyone who is born of the Spirit. . . .*
> *As Moses lifted up the serpent in the wilderness,*
> *even so must the Son of Man be lifted up;*
> *so that whoever believes will in Him have eternal life.*
> *For God so loved the world, that He gave His only begotten Son, that whoever*
> *believes in Him shall not perish, but have eternal life.*[6]

Sanctification

As growth and development are distinguished from birth, so sanctification is distinct from regeneration (Strong, 1907/1976, pp. 869–881; Erickson, 1985, pp. 967–983). It is a life-long process from the point of regeneration. If regeneration/justification is the point, then sanctification is the line. It's an unending line.

It is also a bumpy, often tortured line that proves as challenging as anything in life for those who attempt to walk that line. That is because of several factors: external opposition, internal conflict, and God's discipline.

External Opposition

The world operates according to a naturalistic, mechanistic, secular, and self-serving system. It opposes the kingdom of God. As one Biblical writer put it, "love of the world is enmity with God."

> Do not love the world nor the things in the world. If anyone loves the world, the love of the Father is not in him.[7]
>
> Do you not know that friendship with the world is hostility toward God? Therefore whoever wishes to be a friend of the world makes himself an enemy of God.[89]
>
> Jesus told his disciples before He was crucified, "If the world hates you, you know that it has hated Me before *it hated* you. If you were of the world, the world would love its own; but because you are not of the world, but I chose you out of the world, because of this the world hates you."[10]

Religious persecution is an equal-opportunity scourge. So, is the disdain for Christians just one example of a set that includes Jews, Muslims, Buddhists, and so forth? I don't know, but here are some figures about the persecution of Christians as of 2019:

- 245 million Christians in the world experience high levels of persecution for their choice to follow Christ.
- 1 in 9 Christians worldwide experience high levels of persecution.
- The rise in the number of Christians in the top 50 countries on the 2019 World Watch List (WWL) who experience high levels of persecution (from the 2018 reporting period to 2019's) is 14 percent.
- 4,136 Christians were killed for faith-related reasons in the top 50 WWL countries.
- 2,625 Christians were detained without trial, arrested, sentenced, and imprisoned in the top 50 WWL countries.
- 1,266 churches or Christian buildings were attacked in the top 50 WWL countries.
- In seven of the countries in the World Watch List's top 10, the primary cause of persecution is Islamic oppression.
- 11 countries scored in the "extreme" level for their persecution of Christians. Five years ago, North Korea was the only one.
- For 18 consecutive years North Korea has ranked no. 1 as the world's most dangerous place for Christians.[11]

180 Change, Salvation, and Growth

Almost 50 years ago I sat in an anthropology class in college and the professor asked "How many of you believe in God?" First, why ask that question? It's a form of intimidation.

I was sitting near the front row and I raised my hand. I was told later that I was the only one to raise my hand. I don't believe I was the only one in that large, amphitheater type room who believed in God. The intimidation people feel in social settings as Christians is intense.

In the current decade free speech has been threatened, and the people speaking their minds have been shouted down and eliminated from the conversation on several college and university campuses. Christians have been linked to conservative political perspectives, as if all Christians felt the same about every social and political issue.

So, external opposition means external to one's self, not just external to the church. Judgment and condemnation can arise from within the church toward fellow Christians just as easily as from outside the church toward people who believe in God, or a different God than the prevailing culture. It is not easy to be a thinking Christian and to be transparent about what one believes. One is just as likely to be judged by other believers as one is to be attacked by people who don't know the Lord.

Finally, Satan uses all these means to attack Christians. He has been described as a roaring lion roaming around looking for ways to destroy. He hates the things of God and seeks to undermine the work of Jesus and the Holy Spirit. He is a liar and works his best when he can usurp a bit of truth and twist it into a deception, camouflage and obscure the truth, and lead people away from Jesus. He is a murderous evil.

Internal Conflict

When people are born again, born anew of the Spirit of God, they do not lose their old nature. The old customs, the customary preferences and appetites remain. Whereas the person formerly served him or herself, after regeneration, their concern is how they conform to the image of Christ, how well they fit with His kingdom, how well they serve the Lord. There ensues a lifelong conflict between elements of one's self. Sometimes the figure of interest is obedience to God, believing what He has said and acting in accord. At other times the figure of interest is satisfying one's desires or hungers, bringing pleasure to one's self with disregard or outright rejection of the cautionary input from the Holy Spirit.

Paul said that he at times found himself in this conflict. He said he did not understand how it could be. He was at times not doing the things he wanted to do but doing the very things that he hated.[12] He was not ignorant of what was good and what the Lord wanted for him; he was just determined to do what somewhere in his body, in his being, in his person he desired to do anyway.

This is the internal conflict around which I am certain God interacts with every regenerate person. It will be different for each one. There is no top ten list of

Grace, Regeneration, and Salvation **181**

sins that is the same for everyone. There are terribly sinful, evil things that people can do, but I do not believe that God looks at some sin as not worth quibbling about, and I am certain that he does not lump us all into one basket and treat each one of us exactly the same as others.

In my life I have watched as first sex outside of marriage, then drugs, then certain types of music, then abortion, then sexual preference or same sex intimacy rose to the top of the top ten list of worst possible sins identified by the church. Others could probably make their own similar list. How is it that some sins, some works of the flesh, don't ever seem to make it to the top ten? How often have you seen gluttony or gossip up there? I've seen overweight preachers go on and on about sexual sin, but not about insatiable hunger. I've seen groups of Christians talk about others in the guise of sharing prayer requests, but not really call out anyone for gossip.

We all sin. We all fall short of the glory of God, but I do not believe God attacks the general condition as much as He does one, specific repetitive problem. I think God goes after something likely different with each of us, and since the overall condition is that we are utterly lost, utterly debased and sinful apart from Christ, there is no purpose in going after the problem on a global scale. God picks a fight with a Christian around one of his or her abiding weak spots and there ensues often a life-long "conversation" between God and that Christian about how much they love Him (if you love me you will do as I say), how much they believe Him (the obedience of the faith refers to the influence of faith over behavior; if we believe Him we will do what He says), and so forth. And the purpose is not to condemn but to elevate the believer's perspective on the depths of grace and the need for Christ's sacrifice. It is also to gradually bring about a change in the person so that they increasingly yield to the Holy Spirit and come to resemble Jesus Himself.

We cannot fail in such a conversation. We cannot fail because our failures don't matter. God loves us and sent His son to be a propitiation for our sins. As Jesus said from the cross before He died, "It is finished." We cannot fail, because what God started in us He will complete. We cannot fail, because God turns all things to the good, He makes a profit out of every transaction. We cannot fail because *He has already succeeded.*

The Discipline of God

The discipline of the Lord is not punitive. The punitive part was taken care of at the cross. The discipline is for the purpose of growth. Yet, it is very difficult. It can involve loss, opposition, and criticism. It can include God taking his hand off so that spiritual forces wreak havoc. It can appear as if God has gone silent. Doubt, fear, and confusion can develop.

> Consider it all joy, my brethren, when you encounter various trials, knowing that the testing of your faith produces endurance. And let endurance

182 Change, Salvation, and Growth

have *its* perfect result, so that you may be perfect and complete, lacking in nothing.

James 1: 2–4

and you have forgotten the exhortation which is addressed to you as sons,
"My son, do not regard lightly the discipline of the Lord,
Nor faint when you are reproved by Him;
For those whom the Lord loves He disciplines,
And He scourges every son whom He receives."
It is for discipline that you endure; God deals with you as with sons; for what son is there whom *his* father does not discipline? But if you are without discipline, of which all have become partakers, then you are illegitimate children and not sons. Furthermore, we had earthly fathers to discipline us, and we respected them; shall we not much rather be subject to the Father of spirits, and live? For they disciplined us for a short time as seemed best to them, but He *disciplines us* for *our* good, so that we may share His holiness.
Hebrews 12:5–10

Spiritual depression can be mistaken for simple psychological depression, because it is still depression. However, the cause of spiritual depression is the sense of the absence of God or that God has abandoned a person. It can also arise through an adverse comparison with another Christian, the sense that one has failed in their ministry, or through attempting to live with faulty theology—dismay can result because one's sense of God, the nature of God, is, as J.B. Phillips put it, "too small."[13] Spiritual depression can emerge from slavery—the repetition compulsion, or addiction, to behavior one knows is not okay with God.

Integration

Fritz Perls asserted that curiosity about the way people function in the world leads to "the study of what goes on at the contact boundary between the individual and his environment. It is at this contact boundary that psychological events take place. Our thoughts, our actions, our behavior, and our emotions are our way of experiencing and meeting these boundary events" (Perls, 1976, p. 17).

The experience of self and the experience of salvation are not two unrelated phenomena, because one comes into a new range of self-experience through contact with God, and that occurs at the contact boundary just like any other contact between a person and an other. Contact between the organism and the environment is only a strictly material, physical boundary event if one takes a very reductive and simplistic view of the phenomenology involved in gestalt therapy and a biased perspective—an a priori limited horizon—with respect to spirituality or theology.

Consider the possibilities in Table 16:1.

Grace, Regeneration, and Salvation **183**

TABLE 16.1 Self-Functions and Christian Spirituality

GT Functions of Self	Regeneration/Justification	Sanctification
Id Function	Sense of lightness, curiosity about God; confusion; subtle change of attitude toward the concept of God; vague sense of difficult field conditions; experience of spiritual atmosphere	Diffuse and general dissatisfaction, sense of free-floating guilt or disappointment; general hunger; confusion; spiritual depression; joy; increasing satisfaction in worship
Ego Function	Clear antipathy toward God/clear desire for God; choosing to investigate the possibility of God, believing that the Bible story is true; wanting Jesus.	Beginning the practice of a spiritual discipline such as solitude, fasting, prayer, etc.; desire for confession or accountability to a spiritual mentor; decision to begin systemic study of the Bible, theology, or Biblical languages
Personality Function	Personal identification with Christ; coherent sense of spiritual journey resulting in conversion (I am a person who put my faith in Jesus)	Personal identification with Christ; sense of calling—one is a person called of God for ministry; sense of providence and election; I am a person who follows Jesus—a disciple

What is common in the stories of people who experience conversion/regeneration and then the ongoing growth cycles in the Christian life is the sense of contact with God, which can be a narrative involving God's presence or His absence. It is a give-and-take, a relationship between one being and another and a dialogical process.

People struggle with religious strain, anger toward God or attachment to God, addiction issues and the role of God in recovery, trauma, spiritual meaning, loneliness and isolation, control, death, and impermanence or unpredictability when God is described as loving, all powerful, and all wise (Murray-Swank & Murray-Swank, 2012). One is tempted to doubt that some of that could be true given one's circumstances, one's situation, and one's experience. In such situations, though, doubt is not failure but the way of working through. "The world of Christian faith is not a fairy-tale, make-believe world, question-free and problem-proof, but a world where doubt is never far from faith's shoulder" (Guinness, 1976, p. 16).

It is the gestalt therapist's privilege in such cases to facilitate such working through, but it will entail a third in the room, and the gestalt therapist must be at home with that. It will not be just the "between" of therapist and client, but an "among"—a small group in which the Holy Spirit has access to both client and therapist and things at times seem miraculous. It will also entail the particular

184 Change, Salvation, and Growth

spiritual interruption to contact the Bible calls "hardening." It is a stubborn resistance that turns a deaf ear or a willful disregard toward God. These kinds of things have psychological manifestations, physical and biological repercussions, and social consequences. In dealing with Christian clients the gestalt therapist needs to be alert to such possibilities.

So, do pastors.

Notes

1. The entire organism is a living thing, but the self is personal and subjective—not an *it* but an *I*.
2. Ephesians 2: 8–10.
3. Ruth 2:2, 10, 13.
4. 1 Samuel 1:18.
5. Esther 8:5.
6. John 3: 1–3; 7–8; 14–16.
7. 1 John 2:15.
8. James 4:4.
9. It should be understood that "world" in these contexts means the world system by which people operate and not the physical, environmental planet and its resources.
10. John 15: 18–19.
11. Taken from the web site of Open Doors and downloaded November 2019 from www.opendoorsusa.org/christian-persecution.
12. Romans 7:15.
13. Phillips, J. B. (1967) *Your God is too small.* New York, NY: The Macmillan Company.

Resources

Barabas, S. (1978). Salvation. In J. D. Douglas (Ed.), *The new international dictionary of the Christian church.* Grand Rapids, MI: Zondervan.

Bloom, D. (2012). Sensing animals/knowing persons: A challenge to some basic ideas in gestalt therapy. In T. Bar-Yoseph Levine (Ed.), *Gestalt therapy: Advances in theory and practice* (pp. 79–82). New York, NY: Routledge.

Brownell, P. (2010). *Gestalt therapy: A guide to contemporary practice.* New York, NY: Springer Publishing.

Calvin, J. (1960). *Calvin: Institutes of the Christian religion* (J. T. McNeill, Ed., F. L. Battles, Trans., Vols. 3). Philadelphia, PA: The Westminster Press.

Crocker, S. (1999). *A well-lived life: Essays in gestalt therapy.* Cambridge, MA: Gestalt Institute of Cleveland Press.

Erickson, M. (1985). *Christian theology.* Grand Rapids, MI: Baker Book House.

Esser, H. (1976). Grace, spiritual gifts. In C. Brown (Ed.), *New international dictionary of New Testament theology* (Vol. 2, pp. 115–124). Grand Rapids, MI: Zondervan.

Guinness, O. (1976). *In two minds: The dilemma of doubt & how to resolve it.* Downers Grove, IL: InterVarsity Press.

Mann, D. (2010). *Gestalt therapy: 100 key points & techniques.* New York, NY: Routledge.

Murray-Swank, N., & Murray-Swank, A. (2012). Navigating the storm: Helping clients in the midst of spiritual struggles. In J. Aten, K. O'Grady, & E. Worthington, Jr. (Eds.), *The psychology of religion and spirituality for clinicians: Using research in your practice* (pp. 217–244). New York, NY: Routledge.

Perls, F. (1976). *The gestalt approach & eye witness to therapy*. New York, NY: Bantam Books.

Perls, F., Hefferline, R., & Goodman, P. (1951). *Excitement and growth in the human personality*. London, UK: Souvenir Press.

Robine, J.-M. (2016). *Self: A polyphony of contemporary gestalt therapists*. Bordeaux, France: L'exprimerie.

Spagnuolo Lobb, M., & Lichtenberg, P. (2005). Classical gestalt therapy. In A. Woldt & S. Toman (Eds.), *Gestalt therapy history, theory, and practice* (pp. 21–39). Thousand Oaks, CA: Sage Publications.

Staemmler, F.-M. (2016). Self as situated process. In J.-M. Robine (Ed.), *Self: A polyphony of contemporary gestalt therapists* (pp. 103–112). Bordeaux, France: L'exprimerie (English version).

Strong, A. H. (1907/1976). *Systematic theology: A compendium designed for the use of theological students*. Valley Forge, PA: Judson Press.

Vázquez-Bandín, C. (2016). Like a river flowing, passing, yet ever present: The theory of self in gestalt therapy. In J.-M. Robine (Ed.), *Self: A polyphony of contemporary gestalt therapists* (pp. 21–27). Bordeaux, France: L'exprimerie (English version).

17

RULES, INTROJECTS, AND MATTERS OF CONSCIENCE

One must or must not.
Two ought, but three should not.
Four should, but five could not.
Six caught what seven would not.

Paul of Tarsus wrote, "by the works of the Law no flesh will be justified in His sight; for through the Law comes the knowledge of sin" (Romans 3:20).

Erving and Miriam Polster (1973) wrote about introjection describing it as the most basic form of learning. One simply absorbs from the environment, adopting uncritically what is given. Only until later in life does one question what is given, if then. That is when the "inevitable conflict begins between accepting life as it is or changing it and the conflict lasts as long as one lives" (ibid., p. 74).

Fritz Perls said, "The 'should' mentality is found overtly or covertly in every philosophy and definitely in every religion. . . . Religions are full of taboos, of *shoulds* and *should nots*. I'm sure you all realize that you grow up completely surrounded by what you should and should not do" (Perls, 1970, p. 15).

Accepting what is given means operating in the natural attitude, not questioning the way things seem to be. However, operating on the basis of a system of introjects is more than that. It is being bound by rules, proper procedures, customary rituals—"the way we do it." An introject is a rule or principle, a statement, that acts like a law.

It is also operating according to what one is told.

An introject is a principle that one is given and has adopted as true, thus useful for structuring one's way of living. It is an easy and efficient way of navigating the world.

Examples:

- Immediately wash the frying pan after cooking and before eating.
- Always fold the clean laundry before putting it away.
- Use one slab of butter on the toast.
- Never roll up the pant legs on your denims.
- Don't wear a coat in the house.
- Always say grace and thank God for your food.
- Only use the King James Bible.
- Don't go to movies.
- Only wear dresses that extend at least half-way between the knees and the ankles.
- Don't drink any alcohol.
- Go to church every Sunday.
- Go to the *right* church every Sunday.

In psychotherapy an intrusive, directive therapist who pushes the client into practices, behaviors, exercises, and so on will not build autonomy and personal support in the patient. Rather, the patient will likely "swallow whole," or introject what the therapist advocates (Yontef, 1993), and that will lead to conformity but not personal growth.

Conforming to expectations can be deceiving. If one attends church as expected, does that make him or her a Christian? Some people grow up meeting expectations, and when asked if they are Christians, they say something like, "I've always been a Christian. We always went to church and my parents told us what to do."

The same could be said for a person seeking to grow in their Christian life, their knowledge of God, their spiritual discernment and wisdom. A common practice that is more often simply introjected than anything else is the "quiet time." The quiet time is a space one creates out of the business of one's life in order to pull away and "spend time with the Lord."

I remember hearing among my Christian friends, and advocated from the pulpit by pastors, that a growing Christian and real disciple of Christ would get to a quiet spot, away from the world, and read the Bible and pray. I liked reading the Bible. That was not a chore. Prayer was more difficult. What could I possibly say to God that He did not already know and that I was not already constantly sharing with Him as I went through a typical day? What was I supposed to say? Was I supposed to ask for things? That seemed selfish and small minded. Was I supposed to intercede and ask on behalf of others? Was I supposed to praise God? I fumbled along with trying to do all those things. So, the concrete return, the feedback on observing a quiet time lacked substance. Still, *not to do it* seemed unacceptable. After all, I was called to full-time ministry and I needed to become more spiritual. I felt compelled to develop a quiet time.

188 Change, Salvation, and Growth

So, here is another feature of an introject. It may come with some superficial rationale or reason to it, but the more complex and nuanced factors related to either adhering to it or simply giving it up are never contemplated.

This is also the way law operates. Do it or don't do it because the government says so. The teacher in the classroom says so. The church says so. My pastor says so. Even the Bible says so.

Have you ever wondered why we need to praise God? Is God an insecure monarch who needs the constant adulation of his subjects to make him feel important? Why is it a good thing to praise God? Is it because when we praise God, worship God, we are lifted up and experience a spiritual high? When the worship music gets going and the congregation all raise their hands and some people drop to their knees, and you feel the sweep of ecstasy move through the room, is *that* why we should worship God? So we can get off on God? Or is there some other reason that is consistent with the nature of God? What is there to be gained by questioning, challenging the introject, and working through the complexities that reside in the nature of an infinite Being immanently present among us?

Perls (1947/1992) used the figure of dental aggression—chewing—as a way of advocating that people deconstruct their introjects. Only when food is broken down through chewing does it become best assimilated to the organism. Chewing leads to more effective digestion. It's better for us to chew our food than to swallow it whole. It is more nourishing to deconstruct introjects than to let them rule from the corners of our lives.

Don't misunderstand. I am not claiming that all introjects are based on fallacies or errors. It may be that the common take on these things has developed over time out of the practical knowledge that they are good, that they work. However, for the individual to simply adopt them without asking "why" is to malnourish one's development of wisdom.

Every person must develop his or her own faith in Jesus. Nobody "gets into heaven" based on the faith of their parents. So, people who grow up in Christian families and learn from an early age that they should go to church on Sunday, do that. Without question. When asked if they are Christian, they often indicate that they are, but why are they? In what way are they? Is it cultural? Or personal?

Working Through Legalism

In Paul's letter to the Christians living in Galatia he made it clear that no one is justified by living according to the Mosaic law and attempting to fulfill its mandates. However, legalism is not limited to matters of the Mosaic law. Legalism in Christianity can be understood as any form of a performance-based economy. Use the right Bible. Wear the right clothes. Eat the right food. Do this. Do that. Don't do this, and don't do that.

Legalism produces false shame. I say "false shame" because the shame, which feels real, is based on false premises. No one who has been saved by grace through faith is any longer regarded by God to be within a performance-based economy. They live in a grace-based economy. They are free of the law as any kind of life principle. That is what the term Christian freedom refers to. All things become lawful when law itself has no relevance. The law has been fulfilled and God has been satisfied in Christ. A person's identification with Him is what is efficacious, not the observance of any kind of rules or introjects. Thus, as has been said, if Christ has set one free, then that person is free indeed—free to explore novelty and interest, curiosity, or creativity however and wherever one finds it. Religiosity has no virtue.

Guilt and shame are frequent visitors in the sessions of psychotherapy. For the gestalt therapist working with a Christian, this area of legalism and grace is worth exploring.

Matters of Conscience

Also worth exploring, and surely related, are matters of conscience. Paul dealt with this issue in a couple places. In the fourteenth chapter of the letter to the Christians in Rome, he indicated that people who rejected meat that had been offered to idols were weak because their consciences would not allow them to eat it even though doing so had not been forbidden by God. "Error stirs tensions when the weaker brothers wrongly judge those whose consciences are free. If you have a weak conscience, you can as easily develop a judgmental spirit to form legalistic notions, denying you and others freedom in Christ" (downloaded from Ligonier Ministries, www.ligonier.org/learn/devotionals/weak-conscience, December 2019). Thus, introjects, when triggered, can be a product of a weak conscience that has no support in the Bible, and that can be a useful observation for both gestalt therapists and pastoral counselors. It is a counter-intuitive observation: the weaker conscience is the one with numerous strong prohibitions while the stronger conscience is free, supported for contact wherever interest and creativity invites expression and exploration of novelty.

Resources

Perls, F. (1947/1992). *Ego, hunger, & aggression: A revision of Freud's theory and method*. Highland, NY: Gestalt Journal Press.

Perls, F. (1970). Four lectures. In J. Fagan & I. L. Shepherd (Eds.), *Gestalt therapy now: Theory/techniques/applications*. New York, NY: Harper & Row.

Polster, E., & Polster, M. (1973). *Gestalt therapy integrated: Contours of theory & practice*. New York, NY: Vintage Books, Random House.

Yontef, G. (1993). *Awareness, dialogue & process*. Highland, NY: The Gestalt Journal Press.

18

GROWTH IN SPIRITUAL SENSITIVITY

It whispers, "I'm here."
One wonders at first if it said that.
Then it shouts in the ear, painfully so,
"I AM HERE!"

Michel Henry (2003) wrote, "Only Truth can attest to itself—reveal itself in and through itself" (p. 10). A truth so revealed seems self-evident, obvious.

I have said before to people in various places and at various times that when I became opened up to God it was because He made himself known to me. I had talked to him. I don't know why it seemed okay at the time to talk to a being I was not sure even existed, but I did. I told him that if he was real to make himself known to me. Now, this is the part that may not seem evident. How did I know it was God who suddenly made the Bible so interesting, so compelling? I am aware of a clear difference between what it was like to read the Bible prior to that time and what it was like after I had asked God to make himself known to me. The situation seemed self-evident.

No one else in the world knows what my experience was. I can tell them, but they cannot know it like I experienced it. Only after I'd been in it did I realize what was happening. Suddenly there came a double dose of reality. Not only did I get a response to my prayer, but there was also the revealing, the self-disclosing God making himself real to me. "If you are real, make yourself known to me." That is what happened.

Was it awareness, which seems almost a mundane capacity? Or was it spiritual sensitivity, which seems like a religious thing, something more than the ordinary, temporal, and material. Was it God regenerating me, calling me up to life and granting me the grace to see and hear Him in the words of the Bible?

Growth in Spiritual Sensitivity **191**

Jesus often used the expression of having ears to hear to refer to a capacity to comprehend that was dependent upon sensory input but not limited to sensory input. In that regard awareness is not simply comprehension *of* sensory input; it extends to connections in the person's life, the meaning or significance of what one perceives, the realization of its implications for one's situation, and the sense that it carries overtones of the transcendent:

- Matthew 13:9 He who has ears, let him hear.; Matthew 13:43 Then the righteous will shine like the sun in the kingdom of their Father. He who has ears, let him hear.; Mark 4:9 Then Jesus said, He who has ears to hear, let him hear.; Mark 4:23 If anyone has ears to hear, let him hear.; Luke 8:8 Still other seed fell on good soil, where it sprang up and produced a crop—a hundredfold. As Jesus said this, He called out, He who has ears to hear, let him hear.; Luke 14:35 It is fit neither for the soil nor for the manure pile, and it is thrown out. He who has ears to hear, let him hear.; Revelation 2:7 He who has an ear, let him hear what the Spirit says to the churches. To the one who is victorious, I will grant the right to eat of the tree of life in the paradise of God.; Revelation 2:11 He who has an ear, let him hear what the Spirit says to the churches. The one who is victorious will not be harmed by the second death.; Revelation 3:6 He who has an ear, let him hear what the Spirit says to the churches.
- Paul wrote about spiritual matters being spiritually discerned. 1 Corinthians 2:10–16 For to us God revealed *them* through the Spirit; for the Spirit searches all things, even the depths of God. For who among men knows the *thoughts* of a man except the spirit of the man which is in him? Even so the *thoughts* of God no one knows except the Spirit of God. Now we have received, not the spirit of the world, but the Spirit who is from God, so that we may know the things freely given to us by God, which things we also speak, not in words taught by human wisdom, but in those taught by the Spirit, combining spiritual *thoughts* with spiritual *words*. But a natural man does not accept the things of the Spirit of God, for they are foolishness to him; and he cannot understand them, because they are spiritually appraised.
- John wrote about the relational aspect of such awareness or discernment, that it was directly contingent upon a relationship with God. John 14:17. . . the Spirit of truth. The world cannot receive Him, because it neither sees Him nor knows Him. But you do know Him, for He abides with you and He will be in you.

In gestalt therapy awareness "is the spontaneous sensing of what arises within you in response to your situation" (Mann, 2010, p. 227; PHG, 1951, p. 75). "Awareness is a form of experience. It is the process of being in vigilant contact with the most important event in the individual/environment field with full sensorimotor, emotional, cognitive, and energetic support" (Yontef, 1993, p. 183). Relatedly,

192 Change, Salvation, and Growth

one's "sense of the unitary interfunctioning of [one's self and one's] environment is contact, and the process of contacting is the forming and sharpening of the figure/ground contrast . . ." as a result of meetings between self and other (PHG, 1951, p. 73). Furthermore, in contemporary gestalt therapy awareness is not simply cognizance of sensory experience. It is the aesthetics of contact, but it is more, including also the intentionality inherent to contacting. There is the aboutness of experience, but that aboutness extends from the intentional object or figure of interest to the various connections it has in one's life world. So, in gestalt therapy awareness is not simply mindfulness (the cognizance of current experience); it includes the growing realization of implications, connections, and consequences for self and relational others. This would extend to the transcendent and in Christianity that would be one's awareness of contacting divinity, leading to the experience of spiritual self (Brownell, 2016).

I believe awareness and spiritual sensitivity are cousins. One cannot be spiritually sensitive without being aware, but awareness alone does not make one spiritually sensitive.

Recently, we were invited to a Halloween party. We arrived at the house. Inside were hundreds and hundreds of Halloween decorations and collections of little figures all related to Halloween. Skeletons. Witches. Goblins. Zombies. I am not much for such things, but I tried to be polite.

They had a table with food on it. I got a plate full and sat down on the couch. I started talking to someone I had never met before and before I knew it we were talking about God. I had not started it. I had not gone there on some kind of mission to convert the Halloween revelers. Yet, somehow, as if a trickle had trickled into the mix and contaminated the whole bunch, there we were.

I became aware first of the drift of the conversation. Then, I became aware that there was something else going on and that this was what some people call a "God appointed moment." When those things happen, I can shut it down or I can let the trickle become a flow. The theological term for this is providence.

There are no coincidences. There are windows of opportunity to talk openly about the things of the kingdom of God, and if you don't crawl through those windows, they close. They pass. You cannot create the window, but you can waste it. It takes not only awareness, but also spiritual sensitivity to realize that a providential opportunity has arrived.

Intentionality and Spiritual Sensitivity

Follow me through some connections. Intentionality is the aboutness of experience. In thinking, I am thinking a thought. Atmospheres are pre-reflective, affective, quasi-things that affect people in shared space. The Holy Spirit is a third in meetings where Christians are present.

I believe the Holy Spirit brings a divine atmosphere into a room, and people can identify that if they are trained by experience to identify it for what it

Growth in Spiritual Sensitivity   193

is. In the story of visiting the tombs of the Popes at the Vatican there are several atmospheres encountered: the stark monastery, the nuns watching a street artist, the trinket sellers in St. Peter's square, and then the atmosphere at John Paul II's tomb. Spiritual sensitivity would tell someone that something of a transcendent variety and value was connected with the scene at John Paul's tomb as opposed to the stands of trinkets. Like an atmosphere, a spiritual presence is something a person catches, something that comes over them rather than something a person manufactures or deduces.

Once detected, however, the intentionality involved with spiritual sensitivity carries with it the quality between id and ego function. The experience lacks a clear indication of *what* exactly is going on except that one becomes aware that it is a "God thing" that is taking place and one becomes aware that one is *in it and of it*. One also has the sense of the numinous—attraction and trepidation—and one can decide to yield to it or harden one's heart against it.

What is God doing? What might God want a person to do? That kind of clarity is not given, because the full phenomenon does not appear. What is happening? That is the question that looms large. One doesn't know what, exactly, is taking place or where it is going, but one knows the situation has become changed through the presence and purpose of God and the situation itself has become charged, pregnant with potential.

I have stated that intentionality involves the formation of figures of interest. So, one might think that intentional objects are always things. However, the intentionality can also be focused on processes. The intentionality in spiritual sensitivity is of the process of being in contact with God, of the developing knowledge and experience of God's presence. It is knowing God and not simply knowing things about God (Packer, 1973). The thoughts and feelings in the mind and spirit of someone close to God in this way are "as if God were walking through one's personality with a candle, directing one's attention to things one after the other" (Willard, 1999, p. 102). Sometimes that reveals things about oneself. Sometimes it gives insight into others or reflection of the situation that leads to wisdom. The point is, though, one's awareness is of the pneumenal field, in the spiritual attitude.

Spiritual sensitivity that is of the psychological attitude does not focus on the sacred. It is mundane, and the sensitivity with respect to the pneumenal field is of aesthetic value alone, an end in itself, a turning down into the earth, the natural, or the empirical.

That leads to the observation that spiritual sensitivity is purposeful. It is not simply for pleasure. Adoration of God certainly can be an ecstatic experience, but it doesn't stop there. The Westminster Shorter Catechism asks, "What is the chief end of man?" and answers "Man's chief end is to glorify God, and to enjoy him forever." The glory of God is linked to our enjoyment of God. One cannot glorify God if one is not sensitive *to* God and available for His use.

Availability is taken up in the next chapter.

194 Change, Salvation, and Growth

References

Brownell, P. (2016). Touch of another kind: Contact with God and spiritual self. In J.-M. Robine (Ed.), *Self: A polyphony of contemporary gestalt therapists*. Bordeaux, France: L'exprimerie.

Henry, M. (2003). *I am the truth: Toward a philosophy of Christianity*. Stanford, CA: Stanford University Press.

Mann, D. (2010). *Gestalt therapy: 100 key points & techniques*. New York, NY: Routledge.

Packer, J. I. (1973). *Knowing God*. Downers Grove, IL: InterVarsity Press.

Perls, F., Hefferline, R., & Goodman, P. (1951). *Gestalt therapy: Excitement and growth in the human personality*. Guernsey, Channel Islands: Guernsey Press, Souvenir Press.

Willard, D. (1999). *Hearing God: Developing a conversational relationship with God*. Downers Grove, IL: InterVarsity Press.

Yontef, G. (1993). *Awareness, dialogue & process*. Highland, NY: The Gestalt Journal Press, Inc.

19

GROWTH IN AVAILABILITY

In the moment, this very moment,
Unplanned
Unforced, uncommitted,
Spontaneous,
Not obligated,
Free and available.
The Is-ness of one second
And the consequence of one more.

Grasping the meaning of availability requires that one understand what is meant in gestalt therapy by the term "spontaneity." It is related to creative indifference, openness, and the paradoxical theory of change.

In *Ego Hunger and Aggression*, Frederick Perls (1969/1947) built upon Friedlander's concept of differentiation through creative indifference (better translated "differentiation"). It advocated remaining open to two sides of a given issue rather than building proofs of only one, or as Lagaay (2015) put it, creative indifference is "recognition of the importance of a non-place, a place of neutrality, which lies at the zero point of polar differentiation."

From that place the therapist is able to remain open to whatever arises, and available to whatever that might mean. By paying attention to "what comes up" the therapist is not already committed and is free to move this way or that, according to whatever might seem best. This forms, then, the ground of the "paradoxical theory of change," which asserts that change "occurs when one becomes what he is, not when he tries to become what he is not. Change does not take place through a coercive attempt by the individual or by another person to change him, but it does take place if one takes the time and effort to be what he is—to be fully

196 Change, Salvation, and Growth

invested in his current positions" (Beisser, 1971, p. 77). Truscott (2010) put it this way: "Change then occurs spontaneously and without effort through awareness of what and how we are thinking, feeling, and doing—through awareness of the field of our present moment" (p. 88). Rather than being committed to a given clinical theory, diagnosis, or case conceptualization, the gestalt therapist remains open and available to whatever arises while with the client, taking one moment and one day at a time.

Jesus advocated taking one day at a time, essentially living in the here and now.

> So do not worry about tomorrow;
> for tomorrow will care for itself.
> Each day has enough trouble of its own.[1]

In addition, He advocated an availability, a place of neutrality in which people might be available to God's presence.

> Therefore, just as the Holy Spirit says, today if you hear His voice,
> do not harden your hearts as when they provoked Me,
> as in the day of trial in the wilderness.[2]

That is, do not reinforce a negative interpretation, telling yourself God does not exist, or God could not intend good, etc., which would ignore the zero point of neutrality to a given phenomenon.

> He again fixes a certain day, "Today," saying through David after
> so long a time just as has been said before,
> today if you hear His voice, do not harden your hearts.[3]

Probably most salient, though, is the Christian process of confession, or confessing. It means to agree with, that is, to admit, to accept (i.e., what one is). In order to be able to do that a person must let go of pretending, ignoring, and even striving to be what one is not quite yet in order to agree with God about what one is in the current moment. Traditionally, this has been associated with admitting failures, "sins," but that is not at all the complete understanding of confession.

A confession can be agreeing about one's position in Christ as beloved by God the Father, made in the image of God, cherished as one for whom Christ died, and providentially placed in this world for the purposes of God. It is to acknowledge one's faith in God.

The primary Greek word for "confess" is *homologeo* which basically means "to say the same thing" and then "agree, admit, acknowledge." The context must determine the precise nature, emphasis, and meaning of the word. Thus, it can mean to acknowledge sin or to confess or acknowledge someone as something. A similar and somewhat more emphatic word is *exomologeo*, "promise, consent, admit, confess or acknowledge" and from this, "to praise."

Growth in Availability **197**

In Psalm 32:5, the word for confess or acknowledge is *yada'*, which basically means "to know" or in the hiphil stem, "to make known" as in this context. Another word that looks similar, but is different is *yadah*, "to give thanks, praise," and then, "to confess" as in Lev. 5:5 where it is used in the hithpael stem giving it the idea of "confess." See also 2 Chron. 6:26 where it is used in the sense of "confess God's name." Another word is *nadad*, "to be conspicuous," but in the hiphil stem it means "to make known, declare, tell" (Bible.org, 2017).

Relationship Between Sensitivity and Availability

Being aware and spiritually sensitive, one pays attention to what is going on in any given situation, and as the moment arises when it seems providence has rearranged things, then the person faces a decision.

My wife and I oversee a recovery house for women. We have community meetings in which we discuss life in the house. One day all the residents were gone and the staff was meeting. We were discussing one person in particular who presented some challenging dynamics, both from a psychological and spiritual perspective. The question arose, "What is going on with Jenny?"[4] People offered various theories and each suggested possible responses. Finally, I confessed that I was a fan of adopting a mind-of-not-knowing. The mind-of-not-knowing does not offer theories; it observes. The mind-of-not-knowing doesn't offer suggestions, interventions, models, or solutions. The mind-of-not-knowing does not know. It investigates, and as it does so, the mind-of-not-knowing holds at a distance every temptation to start down the road of one thematization or another. Once someone begins to formulate a theory about another person, one cannot help but be committed to it to some degree, and that limits everything else.

When providence shakes one loose from the normal routine, the best thing a person can do is to adopt the mind-of-not-knowing. It is the zero point. It is a great and freeing place to be, because one does not have to come up with an answer, a solution, a course of action. One is free from urgent crises. Nothing *has to be done*. One has time to learn more about the situation. One can think. And what is more important, one can wait upon God to either work or provide more information, or both.

One of the best places in scripture that addresses this sense of waiting on God at the zero point is in the seventeenth chapter of the gospel of Matthew:

> Jesus took with Him Peter and James and John his brother, and led them up on a high mountain by themselves. And He was transfigured before them; and His face shone like the sun, and His garments became as white as light. And behold, Moses and Elijah appeared to them, talking with Him. Peter said to Jesus, "Lord, it is good for us to be here; if You wish, I will make three tabernacles here, one for You, and one for Moses, and one for Elijah." While he was still speaking, a bright cloud overshadowed them, and behold,

198 Change, Salvation, and Growth

a voice out of the cloud said, "This is My beloved Son, with whom I am well-pleased; listen to Him!"[5]

The question of one's availability depends upon the sensitivity to realize that we live through moments of opportunity that open and then close and that God is active and makes a difference in this world. He is *in* those moments of opening and closing. The best thing a person can do when such a moment opens is to go with it, but one cannot do that loaded down with a priori commitments.

My wife and I once attended a conference in Manchester, England. We decided to spend a few extra days and got a place just outside of London. We brought four large bags with us on that trip. I often tell this story, because I will never forget trying to carry them all through the underground tube that is London's subway train system. At one point I lost one of the duffels, and I can still see in my mind's eye, that bag tumbling in big loops down the escalator between levels of the tube. From that point on we started making do with carry-on luggage.

Holding to a priori commitments, to thematizations of the client, models of therapy, or tenets of theology can burden the process of meeting another living person just as surely as carrying those bags turned our pleasure into our misery. They can also get in the way of what God might want to develop between one person and another. I am not saying that theory of practice and theology are unimportant. I *am saying* that they need to be held loosely so that one can flex this way or that if something new comes along that might change one's theory, theology, or approach to practice in any given moment.

Notes

1. Matthew 6:34.
2. Hebrews 3: 7–8.
3. Hebrews 4:7.
4. Jenny is a fictitious name.
5. Matthew 17: 1–5.

References

Beisser, A. (1971). The paradoxical theory of change. In J. Fagan & I. L. Shepherd (Eds.), *Gestalt therapy now* (pp. 77–80). New York, NY: Harper & Row.

Bible.org. (2017). *What are the Greek and Hebrew words for 'confess'?* Retrieved June 25, 2017, from https://bible.org/question/what-are-greek-and-hebrew-words-%E2%80%9Cconfess%E2%80%9D

Lagaay, A. (2015). Minding the gap of indifference: Approaching performance philosophy with Salomon Friedlander (1871–1946). *Performance Philosophy, 1,* 65–73.

Perls, F. (1969/1947). *Ego, hunger and aggression.* New York, NY: Random House.

Truscott, D. (2010). *Becoming an effective psychotherapist: Adopting a theory of psychotherapy that's right for you and your client.* Washington, DC: American Psychological Association.

Story Five
TIME FOR A CHANGE

He realized no one would understand this.
No one but another servant would comprehend what it was like.

Jack worked as a carpenter to put himself through college. He majored in psychology, but when he graduated, he had to choose between going on to graduate school or continuing to build houses. Building homes paid well, and there was a lot of work to be done. He decided to stick with that instead of assuming college debt to keep going. However, two years into his career as a carpenter the building trade went into a slump. Jack could not find work, and his future no longer looked so good as a carpenter.

It was time for a change. He decided to go back to school, to pick up where he'd left off.

He enrolled in a graduate program for social work with the idea of becoming a clinical social worker and doing psychotherapy. It took him two years for the degree and then a couple more to accumulate enough supervised hours to get his license.

Then he spent the next fifteen years working for the same agency, something rather unheard of, and seeing about thirty clients per week for psychotherapy. It became tedious. He found himself talking to clients more about the theory of doing psychotherapy than listening to them talk about their lives. Then, he found himself falling asleep while they talked. Then he started coming late to get them in the waiting room and ending the sessions just a little too soon. He was burning out.

It was time for a change.

200 Change, Salvation, and Growth

Jack decided to reduce his hours doing psychotherapy and start training psychotherapists. He opened up a gestalt therapy training institute. He paid someone to create for him a good web site, one that would allow him to attract potential trainees from different parts of the world. After all that ran for a few years, and he had become respected as a teacher, he found himself bored with it.

Time for another change. Jack decided to write a book about gestalt therapy. So, he did. It sold a little.

One day Jack was invited to visit a group of gestalt therapists and trainees in Greece. He decided to accept.

Greece was less attractive as a landscape when he saw it than the ethos of Greece had been in his mind. He found himself curious about that disparity. Greece, the land of thinkers, philosophers, progenitors of philosophy, but also the dry, barren, rocky land of sun, light, and heat.

The training group had about thirty people in it. They were young therapists looking for direction. So, Jack talked theory and demonstrated therapy while working with various trainees. He had illustrations and analogies. He pointed out references to seminal literature in gestalt therapy, leading with several well-placed quotes from the seminal book of gestalt therapy by Perls, Hefferline, and Goodman. They all deconstructed the experiential pieces. Near the end of the morning lecture and demonstrations it seemed the group had warmed to him quite a bit. Several invited him to lunch with them, but he told them he needed a break to be alone and think.

During lunch Jack observed a monk. He looked like a monk, with a hooded robe and sandals. Jack asked the waiter about him, and the waiter smiled.

"That is our servant," he said.

Jack could see that the servant was sweeping the ground just outside, at the entrance to the restaurant. He said, "You mean you pay him? He's an employee?"

"Oh no," said the waiter. "He's on his own. He's the servant of all."

"For free?"

"Well, people give him things."

Jack was intrigued. The servant looked to be about forty with short dark hair and a clean-shaven face. He had good posture and did not appear overly muscular, although in the robe it was hard to tell. Jack watched him while he finished his lunch. On his way out he stopped to talk with the man.

He invited him to dinner, and the servant said, "What can I do for you?"

Jack said, "Have dinner with me and tell me about your work as a servant."

The man agreed.

That night, after the training, Jack met the servant back at the same restaurant. When they sat down, he said, "Thank you for meeting with me. I was not sure you'd be here."

"I said I would."

"Yes."

After ordering, Jack said, "Please tell me how you came to be this town's servant."

The man said "I was a journeyman carpenter when the building slump hit in America."

"Been there," said Jack. "Where are you from?" He felt more than curious now.

The servant smiled. He went on, "I liked working with my hands, but to tell you the truth, I liked it more that I was making my living the same way that Jesus made his living. So, the idea of maybe having to find a different job was troubling. I was reading in the Bible one day and I came to the place where Jesus entered Jerusalem and then they were all going to celebrate Passover together. When they were all together, he washed his disciples' feet."

Jack did not follow. He was not familiar with the story. The servant could see it on his face, and he explained.

"So, Jesus had been walking all over Israel and Palestine teaching, meeting with people, talking with people one-to-one, and healing people. A lot of people started following him, and his disciples began to believe that he was the promised Messiah. So, anyway, he goes up to Jerusalem on a holy holiday for everyone and comes into the city with everyone celebrating that he's there. When they get together in a quiet place, he and his small group of most-close disciples, he starts to wash their feet. You see, people walking all over the place in sandals would have dirty feet, and it was the custom to wash your feet before eating, but usually a servant would do that, or a lesser person would wash the feet of a greater person."

Jack said, "I get it."

The servant continued. He said, "So, his disciples complained and said, 'We should be washing your feet.' But Jesus said, 'Unless I wash you, you have no part in me.' So, they let him. For Passover, then, the last one he would have, Jesus became their servant and washed their feet."

"And how does this relate to you becoming this town's servant?"

"Because when I read that, I felt very attracted to Jesus and how he was a servant. So, I started reading about other places where Jesus talked about being a servant, and I found out that he contrasted the religious leaders who liked to be recognized and honored and have their hands kissed in the market, to have people call them teachers and leaders—how he contrasted all that with another way of being. He told them there was one teacher. There was one father in heaven and one leader, Jesus himself. He told his disciples that the greatest among them would be the servant of them all."

"So, you want to be the greatest among people?" asked Jack, with a smile.

"I want to be like Jesus," said the servant. "So, long story short I found a small place where I could serve a whole community. And, I always wanted to live in Greece."

Jack said, "I think there's more to the story."

The servant said, "Another time."

202 Change, Salvation, and Growth

In spite of that the two men talked. Jack told the servant how he'd been a carpenter and then had developed a different career as a gestalt therapist. He told him that he had become a teacher, and he admitted he liked the reverence paid to him as a trainer.

"Yes," said the servant. "I get it."

After they parted and each went their different way, Jack could not get the man out of his mind. He did not sleep well that night. He kept hearing the servant's story about Jesus and about how teachers and leaders liked the attention of their followers. He had a bad dream at one point after falling into a quasi-sleep. He dreamt he was going into a gestalt training group and he was holding out his hand for the trainees to kiss and they were all getting on their knees as he passed them. He sat up from the bed feeling like would throw up.

In the morning he got up in time to take a quick shower. He passed breakfast, got some coffee, and headed for the training session.

As the training group began, Jack stopped. He could not go on with what he had planned, with what he knew how to do. He was stuck, and the familiar words, the going through the motions, would not form in his mouth. With nothing else he could do, it was time for a change.

He took a breath and looked around the room. The trainees were familiar with gestalt people doing that. They all followed suit and breathed deeply themselves.

"When I was in my training group the trainer had a picture on the wall of her trainer. That was Isadore From. She told us that when he would come and do training with her group the people were very appreciative of him. He told them one day, 'I know you like me, but what don't you like about me.' So, I can sense that you appreciate what I've been doing here, but I'm not even going to ask what From asked. Instead, I want to do something else, and I've never done this before, so it's an experiment. I don't know what's going to happen."

The group stirred. They looked expectant, excited. Surely, Jack had something good for them.

Jack said, "Yesterday I met your servant."

Some looked confused.

"He told me a story that touched me, and it convicted me as well. So, I don't want you tell me what you don't like about me. I want you to find a dialogue partner. Right now."

Everyone looked around. They moved around, and eventually everyone had someone they could talk with. The group was evenly divided.

Jack said, "Good. Now, for the next thirty minutes discuss what a gestalt therapist would look like if they were to assume the role of a servant in therapy."

Someone said, "What do you mean by servant?"

Jack said, "Anybody got a smartphone?"

"Yes."

"Google 'Jesus' and 'greatest would be servant of all.'"

The person with the smartphone said, "Matthew 23:1–12."

Time for a Change **203**

"Okay, now look up 'Jesus washed their feet.'"

The person with the smartphone said, "John 13:1–17."

"Okay," said Jack. "How many of you really have your phone with you." Half the group raised their hands. "Each of you pairs, find someone who has a phone." The group reshuffled until every small group had a phone in it.

"Okay, for the next forty minutes, I want your group to read these parts of the Bible. You can find them on your phone, I'm sure. Then do two things: come up with a definition of a servant and then discuss what it would look like for a gestalt therapist to take on the role of a servant in therapy."

One person spoke up. He said, "First I don't feel comfortable reading Bible verses in a gestalt training group, and second, isn't that what we already are— servants to the needs of the client?"

Jack said, "Just go with it. This is an experiment, and this *is* the experiment. Notice everything that comes up when I put it to you as I've done. Notice what you find out from the Bible. Notice how you all handle this charge. Notice what a gestalt therapy servant might be like."

Then Jack turned and left the room. He went immediately into the town, to the restaurant, and into the streets around it looking for the servant. When he found him, he asked him to come with him back to the training group.

"Why?"

"Are you a servant? I need you."

The two of them went back to the training group and the servant stopped before going inside the building. He said, "Will you pray with me?"

Jack said, "I don't pray."

"Will you join me?"

"Okay."

The servant said, "Lord, I am here at your will. I yield myself to whatever you want, to whatever you are doing. Lord, please make me sensitive and aware of what you are doing. Give me ears to hear you so that I might be an instrument of your will, and please come upon Jack to give him the answers he seeks, your words for just him in this situation."

Jack said, "Amen." And they went inside.

The groups were finishing their discussions. They took a break and then came back and Jack asked each group to report on their discussions.

One group said it seemed to them that Jesus was making an ethical statement. We should treat others as we would like to be treated, even though that had not been in the reading. Someone remembered it from somewhere else, some other occasion. They wondered if that is what Jack wanted them to know.

Another group said they had gotten stuck on why they had to read Bible verses and never really did read them; so, they felt lost in the experiment and frustrated.

Another group agreed with the first group on ethics, but they had someone who wanted to add to that. He said there is some question about the veracity of the text in the original languages, because the words "hard to bear" come from

204 Change, Salvation, and Growth

a questionable manuscript tradition. He said the adjective, *dysbástaktos*, meaning "hard to bear," only occurs twice in the New Testament, here in Matthew and then in Luke 11:46 where its use is unquestioned by the manuscript evidence. The trainee added that he had studied the Greek of the New Testament and was taking classes at university because he intended to become a professor and wanted to major in textual criticism.

Jack thanked him, and he sat down. Someone else stood up and said, "It seemed to us that Jesus was telling the Jewish people listening to him to do as their religious leaders said, but not as they did. And that struck us as odd, because usually we hear that someone should not just do as told but as they see others doing. You know. Actions speak louder than words."

The servant broke in at that point. He said, "And what else did Jesus say after that?"

"That their leaders liked to be noticed. They liked adulation. We really laughed about kissing their hands in the marketplace." At which point they all laughed once more.

Jack asked, "What would be today's version, in a gestalt training group, of kissing the trainer's hand?"

There was a stir in the group. The group started offering suggestions. They indicated that asking for autographs, asking to work in experiential work with the trainer, trying to be with the trainer, around them, advocating with others for the trainer's point of view, that these kinds of things were some ways.

The servant said, "For every leader or teacher who extends his hand to be kissed, there is someone wanting to kiss it. But Jesus was saying that there is one worthy of such devotion, one only who is a father, one only who is an adequate leader. Every other pretender is a deceptive distraction. Even this one," at which point he turned to face Jack.

Jack blushed. He said, "Got me."

"Folks," said Jack. "I am very much captured by the idea of trainer or therapist as servant. What if the therapist approached the client with that attitude?"

Someone said, "What would that look like?"

Jack said, "PHG advances faith in the field, that the field would supply the means in any given difficult situation. Here, with me finding this man, this servant, I believe the field has supplied the means for us to consider perhaps a third, and not just that two might meet in dialogue, but that they might meet as somehow in the mix with. . . . Well, I don't know. I haven't gotten far enough with this."

The servant said, "We live, move, and have our being in God. God can be your third, because in fact God *is* your third . . . and your fourth, and your fifth, and so on. He is all in all."

Someone said, "But I don't believe in God."

The servant did not respond immediately. Then, he told the group his story, the story he had told Jack. It seemed to fall flat. Jack expected somehow that there would be some similar fascination as he had experienced, but it did not seem so.

The session faded from that point until they went on break. The servant left. Jack completed his training workshop for this group of people, and he left feeling unfinished, bewildered, and dissatisfied.

Had he been a fool? What had gotten into him to bring someone, a stranger from the town, into that group? Then, he started feeling old shame about being a failure, about people criticizing him, thinking bad things about him. He just wanted to hide, but there was nowhere to go on the plane ride home; so, he had to sit with himself.

So many changes. So many stages of life that he'd been through. He felt tired. He could not quit and go find another career. There was not enough time left in life to start over completely again. But something had to give. He had become sick of himself. In some way he had to find a balance, a new way of being that did not completely reject what he had become. Or was *that even possible!?*

How could he become *servant* as *therapist*? He decided he would not do anymore training of others before he sorted this out for himself. That would be one thing.

Jesus became the other thing. He found a wise, old pastor of a university-based church in town. The church was not part of the university, but many of its people were associated with the university. He called the man up and told him, "I want to come and talk with you about Jesus." Of course, that was a welcome request, and the two men got along. The pastor suggested readings, books by Christian authors, and they discussed them. Inevitably, that led to reading the Bible in places as well. Eventually, Jack found himself reading the gospel of John and it all fell together. "God gave his only, unique son, that whoever would believe in him might not perish but have eternal life."

One night Jack started talking to God as he had seen the servant do. "God," he said, "I would like to have what the servant has. I would like to know you as my pastor friend does. Is that possible?"

A thought came given, "Do you believe that I am?"

He found himself responding without hesitation. "Yes. I believe I do."

"Will you trust me?"

"How do I do that?"

"Will you trust me?"

"You know that I want to."

"More than the servant?"

Jack remembered the servant's prayer. He said, "Not more. But maybe like him?"

One word came given. "Jesus."

"Yes?" said Jack.

"Listen to him."

That was it. He kept talking but there was no more response. Rather, the last thing he had gotten, "Listen to him," echoed all night long.

Instinctively he kept reading the New Testament. He went back and read over and over again sections he'd already consumed. This was not like trying to figure

206 Change, Salvation, and Growth

out "who done it." Jack already knew how the story ended, but then again, as he read, new connections kept appearing. New significations kept weighing on him, astounding him.

One night he was reading, and he suddenly stopped, overcome by the desire building inside. He started talking again to God, and he said, "Jesus, I want you. I want to be yours. I want you to be *my* savior too."

Then a thought came given, "This is my beloved son . . ." It did not go on to tell him again to listen to Jesus. "This is my beloved son," and he knew it was for him. *He* had become God's beloved son too. He had become God's beloved son, and Jack spoke to God, and said, "Father." His heart broke inside and he filled up with love. Tears formed in his eyes. "Father, my father." He felt like he might burst with a new sense of freedom, joy, and a profound, grounded peace.

Time went by and he kept reading the Bible. Days turned into weeks. Weeks turned into months.

One day he was reading about Paul's conversion on the road to Damascus and how Jesus confronted him, and Paul asked him what he wanted Paul to do. Jesus had said, "You will be told what you must do."

The words hung in his mind. He kept replaying them. It seemed to him that they were instructive to him as well as to Paul. How does one become a servant in therapy? One must be available, at the zero point, not committed this way or that, but involved in the situation and aware that God is in the midst and might break in at any moment.

When he went back to doing therapy with that mind set, the process was more vital. He found himself expectant, not making up the presence of God because it was exciting to think of Him there, but simply sensitive enough to keep an ear ready to hear should God provide direction.

One day he was meeting with a patient, a young woman who suffered from depression. She was very reserved. She had been troubled in affect but was not able to mention to what her agitation was connected. Thus, the process was also superficial, and that was making Jack impatient. He quietly, without speaking out loud, told God how he felt, and a thought came given, "Ask about Brad."

"Who is Brad?" he said.

The woman stopped her fidgeting, looked him straight in the eyes, and said, "How do you know about him?"

Now there was contact.

"Who *is* Brad?"

"I *hate* him. He ruined my life."

The woman then proceeded to tell Jack how Brad had humiliated her by not showing up on the day of their wedding so that she was embarrassed and forsaken all at once and how she had gotten revenge, she had thought at the time, by sleeping with quite a number of men. But that only left her disgusted with sex, hating men, lonely, and still angry. While telling him all these things, she began crying, and soon she was sobbing heavily.

The session went over in time.

The session also became a breakthrough in the woman's case, and it became a type that stamped the process going forward for Jack. He could be a servant, he could be the best servant in therapy, by being available to both the client and to the Lord, by being sensitive to both, and by being obedient to what he was told.

He realized no one would understand this. No one but another servant would comprehend what it was like. People struggle to even believe there is a God let alone that that God is present and active in lives if they just don't harden their hearts against Him and have an ear to hear what the Spirit might say.

CONCLUSION

I have asked you to consider being present. I have asked you to consider field dynamics, including the issue of atmospheres and the possibility of a pneumenal field (and what might be involved with that). I have talked some basic phenomenology, which is the backbone of gestalt therapy, but also to Christianity, for no one enters the kingdom of God apart from personal experience. I have raised the issue of contact with God, and what contact is like. I have asked you to consider something basic to the existential aspects of gestalt therapy: risk and trust. I've done so with a view to change, salvation and growth, and I have offered a very brief picture of awareness, which in Christianity is spiritual sensitivity, and availability to God, which in gestalt therapy is spontaneity.

I have spoken Christian to the land of gestaltists and gestalt to the land of Christians, and I have attempted to translate for those having difficulty understanding the idioms of each.

What kind of an age do we live in now? There are various labels for it. One which I have been seeing more lately is "post-secular." We live in a world in which the mirage of secularism no longer shimmers on the horizon. It has faded with the demanding presence of religion, if not radical, forceful, and intrusive religion, in the public square. Religious and spiritual issues are back, having never really left.

Consequently, it is prudent to offer this book, which can take its place alongside Steve Zahm and Eva Gold's book on Buddhist psychology as two offerings for the advancing of gestalt therapy in a post-secular age.

For the Christian who is not a gestalt therapist at all, if you've been reading this book, then you have considered Christianity while standing on a scaffolding, a structural outline inherent to a system you may not have heard about nor even care about. I hope it's been fun. I hope it's been challenging. I hope this take on

Christianity has helped you think with more complexity, because while there is no virtue in complexity for complexity's sake, the gospel may be simple, but our infinite God and His working are quite complex.

I leave you with this:

I read recently that the economic trinity is the immanent trinity. I don't think we can *get* to the transcendent trinity. But there is one.

INDEX

Note: **Boldface** page references indicate tables. *Italic* references indicate figures.

1 Corinthians 60
1 John 60
2 Chronicles 197

Abraham 7
Acts, book of 177
Adam 73
Adame, A. 45
aesthetic criterion in gestalt therapy 13
affective investment 170–171
affective space 88; *see also* atmospheres
affliction 129–130, **130**
aísthēsis ("experience by senses") 13
alterity: critical realist perspective on
 presence and 40–42; divine 48–49;
 God and 48–49; human 49–50;
 intentionality of 50; Levina's concept
 of 40; meeting people and 44, 47–50;
 relationships and 44
anakrino ("examine/investigate") 105
animate things 84–86
anthropology in gestalt therapy 39, 93
antinomies 44
approach-avoidance cycle 156–157
Aristotle 7, 84
Athanasius of Alexandria 148
atmospheres: change in 108–113; clinical
 atmospherics 91–92; defining 35;
 duality of 95; empathy and 88–89;
 enchantment and, 102–103, 106n4;

etymology of 32; givenness and
86; Griffero's concept of 92–93;
hermeneutics and 86; middle voice
of intentionality and 86; objective
genitives of 89–91, **90**; organism-
environment field and 93–94;
perception of 89; quasi-things in 81,
86–93; as representation 86, 103;
spirituality and 92–93; subjective
genitives of 89–91, **90**; synthesis of
94–95; things in 81–86; thinking about
81; usage of term 32–33
attitude: naturalistic 100, 102, 106n2;
personalistic 120; phenomenology and
120, 122; psychological 106, 118, 120,
122–123, **128–130**, 130, 134–135,
193; spiritual 59, 118, 120, 122–123,
128–130, 130, 134–135, 193
attributes 18–19, 26n3, 49; *see also*
relational attributes of God
availability to God 194–198
awareness: animate things and 85; in
Christianity 119; experience and, as
form of 191; gestalt therapy and 150,
191–192; possibility in personal horizon
and 120–122; presence and 29

Bavinck, H. 148
beauty 105–106, **128**
Beisser, A. 166–167

Index 211

belief: in God 101; in Jesus 158–163; non-realist view of 37–38; realism without rational judgment between different 38; trust in religious 37

Bettelheim, B. 99–100

Bible: experience and words of 12–13; God's portrayal in 25; immanence of God in 55, **56**; love in, words for 23, **24**; New Testament 25; Old Testament 25; spirit and, understanding of 92; superlative immanence in 60; *see also specific book*

Biblical counseling 134–135

bisexuality of universe 44

Bloom, D. 13, 39, 85, 175

Böhme, G. 88

Boston Change Process Study Group 170

bottom-up approach to gestalt therapy 81

Brownell, L. 2, 50–51

Brownell, P. 3

Buber, M. 18, 148

Calvin, John 14, 174

Cartesian space 95

case conceptualization 41–42

change: affective investment and 170–171; in atmospheres 108–113; choices and 172; constancy of 166–168; contact with God and 169; contingent universals concept and 168; either-or binary and 172; in gestalt therapy 166–167; healthy living's influence on 168; immanence and 169–172; paradoxical theory of 195–196; personal 167–168; regeneration/conversion and 177–178, **183**; time for 199–207; transcendence and 169–172; in universe 167

charis 176–177

chiasm 49–50, 86, 102

choices and gestalt therapy 172

Christ *see* Jesus

Christianity: awareness in 119; confession and 196–197; conscience and 189; contact with God and 102; development of church and 16; enchantment in 106; experience of 123–124; as experiential approach 116; experiential learning in 155–156; faith and 119, 153; field dynamics and 71; freedom and 189; gestalt therapy and 3, 208–209; God's existence and 6; impasse in 157; introjects and 187; Jesus and 120, 178; legalism and 188–189; meeting ground in 46–47; self-function and **183**; thinking about 208–209; trust and 6, 156

Chun, S. 101

client: approach-avoidance cycle and 156–157; experience of 17; gestalt therapy and eavesdropping on relationship with God 135–137; Holy Spirit accessing in therapy 183–184; therapist and, relationship with 17–18; transference of 45; "whole" 23

clinical atmospherics 91–92

clinical depression 182

clinical practice *see* gestalt therapy

co-constructed 89

Collier, A. 37

commitment 10–11

communicable relational attributes of God 19

concern of God with humans 23–25

confession 196–197

conflict 179–181

conformity 47, 187

conscience, matters of 189

consciousness 85

constructed 38, 89, 102

contact/contacting: boundary 70–71, 78n2; dialogue of 9–10; existence and 6–7; experience of 118; in gestalt therapy 8–9, 20–21, 106n3; with God 21, 102, 118, 123, 169; Merleau-Ponty's conception of 49–50; non-independence and 45; between organism-environment field 182; relational attributes of God and 20–21; shutting down 10–11

contingent universals concept 168

continuity 171–172

conversion 177–178, **183**

Costa, C. 33

Council of Chalcedon (451) 57–58

countertransference 45, 88

creation 73–74

Crisis of the European Sciences (Husserl) 101

Crisp, R. 11

Critchley, S. 47–48

critical realism 40

critical realist perspective on presence: alterity and 40–42; critical realism 40; non-critical relativism 38–40; non-realist view of belief 37–38; realism

212 Index

and 37–40; realism without rational judgment between beliefs 38
Crocker, Sylvia 2, 175
Cvetovac, M. 45

Daniel, book of 76
De Anima (Aristotle) 84
death 63–67
depression 182
Derrida, J. 48
Descartes, R. 94–95, 102–103, 148
dialogical 9–10, 30–32, 151, 183
dialogue: clinical process of 10–11; of contacting 9–10; in gestalt therapy 10–11, 41; presence and 31–32; revelation and 150–151
disenchantment, "crisis" of 100–103
divine alterity 48–49
DMU Group 85
domestic abuse 139–144
duality 95

economic trinity 209
ego function 176, **183**
Ego Hunger and Aggression (Perls) 195
eimi ("being") 7–8
either-or binary 172
eleos 25
embodiment 117
emotional contagion 88–89
empathy 88–89
enchantment: atmospheres and 102–103, 106n4; Bettelheim's book on 99–100; in Christianity 106; disenchantment and, "crisis" of 100–103; immanence and 104–105; life world and 103–104; literature on 99, 106n1; lived body and 103–104; as narrative fantasies 100, 104; pneumenal field and 104–106; transcendence and 104–105
enigma 146–147
Enlightenment 105
Ephesians, book of 60
essence 6–8, 18, 54, 57–58, 81, 147–148
existence: of all things versus God's 7–8; Aristotle's categories of 7; awareness as form of 191; Christianity and God's 6; contact and 6–7; defining 7–8; experience and 6–11; of God 6–8, 17, 71; logical composition and 7; ongoing 8; philosophers and 6; of pneumenal field 73; transitory 168
Exodus, book of 7

experience: author-reader 14; Biblical words and 12–13; of Christianity 123–124; of client 17; of contact 118; Crisp's features of human 11; existence and 6–11; field of 72; in gender dysphoria 118; Heidegger and 8; intentionality and aboutness of 119–120; interpreting 8; knowing by 12–13, 197; of knowing God 14, 46–47; learning from 154–156; limit of 12; lived body and 117–118; of numinous 59; phenomenology and 72, 116–118, 122; reasoning and 116; of self 9; by senses 13; significance of 11–14; of spiritual life 127–130
experiential learning 154–156
external opposition 179–180
Ezekiel, book of 60

fairy tales 99–100; *see also* enchantment
faith: Christianity and 119, 153; commitments of gestalt therapists 37; communities 120; developing 188; doubt and 183; experiential learning and 154–155; gestalt therapy and 153–154; in God 21, 149, 155, 196; grace and 176–178, 188–189; horizon of personal possibility and 122; in Jesus 22–23, 100, 120, 130, 188; Paul and 154; perceptual 122–123; salvation and 44; scripture and 128; of Stein 15n2; tenets of church and 16; testing 181; trust and 153–155; works and 44, 153–154
fear 9, 105, 156, 172, 181
feeling of life (*Lebensgefühl*) 117
field dynamics: Christianity and 71; gestalt therapy and 71; ontical conceptualization of 71–73; personal change and 168; phenomenal conceptualization of 72–73; pneumenal conceptualization of 73–77; story 77–78; *see also* organization-environment field; phenomenology; pneumenal field
Figal, G. 86, 94
figures of interest 168
Francesetti, G. 71, 78n2, 91
freedom 39, 119, 189
Fuchs, T. 87, 117

Gaffney, S. 70
Galileo 101
Gefühlston ("feeling-tone") 87

Gegenständlichkeit ("standing in opposition") 86, 94
Geller, S. 28–29
Gelso, C. 45
gender dysphoria 118
Genesis 74
gestalt therapy: aesthetic criterion in 13; anthropology in 39, 93; author's note about 3–4; awareness and 150, 191–192; Biblical counseling versus 134–135; bottom-up approach to 81; case conceptualization in 41–42; change in 166–167; choices and 172; Christianity and 3, 208–209; contact/contacting styles in 8–9, 20–21, 106n3; dialogue in 10–11, 41; disenchantment in, "crisis" of 100–103; eavesdropping on client's relationship with God and 135–137; experience of client and 17; as experiential approach 116; experiential learning in 155; faith and 153–154; field dynamics and 71; health in 9, 119, 168; Holy Spirit accessing client and therapist in 183–184; impasse in 156–157; inter-personal attitude and 120; introjects and 187; legalism and 189; meeting people and 61–62; non-independence in 46–47; ongoing existence and 8; ontological questions and 40; organism-environment field and 78n2, 93; patient-therapist relationship in 17–18; perception of direct affect and 90–91; personal change and 166–167; personal experience with 133–134; personalistic attitude and 120; phenomenology and 116; in post-secular age 208; presence in 28–30, 33–34; revelation and 150; risk and 208; self-disclosing in 34, 150; self-theory 175–176; situational unit in 12; spiritual dimension of 22; spiritual rationale for 25; tenets, various 81; trust and 208; "whole" people and 23
ginōskō ("knowing through senses") 13
givenness 82, 86
God: adoration of 193; affective investment and 170–171; alterity and 48–49; amenability to being known and 148; attributes of 19, 49; availability to 194–198; belief in 101; Bible's portrayal of 25; call of 76; change and 169; concern with humans 23–25; constancy of 168;

contact with 21, 102, 118, 123, 169; continuity and 171–172; difference made by 102; discipline of 181–182; enigma of 146–147; essence of 18, 54, 148; existence of 6–8, 17, 71; experience of knowing 14, 46–47; faith in 21, 149, 155, 196; Holy Spirit and 60; immanence of 54–55, **56**, 57–60; ineffability of 148–149, 151; infiniteness of 12; Jesus and 58, 76, 118; kingdom of 76–77; as love 23, **24**; meeting people 58–60; mercy of 25; mystery of 18, 48–49, 146–147; Paul and 74; praising 188; priority of person and 171; relationship with humans 18, 20; revelation of 149; self-disclosure of 24–25; as spirit 21–22; transcendence of 48, 54–55, 57–59; trust in 19, 60, 137, 154; truth of 19; as whole 23; Word of 3, 22–23, 127, 150–151; *see also* relational attributes of God
Gold, E. 208
Goldberg, S. 45
Goldstein, K. 74
Goodman, P. 94; *see also* PHG
grace 176–178, 188–189
Greenberg, L. 28–29
grief 63–67
Griffero, T. 32, 81, 91–93

"hardening of the heart" 10–11, 184
Hass, L. 49–50
Hayes, J. 45
health in gestalt therapy 9, 119, 168
healthy living's influence on change 168
"heart" 95
Hefferline, R. *see* PHG
Heidegger, M. 8, 41, 81
Henry, M. 190
hermeneutics 25n1, 86
Heschel, A. 16–17, 146–147
ḥeseḏ 25
Hoffman, M. 133
holy, idea of 59
Holy Spirit 59–60, 76, 92, 151, 156, 183–184
homosexuality 158–163
horizon, possibility in personal 120–122
House Un-American Activities Committee 47
human alterity 49–50
human-god relationship 17–18
humility 59

214 Index

Husserl, E. 15n2, 41, 100–101, 103, 116–117, 121, 148
hypostasis 57–58

Ideas I (Husserl) 101
id function 175, **183**
imagination 120–121
immanence: big 54; change and 169–172; defining 54; enchantment and 104–105; of God 54–55, **56**, 57–60; ontical field and 59; pneumenal field and 58–59; small 54; superlative 59–60; transcendence versus 54; trinity of 209
immanent frame 54, 61, 105, 169, 172
impasse 156–157
inanimate things 83
incarnation 57–58
inclusion 10
ineffability of God 148–149, 151
ineffable, response to 129, **129**
infiltration 90
intentionality: of alterity 50; defining, 51n1 30; divine 58; experience and, aboutness of 119–120; middle voice of 30, 86; phenomenology and 119–120, 122; rational thought and 7; spiritual sensitivity growth and 192–193
intentional object 7, 29, 43n1, 119, 122, 168, 176, 192–193
internal conflict 180–181
inter-personal attitude 120
introjects 186–189
intuition 75

James (apostle) 153–154
Jani, A. 73
Jeremiah (prophet) 53–54
Jesus: atonement of 178; belief in 158–163; Christianity and 120, 178; divinity and, imprint of 127; ears for hearing for comprehension and 191; essence of 57; faith in 22–23, 100, 120, 130, 188; God and 58, 76, 118; living in the present and 196; love of 171–172; rebuke of storm by 9; Sabbath and 75; sermon on the mount and 25; sins of the world and 158; trust in 123, 135, 137, 162–163; as truth 123
John (apostle) 191
John, gospel of 7, 60, 123
justification 178
Justin Martyr 147–148

Kant, I. 117, 148, 154
Kierkegaard, S. 154
kingdom of God 76–77
Kivlighan, D. 45
koinonia ("community/partnership/ contact") 61, 121
Körper (physical bodies) 84–85, 96n3, 103

Lagaay, A. 195
learning, experiential 154–156
legalism, working through 188–189
Leib (lived body) 84–85, 92, 96n3, 103–104, 117–118
Levinas, E. 17–18, 40, 47–49, 86, 150
Leviticus, book of 197
Lewin, K. 71
Lewis, C.S. 80
life, pneumenal field infused with 73–74
life world 103–104, 121–124
lived body (*Leib*) 84–85, 92, 96n3, 103–104, 117–118
lived experience (*Erlebnis*) 117
living in the present 196
Logical Investigations (Husserl) 101
Logos, incarnation of 57
love 23, **24**, 25, 60, 156, 159–160, 171–172, 179, 181
loyal love 25

Mackinlay, S. 86
Marion, J.-L. 82, 86, 94, 149
Matthew, gospel of 75, 191, 197–198
McCarthy, Joe 47
meeting people: alterity and 44, 47–50; defining *meet* and 44–45; example of 50–51; gestalt therapy and 61–62; by God 58–60; non-independence and 45–47; possibilities of 61–62
mercy 19, 25
Merleau-Ponty, M. 49–50, 86, 101–102, 122, 148–149, 154
Michael (angel) 76
middle voice of intentionality 30, 86
mindfulness 29
Möller, E. 101
Moran, D. 101
Moses 7, 57
Müllen, R.O. 32
mysterium fascinans 20, 59, 92
mysterium tremendum 20, 59, 92
mystery 9, 18, 48–49, 60, 105–106, 129, 146–147
myths 99–100; *see also* enchantment

narrative fantasies *see* enchantment
narratives *see* stories
"naturalistic" attitude 100, 102, 106n2
nature (essence) 57
nature, appreciation of 127–128, **128**
New Testament 25, 61, 73, 127, 177;
  see also specific book
Noah 177
non-Cartesian space 95
non-critical relativism 38–40
non-independence 44–47
non-realist view of belief 37–38
Nordling, W.J. 85
numinous, experience of 59

objective genitives of atmospheres
  89–91, **90**
oida ("to see so as to understand fully") 13
Old Testament 25, 73, 95, 177; *see also*
  specific book
O'Neill, B. 70
ontical field 59, 71–73, 168
opposition, external 179–180
organism-environment (O-E) field:
  atmospheres and 93–94; contact
  between 182; contact-boundary in
  70–71, 78n2; defining 39, 70; gestalt
  therapy and 78n2, 93; grammatical
  structures of 43n1, 78n2
otherworldly, response to 129, **129**
Otto, R. 20, 59
ousia ("being/essence") 7, 57

Packer, J.I. 14, 46–47
Pantheism 57
paradoxes 44, 195–196
Pargament, K. 59
Parlett, M. 71
pathos 129–130, **130**
patient-therapist relationship 17–18; *see*
  also client
Paul (apostle) 74, 105, 123, 131, 146, 154,
  169, 171, 180, 186, 188–189, 191
peace 139–144
perceived 13, 50, 73, 75, 82, *84*, 87–91,
  93–95, 101–102, 121, 157
perceptual faith 122–123
Perls, F. 182, 186, 188, 195
Perls, Hefferline, and Goodman (PHG) 39,
  70, 122, 154–155, 174
persecution, religious 179–180
person 57
personal change 167–168

personalistic attitude 120
personality function 176, **183**
personal space 8–9
personhood 22
perspectivalism 39
phenomenology: attitude and 120, 122;
  awareness and 120–122; experience and
  72, 116–118, 122; in field dynamics,
  conceptualization of 72–73; gestalt
  therapy and 116; imagination and
  120–121; intentionality and 119–120,
  122; life world and 121–124; lived body
  and 117–118, 122; ontical field and 72,
  168; possibility in personal horizon and
  120–121; spiritual life and Christian
  131–132
phenomenon 82, 86
PHG (Perls, Hefferline, and Goodman) 39,
  70, 122, 154–155, 174
Philip (apostle) 123
Phillips, J.B. 18
physical bodies (*Körper*) 73, 84–85, 90,
  96n3, 103
pity 25
pneuma ("spirit") 21–22, 33, 58–59, 73, 105
pneumenal field: enchantment and
  104–106; existence of 73; field
  dynamics and, conceptualization of
  73–77; immanence of God and 58–59;
  intuition and 75; life and, infused with
  73–74; operation of 73; spirit and,
  driven by 74; story and, characterization
  by 75–76; transcendence and 75
Polster, E. 186
Polster, M. 186
possibility in personal horizon 120–121
post-secular age 208–209
power of living 175
presence: awareness and 29; in clinical
  process of dialogue 10; consequences
  of 29; defining 28–29; dialogue and
  31–32; as field dynamic 32–33; fluidity
  of 30–33; in gestalt therapy 28–30,
  33–34; in middle voice of intentionality
  30; personalness of 31; self and, use of
  29, 34–35; *see also* contact/contacting;
  critical realist perspective on presence
priority 171
Psalms 55, 76–77, 197
psychikos ("psychological") 106
psychological attitude 106, 118, 120,
  122–123, **128–130**, 130, 134–135, 193
psychotherapy *see* gestalt therapy

216 Index

qualities ascribed to things 82–83, *83*, *84*
quasi-things: atmospheres and 81, 86–93;
   defining 81; empathy and 88–89;
   ontological status of 87–88; *see also*
   things

realism: critical 40; non-critical relativism
   38–40; non-realist view of belief 37–38;
   without rational judgment between
   beliefs 38
reason/reasoning 116
regeneration 177–178, **183**
relational attributes of God: communicable
   19; contact and 20–21; contact
   with God versus other people and
   21; examples of 21–25; relative 20;
   transitive 19–20
relationships: alterity and 44;
   eavesdropping on client-God 135–137;
   with God 18, 20; non-independence in
   44; patient-therapist 17–18; revelation
   in 150–151
relative relational attributes of God 20
relativism 38–40
religious persecution 179–180
representation, atmosphere as 86, 103
res cogitans ("thinking thing") 94–95
res extensa ("extended thing") 94–95
revelation 149–151
Revelation, book of 75
Riedel, F. 93–94
risk 154, 156–157, 208
Robine, J.-M. 174
Romans, book of 60
ruah ("spirit") 73, 95

Sabbath 75
St Peter's Basilica 108–113
salvation: faith and 44; grace and 176–177;
   integration and 182–184; regeneration
   and 177–178; sanctification and
   178–182; theology of 174; topic of 176
sanctification 178–182, **183**
Satan 180
saturated phenomenon 76
saturation 149–151
Schaff, P. 16
Schmitz, H. 32, 88
science of psychology 40; *see also* gestalt
   therapy
scripture, approach to 128, **128**; *see also*
   Bible
self: experience of 9; presence and use
   of 29, 34–35; sense of 119; theory in
   gestalt therapy 175–176

self-disclosing 34, 150
semantic realism 43n2
senses, experience by 13
Silsbe, D. 29
Siminovitch, D. 29
sin 60, 74, 131–132, 135, 158–159,
   181, 196
Slaby, J. 32
Slife, B. 101
soul 73, 84
spirit (*pneuma/ruah*) 21–22, 33, 58–59,
   73–74, 92, 95, 105
spiritual atmospheres 92–93
spiritual attitude 59, 118, 120, 122–123,
   128–130, 130, 134–135, 193
Spiritual Competence in Psychotherapy (P.
   Brownell) 3, 73
spiritual depression 182
spiritual life: appreciation of nature
   example 127–128, **128**; Christian
   phenomenology of 131–132;
   experience of 127–130; God-
   inclusiveness and 130; personal
   experiences of 126–127, 131–132;
   response to other-worldly and ineffable
   example 129, **129**; scripture approach
   example 128, **128**; tragedy/affliction/
   pathos example 129–130, **130**
spiritual sensitivity: availability to God and
   197–198; awareness and 119; growth in
   190–193
spiritual things 104
spirituality 3, 59, 93–94, 106, 123, 124n3,
   130, 136, 150, 154, **183**
Stein, Edith 7, 15n2, 73
stories: belief in Jesus and homosexuality
   158–163; change in atmospheres
   108–113; field dynamics 77–78; grief/
   death 63–67; peace from domestic
   abuse 139–144; pneumenal field 75–76;
   rationale of 4; St. Peter's Basilica/tombs
   of the Pope's visit 108–113, 193; time
   for change 199–207; trust 158–163
subjection/subjugation 47
subjective genitives of atmospheres
   89–91, **90**
synthesis of atmospheres 94–95

Taylor, C. 54–55, 100, 104
theism, critique of 117
things: animate 84–86; in atmospheres
   81–86; givenness and 82; inanimate
   83; phenomenon and 82; qualities of
   82–83, *83*, *84*; spiritual 104; *see also*
   quasi things

Index **217**

Timothy 123
Titus, C.S. 85
Tolkien, J.R.R. 80, 104
tombs of the Popes 110–113, 193
Toms, Lee 29
"touch of another kind" 14, 21, 75, 102, 118, 123
tragedy 129–130, **130**
transcendence: big 54; change and 169–172; defining 54; enchantment and 104–105; of God 48, 54–55, 57–59; between humans 18; immanence versus 54; pneumenal field and 75; small 54; trinity of 209
transference of client 45
transitive relational attributes of God 19–20
transitory existence 168
transparency 2, 82
trinity 209
Truscott, D. 196
trust: Christianity and 6, 156; faith and 153–155; gestalt therapy and 208; in God 19, 60, 137, 154; in Jesus 123, 135, 137, 162–163; in religious belief 37; story of 158–163
truth: of God 19; Henry's idea of 190; Holy Spirit and 156; Jesus as 123; as person 158, 163; personal versus

universal 17; relative 38–39; Satan and 180; Spirit of 60, 76, 191; values 38

Updike, J. 99

Visible and the Invisible, The (Merleau-Ponty) 101–102
Vitz, P.C. 85

water's attributes 18–19
Weber, M. 100
Well-Lived Life, A (Crocker) 2
Westminster Shorter Catechism 193
Wheeler, G. 71
Willard, D. 10
Wojtyla, Karol Józef (Pope John Paul II) 108
Word of God 3, 22–23, 127, 150–151
worship 20, 58, 93–94, 118, 188
Wright, N.T. 40

yada ("knowing by experience") 12–13, 197
Yontef, G. 71

Zahm, S. 208

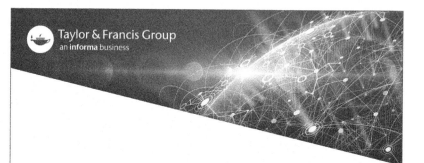